THE COMPLETE IDIOT'S GUIDE® TO

Early Christianity

For Bishop Ed,
Many blessings on
your leadership.
J. Michael Matkin

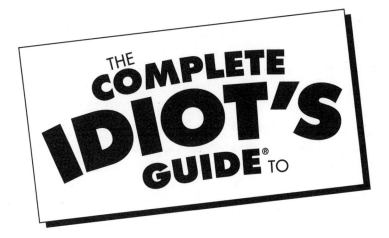

Early Christianity

by J. Michael Matkin

ALPHA

A member of Penguin Group (USA) Inc.

ALPHA BOOKS

Published by the Penguin Group

Penguin Group (USA) Inc., 375 Hudson Street, New York, New York 10014, USA

Penguin Group (Canada), 90 Eglinton Avenue East, Suite 700, Toronto, Ontario M4P 2Y3, Canada (a division of Pearson Penguin Canada Inc.)

Penguin Books Ltd., 80 Strand, London WC2R 0RL, England

Penguin Ireland, 25 St. Stephen's Green, Dublin 2, Ireland (a division of Penguin Books Ltd.)

Penguin Group (Australia), 250 Camberwell Road, Camberwell, Victoria 3124, Australia (a division of Pearson Australia Group Pty. Ltd.)

Penguin Books India Pvt. Ltd., 11 Community Centre, Panchsheel Park, New Delhi—110 017, India

Penguin Group (NZ), 67 Apollo Drive, Rosedale, North Shore, Auckland 1311, New Zealand (a division of Pearson New Zealand Ltd.)

Penguin Books (South Africa) (Pty.) Ltd., 24 Sturdee Avenue, Rosebank, Johannesburg 2196, South Africa

Penguin Books Ltd., Registered Offices: 80 Strand, London WC2R 0RL, England

Copyright © 2008 by J. Michael Matkin

International Standard Book Number: 978-1-59257-756-9
Library of Congress Catalog Card Number: 2007941481

10 09 08   8 7 6 5 4 3 2 1

Interpretation of the printing code: The rightmost number of the first series of numbers is the year of the book's printing; the rightmost number of the second series of numbers is the number of the book's printing. For example, a printing code of 08-1 shows that the first printing occurred in 2008.

Printed in the United States of America

Most Alpha books are available at special quantity discounts for bulk purchases for sales promotions, premiums, fundraising, or educational use. Special books, or book excerpts, can also be created to fit specific needs.

For details, write: Special Markets, Alpha Books, 375 Hudson Street, New York, NY 10014.

Publisher: *Marie Butler-Knight*
Editorial Director: *Mike Sanders*
Senior Managing Editor: *Billy Fields*
Acquisitions Editor: *Michele Wells*
Senior Development Editor: *Phil Kitchel*
Production Editor: *Megan Douglass*
Copy Editor: *Krista Hansing*

Cartoonist: *Steve Barr*
Cover Designer: *Bill Thomas*
Book Designer: *Trina Wurst*
Indexer: *Joan Green*
Layout: *Ayanna Lacey*
Proofreader: *John Etchison*

For Emily & Elaina. Yes, Daddy can play now.

Contents at a Glance

Contents

Introduction

Welcome to *The Complete Idiot's Guide to Early Christianity*. By "early Christianity," we are referring to the first 300 years or so of the existence of the Christian faith. This period begins with the life of Jesus of Nazareth, on whom Christianity is based, and ends with the rise of the Roman Emperor Constantine, under whose leadership Christianity became a favored religion.

How to Use This Book

While we'll try to cover all the bases, any book of this size can only hope to orient the reader to the amazingly complex and sometimes baffling world of early Christianity. Think of this book as a map. At nearly every point along our journey, there will be room for you to explore more deeply areas of this history that catch your eye. My hope is that what you read here will help to orient you, and as we go, I will point you to further resources that can assist you.

The Path Ahead

We've got a lot of ground to cover, so I'm going to make this as easy as possible. I've broken the book down into five parts to make this more manageable for you.

Part 1, "Beginnings," will get us familiar with the background that we'll need to understand Jesus and his earliest followers. If you've ever read the New Testament and felt like you were getting only part of the story, this will interest you.

Once we've got that foundation going for us, **Part 2, "Conflict and Crisis,"** will delve into the ways that Christians began to define themselves as their numbers grew larger and more diverse. This is where we'll look at folks like the gnostics, who have been getting so much press recently.

Sometimes we can get so focused on the big names and big arguments in history, we forget about the little guy. We'll take a more thematic approach in **Part 3, "Church and Culture,"** and ask what daily life was like as a Christian in the Roman Empire.

When we get back to the action in **Part 4, "Kingdom and Empire,"** things are really beginning to heat up between Christians and the Roman Empire. At the same time, the Church is getting stronger and more assertive. As we'll see, just when it seems like there's no end in sight, a series of events brings Constantine, a Christian emperor, to the throne. That, of course, changes everything. Christianity went from being an illegal religion to being the favored faith of the empire. We'll wind up our time together by looking at how those changes impacted Christianity and look at how current, momentous changes in the Christian world make our exploration of early Christianity very relevant.

Clues for the Journey

All through this book, you will find these little gems that we call sidebars. They're designed to provide you with information that doesn't fit well into the flow of the story.

From the Source

There's nothing quite like hearing it straight from the horse's mouth. In these sidebars, I'll share with you selected quotations from ancient writers.

Word to the Wise

Just as we'll hear from ancient writers, occasionally I'll share with you an insightful remark from a modern scholar.

In Depth

Late antiquity was a very different place and time. Here's where I'll highlight significant people, events, and discoveries that enhance our understanding of early Christianity.

Word Knowledge

I promise to use plain language as much as possible, but sometimes we have to use new terms. When that happens, I'll have a handy definition so you can keep on reading without wondering what I'm talking about.

Acknowledgments

A book doesn't write itself, much as I have wished that it would at times. Every author owes a debt of gratitude to those who make the work possible. In particular, I have relied a great deal on the patience of those around me as this project came to completion.

First, to Michele Wells and the editors at Alpha Books, my deepest thanks for their skill and energy, and especially for their incredible patience with me through this process.

I am surrounded by a "great cloud of witnesses" who remind me who I am and what I'm about, and who are patient with me when I too frequently forget. To Dale and Diane Pollard, Deb Steinkamp, Adam Foy, and all of my friends with Eighth Day Community; to Baron and Cristina Miller (I got it right this time!) and the folks at Roosevelt Community Church; to Brett Desper, Chris Bickert, Josh and Jessa Parrish, and Rob Haskell, my deepest thanks. I want to especially thank two men, Fr. Dale Caldwell and Dr. Jonathan Wilson, for their friendship and for graciously sharing their time and wisdom with me. I treasure you both.

To my wife, Christine, thanks are not enough. She is the glue that keeps my world together. Without her, none of this would be possible. Thank you, dearest.

Finally, to my little girls, Emily and Elaina, Daddy says, "Thank you." This book was an unexpected project, and Dad had to do a disappearing act more times than he found comfortable. Emily and Elaina are the ones who gave up the most so that I could complete this book, often without understanding why. It is to them and their patience that this work is dedicated.

Special Thanks to the Technical Reviewer

The Complete Idiot's Guide to Early Christianity was reviewed by an expert who double-checked the accuracy of what you'll learn here, to help us ensure that this book gives you everything you need to know. Special thanks are extended to James S. Bell.

Trademarks

All terms mentioned in this book that are known to be or are suspected of being trademarks or service marks have been appropriately capitalized. Alpha Books and Penguin Group (USA) Inc. cannot attest to the accuracy of this information. Use of a term in this book should not be regarded as affecting the validity of any trademark or service mark.

Part  Beginnings

Before there was Christianity, there was Christ. Before there was a church, per se, there were the women and men who knew Jesus of Nazareth. Jesus left us no writings of his own, so we have to rely on what his followers tell us about him. Who were they, and how did they interpret Jesus' life?

In this first part, we'll get acquainted with the world that Jesus and his earliest followers occupied. Once we have a snapshot of late antiquity in our mind's eye, we'll be ready to consider the life of Jesus of Nazareth. We'll listen to his teachings through his contemporaries and explore the impact of the stories about his death and alleged resurrection. When his followers shift into high gear, we'll head out with them as they spread his word. Cataclysmic events and the passing away of the first generation of Christians forced the emerging Christian community to relate to Jesus differently, and that's where we'll end up.

1

"In the Fullness of Time ..."

In This Chapter

- We have to begin with the Big Story

- Communication is easier when it's all Greek to everyone

- What do you call a man who thinks he's a god?

If you're going to understand early Christianity, you'll have to grapple with the meaning and significance of Jesus of Nazareth. Nearly every question that roils beneath the surface of the emergence of the Christian faith, especially during these first volatile centuries, revolves around understanding the life of this one man. Neither Jesus nor his early followers existed in a vacuum. Jesus lived, ate, taught, slept, labored, and loved in a world that was at once very similar to and yet very different from our own. If we're going to make sense of Jesus, we'll have to start by getting to know his world.

The first great missionary of the Christian faith, Paul of Tarsus, wrote, "When the time was fully come, God sent his Son ...." Early Christians believed that Jesus had come at just the right time in human history. This confidence in the guiding hand of God shaped the way that they interpreted not only Jesus' life, but also their own lives. Taking the time to understand the world that the early Christians inhabited will help us to understand them as well.

So before we begin our look at early Christianity, let's back up and get a running start by taking note of the three defining realities of Jesus' world. First, we'll listen in on the Jewish story that Jesus grew up hearing, the history of the people of Israel and their often tempestuous relationship with their God. Second, the culture of Jesus' day was indelibly stamped by the philosophy and language of Greece, so we'll talk about that. Third, Jesus was born into the Roman Empire, which dominated the political and economic life of late antiquity. That will give us the background we need for the next chapter. All set? Then let's go.

The Jewish Story

Every thriving society has a Big Story. It's the story that we tell to make sense out of the chaos of daily living. The Big Story helps us understand who we are, individually and collectively, and shapes what we value and how we pursue what is most important to us. If you want to know what drives a person or an entire civilization, figure out the Big Story they are telling.

For Jesus and the early Christians, the Big Story was Israel's story. It was a story of God's covenant with their ancestors—the wandering bedouin Abraham, his son Isaac, and Isaac's son Jacob (who was also called Israel)—an eternal agreement to give them descendants and a land in which to live. It was the story of how their descendants, the twelve tribes of Israel (one for each of Jacob's sons), left behind slavery in Egypt to become a nation; and how, through Moses, they received from God a Law to live by that would distinguish them from all other people on earth. It was the story of how the Israelites conquered the Promised Land, built a Temple for God to live among them, and appointed kings to rule them. It should have lasted forever.

But the Israelites failed to hold up their end of the covenant, taking God and His blessings for granted. Israel split into two, with ten tribes forming a kingdom in the north while the other two continued to rule in the south. So along came the Assyrian Empire, which took over the northern kingdom and relocated its people. It was followed by the Babylonians, who in 587 B.C. ransacked Jerusalem, burned down the Temple, and took the best and brightest of Israel back to Babylon. So the Jewish story was also a story of a people exiled, and why, despite the fact that they had returned to the land some two generations later and rebuilt the Temple, things still didn't feel quite right.

From the Source

When the Lord brought back the captives to Zion,
we were like men who dreamed.

Our mouths were filled with laughter,
our tongues with songs of joy.
Then it was said among the nations,
"The Lord has done great things for them."

The Lord has done great things for us,
and we are filled with joy.

Restore our fortunes, O Lord,
like streams in the desert.

Those who sow in tears
will reap with songs of joy.

He who goes out weeping,
carrying seed to sow,
will return with songs of joy,
carrying a harvest with him.

—Psalm 126

We have to be attentive to that unease when we meet Jesus and listen to his teachings. God had promised Israel a return from exile, a new Exodus out of a different kind of bondage. It would be a new heaven and a new earth, Isaiah said, where the wolf would lie down with the lamb. Men would beat their weapons of war into hoes and plows, prosperity and safety would hang in the air, and all the foreign nations that once oppressed Israel would come streaming up Mt. Zion in Jerusalem to God's Temple, begging for a chance to learn his ways.

Except, none of that happened. Oh, the Jews came back from their captivity in Persia (modern-day Iran), but only a relative handful. And they were still under the thumb of others: first the Persians, then the Greeks, and now the Romans. The Temple had been rebuilt, but it was a small and unimpressive structure. The promises seemed rather hollow. The new earth looked far too similar to the old one: wolves snacked on lambs, the weapons of war were still brandished frequently, and the nations of the world certainly weren't knocking on the Temple's door. Like Ezra, who helped lead the return from exile, the average Jew in Jesus' day often felt like he was still a slave, even in his own homeland.

While there was a good deal of anxiety, there was also a great deal of anticipation. The Gospel of Luke introduces us to old Simeon, who "was waiting for the consolation of Israel." There were many more like Simeon, women and men who were standing on tiptoe, as it were, and straining to embrace the salvation that they were certain was coming.

Greek Culture

Israel remained under Persian control for a little more than a century, until Alexander the Great and his army of Greeks crossed the Dardanelles Straits. Soon Alexander was master of the Middle East, including Palestine. Alexander wasn't out to conquer the world simply through military might. More than anything else, Alexander dreamed of an empire united not merely by conquest, but by a common culture: *Greek* culture.

So, along with his army, Alexander brought scholars, artisans, engineers, and historians. He founded new cities—usually named for himself—and remade old cities in the image of the Greek city-state. All along the route of his conquests, he established colonies of Greek soldiers whose purpose was to intermarry with the local population and tie them more closely to Greece. Over time, the Mediterranean, the Middle East, and Asia were all drawn together into a new level of proximity, united by the core elements of Greek civilization. Scholars refer to this process as *Hellenism*.

Urbanization

The heart of Hellenistic culture was the *polis*, the city-state. More than just a center for commerce or a hub of military power, the city was a place of cultural formation. Public spaces and buildings, both in number and in their design, existed intentionally to invest the residents of the city with a common cultural identity shaped by Greek ideals.

Word Knowledge

Hellenism literally means "to make Greek." In practice, it refers to the way that the Mediterranean world, in the aftermath of Alexander the Great, absorbed or was absorbed by core aspects of Greek ideals.

Polis is usually translated into English as "city" or "city-state." It is the basic unit of Greek political identity. From it we get English words like political and politician.

Among these ideals was the notion of the city as a kind of living organism encompassing all of human experience. In the Greek view, there was the city and there was the wilderness. The Greeks referred to the assembly of the citizens as the *ecclesia*. Far from being simply political in nature, the ecclesia was an expression of the spiritual unity of the city-state. Small wonder, then, that Christians would later use *ecclesia* to refer to their own gatherings, the church. It perfectly expressed the Christian sense of their communities as a kind of alternative polis.

Word Knowledge

The Greek word **ecclesia** originally referred to the popular assembly in Athens where citizens made communal decisions about law and government. It was adopted by Christians as a term for the body of people who gathered together to worship Jesus, and it translates into English as "church."

Religion

Hellenism also sought to universalize religion. It used to be that when one tribe or nation defeated another, the winner effectively said, "My god is bigger, stronger, and better looking than your god. Bow down!" The Greeks took a slightly different tack. They were fine with the whole military conquest thing, but their message was more, "Hey, you worship a god of thunder? So do we. He's probably the same god." By attaching or identifying a local god or goddess to its Greek equivalent (if she's Isis in Egypt, she's Aphrodite in Greece), the Hellenists sought to break down loyalty to merely local beliefs and to get people thinking of themselves as part of one big happy empire. It's hard to hold on to an "us" versus "them" mentality if you can convince everyone that "us" and "them" are pretty much the same.

This flattening of religious differences had the odd effect of making many people hungry for something more, something utterly transcendent and untamed. In the long run, making all gods alike only cheapened them and made them seem less real. The ancient world was a dangerous place. War, drought, and famine were bad enough. Combine them with epidemics and natural disasters like earthquakes and fires, and then add a dash of daily life without antibiotics, disinfectants, or modern hygiene. It's easy to see why many people expressed a feeling of powerlessness and longed to have security and be part of a community of like-minded folks. Ecstatic spiritual experiences were much sought after, and mystery religions became very popular.

> In Hellenistic cities, you could find a shrine to some deity on almost every street corner and in almost every back alley. They were open to anyone and required no commitment. Mystery cults, on the other hand, were very exclusive religious groups. In order to be a part of one, you had to undergo an initiation process. Some modern groups like the Masons preserve elements of this process, though it has lost nearly all of its religious seriousness.

For others, the schools of Greek philosophy offered a pattern for living well, something not available through the regular worship of the gods. *Philosophy* literally means "love of wisdom," and in the ancient world, wisdom was about how to make your way through daily life, making decisions and living in ways that are sound and right. Philosophy wasn't so much about abstract principles (though they certainly play a part) as it was about learning how to live life properly. How many of us got that impression from Philosophy 101 in college?

So city dwellers in the Hellenistic world had a choice of a worship of gods that could easily become about making a transaction ("Give me health and I'll give you my worship"), the ecstatic experience of the mystery cults, or the ethically concerned schools of philosophy. One of the geniuses of early Christianity was its ability to meld the last two in one faith. Christianity would be a religion with both cultic ritual and compassion for the neighbors.

Language

The glue holding all of this together was the widespread use of Greek as the language of diplomacy and trade. Languages naturally embody the assumptions of the culture they come from, and Greek is no different. Certainly, the Hellenistic view was that the first step toward thinking like a Greek was to talk like one. The language became so deeply embedded and so widely used that, even under the Roman Empire, where Latin was the language of the state, Greek remained the preferred tongue for travel, trade, and intellectual dialogue.

As Greek became the language through which ideas were shared, local beliefs and philosophies had to be translated into Greek, and this sometimes changed the meaning of words and images—sometimes drastically. Even the Jews, deeply committed to their Hebrew Scriptures, eventually needed to translate them for the vast numbers of their fellows living throughout the Mediterranean who spoke Greek more fluently than they did the Hebrew and Aramaic languages of Palestine. By the middle of the second century before Christ, the Septuagint began to be widely distributed throughout the *diaspora*, or dispersed Jewish communities. For many *Hellenistic Jews*, it literally was the Bible.

Word Knowledge _____

The Greek word **diaspora** means "dispersion," like a farmer scatters seeds in a field. In terms of Jewish history, it refers generally to all of the Jewish communities located outside of Palestine.

Hellenistic Jews distinguishes Jews native to Palestine from those who were rooted in the diaspora. Hellenistic Jews were far more comfortable with the Greek language, and generally had a better relationship with non-Jews.

Hellenism survived Alexander's untimely death in 323 B.C. His empire did not, breaking up into four sections. The Jews and their homeland came under the control of the Seleucids, along with most of what used to be the Persian Empire. The Seleucids were passionate Hellenists and tried to Hellenize Jewish culture, by persuasion at first and then by force. In one famous incident, the Seleucid Antiochus IV ransacked Jerusalem and sacrificed a pig on the altar in the Temple. Jewish religious law regarded pigs as ritually unclean and unfit for consumption. Antiochus's act was a vile insult and a desecration of the Temple.

In Depth _____

The **Septuagint** is the Greek translation of the Hebrew Scriptures produced in the second century B.C. and widely used by Greek-speaking Jews. The name, odd as it may sound, is Latin for "seventy," often abbreviated LXX (the Latin numeral 70). The title is a reference to the 72 scholars who supposedly produced the original version, a Greek translation of the first five books of the Bible, called the Pentateuch. Other scriptural texts were added over time. The Septuagint was held in great esteem. Jews and, later, Christians considered it as inspired as the original. Both the Jewish historian Josephus and the Christian apostle Paul used the Septuagint in their writings when they quoted from Scripture. In Western Christianity, the Septuagint was finally displaced by the Latin translation called the Vulgate, but Eastern Orthodox Christians, for whom Greek has remained a living language, still use the Septuagint.

The viciousness of Antiochus's behavior sparked a revolt in 167 B.C., led first by a priest named Mattathias and then by his son Judah the Hammer (Judah Maccabeus) and Judah's four brothers. After three years of brilliant fighting, Judah's forces captured Jerusalem and purified the Temple. Conflict continued with the Seleucids, and Judah was eventually killed in battle. His brothers eventually broke the back of Seleucid control and established the Hasmonean dynasty.

Roman Rule

Jewish home rule didn't last very long. Within 60 years, the Hasmoneans had descended into civil war. Both sides appealed for help to the Roman Republic, which was flexing its muscles in the region. The Roman general Pompey was happy to oblige, setting aside the Hasmonean dynasty and taking Israel under Rome's wing as a protectorate.

Rome: The Upside

Life in the Roman Empire had its benefits. For two centuries, from the beginning of the empire under Augustus in 27 B.C. at least until the death of Marcus Aurelius in 180, the *Pax Romana* held sway over the Mediterranean world. It created a bubble of relative calm and stability that allowed travel and trade to flourish.

> **Word Knowledge**
>
> **Pax Romana** is Latin for "peace of Rome" and refers to the period of Roman history between the rise of Augustus Caesar in 27 B.C. and the death of Marcus Aurelius in A.D. 180. It was roughly 200 years of relative peace and predictability in the lives of most of the residents of the Empire.

> **Word to the Wise**
>
> "All right, but apart from the sanitation, the medicine, education, wine, public order, irrigation, roads, a fresh water system, and public health, what have the Romans ever done for us?"—From Monty Python's *Life of Brian*

Empires require armies, and armies need infrastructure. Wherever Roman armies went, sturdy Roman roads followed, with Roman garrisons to patrol them and keep down bandits. Roman navies cruised the Mediterranean in search of pirates. As a consequence, whether by land or by sea, travel in the first century was safer and more common than it would be again until the nineteenth century. As a result, both information and goods flowed freely and, in most cases, quickly. This ability to travel safely and swiftly throughout the Roman Empire and beyond contributed greatly to the church's early growth.

It was possible to become a citizen of Rome and enjoy the benefits that came with that status. Principle among these was the freedom from especially humiliating forms of punishment and the right to appeal the decisions of local government or of regional governors to Rome itself. The ability to exert some level of oversight allowed Rome to extend a relatively fair system of laws throughout the empire. With the laws came the governmental apparatus necessary to dispense them.

Rome: The Downside

All of this stability came at a high price. Empires are built on the use of force, and Rome is the classic example. The Pax Romana was frequently interrupted by border skirmishes, revolts, and wars of conquest. You could be friends with Rome as long as you obeyed, but if you got out of line, you could expect the boot heel of the empire to come down on your throat. At the same time, because empires fix their problems by constantly expanding, Rome was frequently launching military adventures. That was bad news for Rome's neighbors, but even worse news for those living in the empire.

It takes a lot of money to run an empire, so taxes were high, especially out in the provinces. Numbers are hard to come by, but taxes to Rome alone could cost a peasant in Palestine a quarter of his income. On top of that were the regional and local taxes—and it wasn't uncommon for the tax collector to inflate the amount owed and skim money off the top for himself. (They were not the most popular people in the neighborhood.)

From the Source

"Whenever I consider the origin of this war and the necessities of our position, I have a sure confidence that this day, and this union of yours, will be the beginning of freedom to the whole of Britain. To all of us slavery is a thing unknown; there are no lands beyond us, and even the sea is not safe, menaced as we are by a Roman fleet. And thus in war and battle, in which the brave find glory, even the coward will find safety. Former contests, in which, with varying fortune, the Romans were resisted, still left in us a last hope of succor, inasmuch as being the most renowned nation of Britain, dwelling in the very heart of the country, and out of sight of the shores of the conquered, we could keep even our eyes unpolluted by the contagion of slavery. To us who dwell on the uttermost confines of the earth and of freedom, this remote sanctuary of Britain's glory has up to this time been a defense. Now, however, the furthest limits of Britain are thrown open, and the unknown always passes for the marvelous. But there are no tribes beyond us, nothing indeed but waves and rocks, and the yet more terrible Romans, from whose oppression escape is vainly sought by obedience and submission. Robbers of the world, having by their universal plunder exhausted the land, they rifle the deep. If the enemy be rich, they are rapacious; if he be poor, they lust for dominion; neither the east nor the west has been able to satisfy them. Alone among men they covet with equal eagerness poverty and riches. To robbery, slaughter, plunder, they give the lying name of empire; they make a place desolate and call it peace."

—Calgacus, a British leader in the first century, talking to his men about the Roman Empire. From Tacitus's *Agricola*.

Rome's economic prosperity was borne on the backs of slaves, many of them captured during conflicts. A slave, to follow Aristotle's thinking, was nothing more than an object, a tool to be used at will. Masters had near absolute authority over their slaves and could do with them what they willed within certain very broad limits. Many slaves were understandably unhappy with their lot in life, and the Romans were very conscious of the possibility of slave uprisings. We will see that the apostle Paul, whose communities were attractive to slaves, had to navigate some pretty dangerous social waters in his dealings with and about slaves. Attacking slavery would have been an attack on one of the foundation stones of the Roman economy and would have been dealt with accordingly.

> **In Depth**
>
> When a law came before the Senate requiring slaves to wear distinctive clothing so that they could be more readily identified, it was defeated because senators feared what would happen if slaves could see how numerous they really were.

The population of the empire moved more and more into the cities. Overcrowding, dangerously poor hygiene, and scarce food combined with ethnic conflicts and the general frustration that comes from never having what you really want out of life. Public support was a way of life in the cities. Food was distributed by the government. Rome, for example, was almost entirely dependent on the shipments of grain coming in by sea from Egypt. If a grain boat was delayed, riots could and did break out. In Chapter 14, we'll take a much closer look at the cities in the empire and how Christianity took root and grew in them.

The Worship of Rome

By and large, Roman worship was not distinctly different from that of the Greeks. In fact, the Greeks taught the Romans a thing or two. Alexander had adopted the Eastern practice of worshipping the ruler as a god, and those who ruled the fragments of his empire followed in his footsteps. Rome also picked up the notion of a ruler whose soul was somehow marked differently from the rest of us, but elevating a single individual in that way went against the grain of Roman culture. So the emperor became a symbol of the empire itself. As such, beginning with Julius Caesar, but especially with Augustus, divine honors were accorded to the emperor as a way of submitting to the rule of the empire.

Rome wasn't setting out to repeat Alexander's empire of culture. There is no Roman equivalent to Hellenism, unless it is the long-standing legacy of the Roman legal system. And that may tell us something. Rome was a pragmatic empire interested in results more than philosophical debates. Romans worshipped the state, vested in the emperor, and worship of the emperor became part of the glue holding the empire together. You could believe almost anything you wanted, as long as you burned a pinch of incense and called Caesar "Lord and Savior."

In a sense, Caesar was like a flag, something for people to identify with their collective identity and patriotism. Residents of the Roman Empire were no different in that regard. And you don't insult someone's flag unless you're looking for a fight. We'll see later in the book how the Christian confession of Jesus as "Lord and Savior" managed to do exactly that.

The Least You Need to Know

- Jews in Jesus' day were looking for something to make sense of their continued experience of exile.

- Greek language and culture permeated the first century, shaping religion, government, and trade.

- Rome demanded that everyone bend his knee to Caesar.

2

The Carpenter's Son

In This Chapter

- ◆ How do we know what we know about Jesus?
- ◆ What a difference a little water makes
- ◆ There's a new kingdom in town
- ◆ You can't keep a good man down

If you want to get to know early Christianity, there's just no getting around Jesus of Nazareth. Jesus and Christianity are integrally and inextricably linked together. On the other hand, they are not synonymous. While a critical study of the life of Jesus is a worthwhile endeavor, the purpose of this book is to familiarize you with the *movement* that Jesus began: the earliest stages of the religion based on him and his teachings. Accordingly, our swift tour of Jesus' life will focus on the way that he was understood by those who followed him.

Sources for the Life of Jesus

Before we go looking at the life of Jesus, we have to very briefly look at how we know about him. Where does our information about the life and teachings of Jesus come from, how reliable are those sources, and how do we go about interpreting them?

The natural response would be to turn to the New Testament, particularly the four Gospels of Matthew, Mark, Luke, and John. In Chapter 10, we'll go into greater depth about just exactly how we got the New Testament. For right now, we'll assume with the vast majority of scholars that the New Testament still constitutes the best source for sound evidence about the life of Jesus, and it will form the primary foundation for this sketch of his life and teachings.

In addition to the Gospels, however, in recent years some historians have referred to a larger body of writings and evidence not found in the New Testament. These include references to Jesus in some Jewish and Roman historians. There are hints of Jesus in the Jewish Talmud, as well, and a host of *apocryphal* Christian writings such as the Gospel of Thomas and the Gospel of Peter, which are not included in the New Testament but purport to reveal details about Jesus.

Word Knowledge

Apocryphal writings are Jewish and Christian writings that were not included in either the Old or New Testament.

Agrapha are individual sayings of Jesus not found in the New Testament Gospels.

A tremendous amount of speculation has surrounded the so-called Gospel of Thomas ever since it was unearthed in Egypt in 1945. Thomas differs from the New Testament Gospels, in that it is almost entirely a collection of sayings of Jesus. Thomas opens with the line, "These are the sayings that the living Jesus spoke and Didymos Judas Thomas recorded." The sayings are kind of like punch lines without the joke, as they lack any sort of narrative or storyline to give them context. Instead, the sayings are intended to spark insight or enlightenment. The message of Thomas is that the kingdom of God is not something that is coming in the future, but is present right now. Jesus serves not as a savior to be honored or worshipped, but as a teacher to be imitated, whose words make the divine life available. The names Didymos and Thomas (the first Greek, the second Hebrew) both mean "twin," which might mean that the person who hears Jesus is supposed to become his twin, a spiritual equal.

In Depth

The Gospel of Thomas was probably written in Syria, where traditionally the apostle Thomas passed through on his way to India in the first century. The real fight is over how old it is and whether it contains an independent witness to the teachings of Jesus. Some scholars believe that Thomas may predate the New Testament Gospels and thus give us a very different perspective on Jesus. Others date Thomas much later, sometime in the second century, due in large part to evidence that it demonstrates knowledge of many of the New Testament writings. At this point, there's no consensus.

Finally, there are some scattered sayings of Jesus, called *agrapha*, that appear in documents here and there but that do not appear in the canonical Gospels. One that will be immediately recognizable to Christians is Paul's comment in Acts 20:35, "... remembering the words the Lord Jesus himself said: 'It is more blessed to give than to receive.'" Several early Christian writers such as Justin Martyr and Irenaeus (we'll meet these guys in later chapters) also preserve sayings of Jesus that don't appear in the Bible.

Certainly, outside sources can be helpful, but with the exception of the Jewish historian Josephus, non-Christian historians really have little to tell us about Jesus himself other than what the early Christians were saying about him. The agrapha are thought-provoking and, at times, illuminating. Many may be legitimate memories of something that Jesus said. However, without some kind of context or backstory, it is very difficult to determine what they reveal about Jesus that we don't already know.

Last of all, the use of apocryphal writings is fraught with all kinds of difficulties. Most were written in the second century, much later than the New Testament Gospels, and therefore tell us more about their own concerns and beliefs than they do about Jesus. Ultimately, after evaluating all this evidence, most scholars have concluded that the four New Testament Gospels, read critically, are still the best evidence we have for the life of Jesus.

Word to the Wise

"For all practical purposes, then, our early, independent sources for the historical Jesus boil down to the Four Gospels, a few scattered data elsewhere in the NT [New Testament], and Josephus .... It is only natural for scholars—to say nothing of popularizers—to want more, to want other access roads to the historical Jesus. This understandable but not always critical desire is, I think, what has recently led to the high evaluation, in some quarters, of the apocryphal Gospels and the Nag Hammadi codices as sources for the quest. It is a case of the wish being father to the thought."

—John Meier, *A Marginal Jew*

Main Street, Nazareth

First-century Palestine was divided up into smaller regions, three of which concern the story of Jesus. In the south, Judea was the site of Jerusalem, where the Temple was in a constant state of renovation and beautification, a decades-long project begun by Herod the Great. In the north, Galilee was a more rough-and-tumble kind of place.

The area had been recaptured by the Hasmonaeans almost 100 years before Jesus was born, and they had instituted a project of resettlement. That may explain why Jesus' father, Joseph, was from Bethlehem in Judea but now lived in Nazareth.

Palestine in the first century A.D.

All four of the New Testament Gospels tell us that Jesus hailed from the town of Nazareth in Galilee, though Matthew and Luke tell us that he was born in his father's hometown of Bethlehem. Prior to the third century A.D., Nazareth isn't mentioned in any Jewish sources. The Jewish historian Josephus, who lists more than 60 Galilean towns by name, also makes no reference to Nazareth. The modern site of Nazareth seems to pose some difficulties for the Gospel accounts as well. Luke's Gospel describes how the townspeople attempt to throw Jesus off a cliff in response to his teaching, but no suitable cliff exists. For these reasons, many scholars dismiss the notion that Jesus was from Nazareth.

Defenders of the tradition note, however, that Nazareth in the first century was a very small village, with perhaps 200 or 300 families. This could easily have escaped comment in contemporary sources. It is interesting that John's Gospel, which demonstrates a high degree of knowledge about the geography of Palestine during the first century, calls Jesus a native of Nazareth. Last, it is certainly possible that Jesus' Nazareth may not have been located on the traditional site.

The Family

Joseph was engaged to a young woman named Mary. According to Luke's Gospel, Mary was told by an angel that she would conceive and give birth while still a virgin. Matthew's Gospel tells a parallel story focusing on Joseph, who discovers Mary's pregnancy and is tempted to divorce her, only to be stopped by a dream in which a divine messenger reveals to him the identity of Mary's unborn child. Both are told that Mary is carrying the Messiah.

Both Matthew and Luke make it clear that Jesus was born shortly before the death of Herod the Great. It seems that Jesus was perhaps a year or two old when Herod died in 4 B.C. But wait a minute—doesn't the Common Era begin with the birth of Jesus? Well, it was supposed to be that way, but the monk who came up with the whole dating system that we still use got a few things wrong, so it turns out that Jesus was actually born five or six years before we all thought he was. Go figure.

 **In Depth** _____

You're probably used to using B.C. and A.D. to tell the date, right? B.C. means "Before Christ," while A.D. is from the Latin phrase *anno domini*, or "year of our Lord." Because the use of these terms is religiously loaded, scholars have increasingly used the more neutral B.C.E. ("Before Common Era") and C.E. ("Common Era") in their place. The dates are exactly the same—just the references have changed.

The Neighborhood

Jesus grew up in a region that was facing significant economic and political pressure. Shortly after his birth, a Galilean named Judah had launched a tax revolt. The uprising was quickly squelched by the arrival of Roman troops from Syria. They destroyed the city of Sepphoris, about an hour's walk from Nazareth. When Jesus was in his early 20s, however, Herod Antipas began to rebuild Sepphoris on a grand scale. Curiously, the Gospel accounts never mention Jesus ever going to Sepphoris during his later ministry, but odds are good that at some point he had worked as a builder and tradesman in the reconstruction of Sepphoris. His acquaintance with the city might have fueled his later criticisms of the wealthy who occupied the urban areas and sponged off the countryside.

Taxes in Galilee were high. In addition to the Roman taxes, Jews had to pay a tithe (one tenth) of their income to the Temple in Jerusalem. Economic distress managed to drive more than one farmer off his land. These landless peasants flooded the ranks of day laborers who lived almost hand-to-mouth. Many of Jesus' later parables would have great significance for this crowd.

Several factions were active in Palestine during Jesus' lifetime, and it's important for us to be familiar with them. Probably the most visible were the Pharisees. Successors to those Jewish groups that formed to resist the introduction of Hellenism during the reign of the Seleucids, the Pharisees were noted for their commitment to purity in their practice of the religious law. They were masters of the Scriptures, but also believed in a tradition of oral teaching that was given by God to Moses to accompany and help interpret the Scriptures. Of course, the Pharisees are best known today to most people because of their frequent clashes with Jesus in the pages of the New Testament. Strangely enough, Jesus had more in common with the Pharisees than he did any of the other groups, especially the Sadducees.

The Sadducees were the elite Temple priests and their supporters. Their entire religious focus was on the rituals and ceremonies of the Temple. The Sadducees were strict literalists when it came to the Scriptures, rejecting as authoritative anything except the Torah. So, for example, they did not believe in an afterlife because there is no mention of it in the Torah. In contrast to the Pharisees, the Sadducees were comfortable with Hellenistic influences. The power and prerogatives of the Sadducees were largely what Jesus would confront in the final week of his life, and the priests did the most to have him executed. The Sadducees essentially disappeared from Jewish life after the destruction of the Temple in A.D. 70.

The Essenes probably started as a small splinter group of Temple priests who became convinced that the dabbling of the Hasmonaean kings in the activities of the Temple had defiled it. As a consequence, they retreated into the desert to establish a pure community of genuine priests. We do not know if Jesus or anyone else in his circle knew or were influenced by the Essenes, because they are never mentioned by name in the New Testament. Like the Sadducees, the Essenes largely disappeared after A.D. 70. A group of Essenes living in Qumran are generally thought to be responsible for the famous Dead Sea Scrolls.

Finally, there were the revolutionaries. These ultranationalists, sometimes called Zealots, were committed to removing Roman influence and institutions from Palestine by force. They frequently attempted to instigate uprisings, finally succeeding in A.D. 66, an event which led ultimately to the destruction of Jerusalem and the Jewish state in Palestine. It is possible that one or more of Jesus' closest disciples had Zealot connections, but Jesus' message was in clear contrast to what the Zealots wanted to accomplish.

The King

The Herod family and early Christianity go hand in hand. Over three generations, the Herods had an up-close-and-personal view of the beginning of the Christian faith. Here's a helpful breakdown of those members of Herod's household who had the most significance for early Christians.

Herod the Great (74–4 B.C.)   Rome's client-king of Judea, Herod was a brutal fellow who managed to kill, among many others, three of his own sons in order to maintain his hold on the throne. Matthew's Gospel says that, tipped off to the birth of a rival to the throne, Herod had every boy toddler in Bethlehem murdered. Shortly afterward, he died, leaving behind instructions that certain high-ranking prisoners were to be killed so that someone would be mourning in wake of his passing.

Herod Antipas (20 B.C.–A.D. 40)   Ruler of Galilee while Jesus was growing up there, Antipas launched a building boom that managed to deplete the countryside. He is responsible for the death of John the Baptist. Rome exiled him in A.D. 39.

Herod Agrippa I (10 B.C.–A.D. 44)   A grandson of Herod the Great, Agrippa was appointed king of Judea by the Emperor Claudius in 41. In order to cement relations with the Jerusalem authorities, including the high priest's family, he executed the apostle James Zebedee and arrested Peter, who escaped. In 44, he died an extremely painful death, struck down suddenly by a disease.

Herod Agrippa II (27–100 A.D.)   The son of Agrippa I, he presided over a hearing regarding the apostle Paul's arrest in A.D. 59.

John the Baptist

The crucial turning point in the life of Jesus was his *baptism* by John. John was a wilderness preacher who lived around the Jordan River. Sometime in the late '20s A.D., he began calling the Jewish people to repentance, and as a sign of their repentance, he baptized them in the Jordan as a kind of reenactment both of their deliverance from Egypt in the Exodus and of their crossing over into the Promised Land under the leadership of Joshua. In other words, John was re-creating with each person individually two of the most paradigmatic moments in Israel's history.

Word Knowledge

Baptism means to immerse in water. Many religions have such a ritual act.

Jesus came to John to be baptized. All four New Testament Gospels attest to that fact. All four Gospels tell us that John identified Jesus as a Messianic figure. All four also indicate that Jesus experienced something in that event, a calling or summons that set him on the path that led eventually to the cross. Prior to his baptism, there seems to have been nothing about Jesus that made him stand out as a would-be religious leader. Most of his friends and family later seem shocked at his behavior and the things that he says. All evidence points to the moment of baptism as the inaugural event in Jesus' ministry.

The Jesus Project

Following his baptism by John, Jesus briefly worked with him baptizing people in the Jordan River. It's not known how long this stage lasted, but at some point, Herod Antipas arrested John for condemning Herod's marriage to his sister-in-law, Herodias. Herod later had John beheaded. Jesus, on the other hand, seems to have seen John's arrest as a release to begin pursuing his own vision of the kingdom of God.

The Kingdom of God

Mark's Gospel tells us that Jesus came preaching the kingdom of God. "The time has come," Jesus declares. "The kingdom of God is near. *Repent* and believe the good news." Historians and theologians across the spectrum agree that "the kingdom of

God" formed the central point of Jesus' message. But what the kingdom of God might be is a matter of much debate.

> ### Word Knowledge
>
> **Repent** in the New Testament is a translation of the Greek word *metanoia*, which literally means "to change your mind." The emphasis is not on guilt or sorrow, though these may accompany repentance. Instead, the summons to *metanoia* is an invitation to reconsider the direction of your life and thinking. The presumption that one's way of living will change as a consequence of this self-reflection is also implied.

The phrase "kingdom of God" (in Matthew's Gospel, sensitive to Jewish feelings about throwing the name of God around, the equivalent phrase is "kingdom of heaven") is not unique to Jesus, but it is so rarely used either before him (in the Hebrew Scriptures, for example) or after him (in the New Testament writings) that it's clear we're touching on something that was a profound part of Jesus' own sense of God and God's interaction with human beings.

While the language Jesus uses may not be typical, the idea that he was pointing to comes straight out of the Jewish experience with God. Because God operated in history, he was regarded as the Lord over history. Consequently, history is not aimless or random, but has a purpose and a goal. That this divine purpose was meaningful grew out of Israel's understanding of God as the one who saves His people. The Exodus story is hard at work here defining Jewish expectations about who God is and what God will do. God is faithful, the Hebrew prophets assure us, and therefore he will not leave us to the whims of time.

The Jews, then, looked for a divine visitation, what the prophets called the Day of the Lord, when God would rule not just behind the scenes of history, but plainly and openly. The kingdom language of Jesus comes right out of this expectation and, frankly, this longing that God would personally come and take charge. It was this expectation that was so much at odds with the Jews' current situation, and the cause of that anxiety that I talked about in the previous chapter. *When will God return to us? When will God's promises finally be fulfilled?*

A critical result of this *eschatological* view was its demand for a response. Prophecy, at least in the Hebrew Scriptures, isn't primarily about predicting future events so much as it is about revealing the meaning of all events—past, present, and future. Essentially, the Hebrew prophets were asking, "If this is who God is, and if this is what God will do, how ought we then to live?" Their proclamation demanded obedience or rejection. Detached indifference was not an option. This same spirit of demand was present in Jesus' teachings. Repent, he says, because the kingdom of God is here. As we will see, this same call for decision was a core principal of the early Christian preaching.

> ### Word Knowledge
>
> **Eschatology** is one of those big theological words that carries a lot of conceptual weight. It literally means "the study of last things." Generally, it refers to the ultimate purpose or end of all things and particularly the human race. That meaning also tends to include the events that will bring about that ultimate end, so you get a lot of end-of-the-world kind of talk in eschatology.

More to the point, Jesus puts himself at the center of God's purpose and goal for all things. Over and over again, Jesus claims that those who are hearing him are witnessing in his own actions the fulfillment of the expectations of the prophets. In other words, in the mission of Jesus, God has entered into history and is putting an end to the Exile.

Healings and Exorcisms

But how does the kingdom of God come about? What does it look like when it gets here? How will we know when it arrives? Jesus' contemporaries were asking these kinds of questions. Even John the Baptist, now imprisoned, began to wonder if he had tagged the wrong fellow as Messiah. When some of John's followers came to see Jesus with John's concern, Jesus reassured them in an extraordinary manner. He started healing people and exorcising demons from those who were possessed.

Jesus clearly had a reputation as a healer and a wonder worker. One of his followers, the apostle Peter, later described Jesus as a man who "went around doing good and healing all who were under the power of the devil." In this he was not alone. There were many such miracle workers active in Palestine before, during, and after Jesus' day. What seems to have set him apart is that Jesus pointed to these acts of power not as ends in themselves, but as signs pointing to his identity and to the presence of the kingdom of God. He remarked at one point, "But if I drive out demons by the finger of God, then the kingdom of God has come to you." (Luke 11:20)

He also indicated that his actions pointed to his actual enemy. The Jewish Messiah was expected to defeat the enemies of the people of God and deliver them from their bondage. For most Jews in Jesus' day, that meant the Romans. For a handful of others, the enemy was the high priest's family and a corrupt Temple hierarchy. Jesus looked past all of those, addressing his efforts at the spiritual darkness that he saw standing behind all of these destructive forces.

Table Fellowship

Palestine was in the grip of what Marcus Borg has called "the politics of holiness." In an effort to be entirely faithful to Torah, many Jews had begun to accentuate the need to separate themselves from contamination. Right standing with God increasingly became a matter of keeping oneself unstained by actions, by things, and, yes, by people who did not adequately keep Torah. You didn't gather with them, you didn't consort with them, and you most certainly did not eat with them.

So if you were proclaiming a kingdom not about separation but about reconciliation, how would you go about doing that? Well, you could start by having dinner with people. Jesus became famous for eating with "tax collectors and sinners." In doing so, he clashed head-on with a culture obsessed with honor and shame, which considered eating with the disreputable as a blow to one's own standing.

Jesus constantly stepped around the politics of holiness, daring to interact with the unclean, the degenerate, and the disenfranchised. He did so with the presumption not that their uncleanness would taint him, but that his purity would renew them. He frequently did an end-run around the Temple system, offering forgiveness in God's name freely to those who came to him.

By eating with the marginalized, Jesus presented a God who didn't want people to come to the table with hat in hand. To eat at his table was to be his friend, was to be forgiven already. Table fellowship became a moment of the kingdom breaking into the present moment. Neither Temple nor Torah mattered any longer—or, rather, both were superseded by Jesus, a point not lost on those whose power and livelihood were dependent on those centers of Jewish religious life.

Parables

The same was true of the parables. Jesus taught by using stories that had double meanings. Jesus always seemed to be looking for that moment of heart-change, of transformation. His famous Sermon on the Mount in Matthew's Gospel calls for more than external morality. Sure, don't kill, Jesus says, but start by not hating. Yes, don't commit adultery, but start by not lusting. If the heart is clean, then the life will be as well.

That makes parables a perfect medium for Jesus. Parables invite the hearer to reflect, to grapple with their meaning. They invite dialogue. They don't just inform, they reshape the imagination. The parables were designed to elicit that "A-ha" moment, like when your eyes finally adjust and you see one of those 3D pictures for the first time. Again, for Jesus, parables were a place for the kingdom to make its presence known because they required a response from the hearer.

Israel Renewed

A response was exactly what Jesus was after. He wasn't proclaiming a set of universal religious truths, but instead he had set about renewing Israel. Included in that mission was a need to create a new organizing structure. Jesus selected twelve of his closest followers to form the heart of his renewed Israel.

The symbolism of the Twelve is deeply grounded in the Jewish story. The Jewish patriarch Jacob had twelve sons, regarded by the Jews as the founders of the twelve tribes of Israel. Jesus drew on that history in establishing his new Israel, reconstituted and organized around himself rather than the Temple and Torah.

The choosing of the Twelve is one of those details that wouldn't have been invented later, after the Christian community became less Jewish. It gives us a momentary glimpse into the mind and motivations of Jesus. He was clearly concerned that the community that had formed around him in life would continue after his death.

The Passion

Biblical scholars are fond of Martin Kähler's phrase, "To state the matter somewhat provocatively, one could call the Gospels *passion* narratives with extended introductions." What Kähler was alluding to is that, in each of the four New Testament Gospels, the accounts of Jesus' arrest, trial, and execution take up an inordinate amount of the text. No other period of Jesus' life receives such detailed treatment. Clearly, for the Gospel writers, the events leading up to the death of Jesus are of surpassing importance.

Word Knowledge

Passion is one of those words that has layers of meaning. We use it these days to refer to strong feeling or desire. Deep love and affection, sexual attraction, and the like fall into that category. Obviously, that's not what Christians are talking about when they refer to the death of Jesus as his "passion." *Passion* comes from a Latin word that means "suffering," with the sense of being acted upon. Passion involves vulnerability to harm. Words like *passive* and *patience* belong to the same family of words.

That assessment is strengthened when we look at the accounts themselves. Until the final week of Jesus' life, each New Testament Gospel has its own literary style and approach to painting the portrait of Jesus' life and teachings. However, once we get to that final week, what Christians call Holy Week, the differences between the Gospels become much smaller, the correspondences tighter. It looks as if that part of the story, the Passion narrative, solidified very early on in the church's history.

A Week of Conflict

A few days before the Passover feast, Jerusalem was filled with pilgrims from all over the world. Her normal population of 40,000 or so had swelled to nearly half a million. Religious festivals, particularly Jewish religious festivals, were often times for violent outbreaks, and the Romans had learned to show the flag early and try to head off any problems before they started. Entering in the west gate of Jerusalem, the Roman governor Pontius Pilate would have paraded his troops in full Roman splendor, all designed both to insult and to cow the watching crowds.

At the same festival, perhaps even on the same day, another entourage was entering the city from the east. Jesus of Nazareth was being escorted into Jerusalem by a group of his followers. It's not known how many were present or how much of a spectacle they created; it was certainly less impressive than the one the Romans had put on. But the symbolism has weight because the kingdom of God and the empire of man were about to collide head on.

Jesus spent the next few days like a man with a death wish. He antagonized the Temple authorities, debated the Pharisees to a standstill, and seemingly did everything in his power to stir up a hornet's nest. At the end, the event that set everything else in motion and led to his death was his assault on the moneychangers in the Temple.

The family of the former high priest Annas was known to be particularly corrupt. Their behavior contributed to a widespread disregard for the Temple among the lower classes in Palestine, as they were seen as part of the whole oppressive system (remember that Jews paid a tithe, like a tax, to the Temple). The Temple was the residence of God on earth, the holiest place on earth to a Jew. And out in the courtyard, the high priest had a small market where visitors could purchase animals for sacrifice or exchange their currency for the Temple shekel, the only form of currency accepted by the Temple authorities—at an exchange rate presumably favorable to the authorities.

Jesus tossed over the tables where the moneychangers worked, and chased them from the courtyard. When he was confronted by the authorities and asked his reason for doing this, he responded, "It is written," he said to them, "'My house will be called a house of prayer,' but you are making it a den of robbers." Jesus picked up on two of the Hebrew prophets, Jeremiah and Isaiah, both of whom had described God's judgment on the Temple for Israel's failure to live up to its covenant with God.

Some see here a cleansing of the Temple, an attempt to restore the Temple to its original purpose. In the view of many scholars, however, Jesus was acting out a symbolic destruction of the Temple. Essentially, he was saying, "This place is so corrupt that the only way to fix it is to get rid of it." When he was finally arraigned before the court, charges laid against him included threatening to destroy the Temple. If that's what he was trying to communicate, he definitely got the message across.

Gethsemane

His time running out and his enemies looking for an opportunity to get rid of him quietly, Jesus spent one final evening alone with his closest followers. This "last supper" was an opportunity for Jesus to establish a new ritual for his followers to keep. Taking bread and wine, he instructed them to remember his death each time they ate together. His intent was to draw a connection between the Passover event, which occasioned the deliverance of the Israelites from Egypt in the Exodus, and his own impending death.

After the meal, Jesus and his followers walked out of the city and across the valley to the Mount of Olives, where they customarily spent the night at an olive orchard overlooking Jerusalem. Here, in one of the most moving moments of Jesus' life, he moves off by himself to pray. He had come to Jerusalem intent on dying, to give his life as an offering that would pay the price for Israel's sins. Confronted now with the very real prospect of his death, Jesus balked. "He plunged into a sinkhole of dreadful agony,"

Mark's Gospel informs us. The next few hours were spent in wrenching prayer, asking God to "let this cup pass from me." Events were already in motion, however. When the soldiers arrived to arrest Jesus, led by his traitorous disciple Judas, he calmly accepted what was coming.

Word to the Wise

"The scene in Gethsemane, involving Jesus in weakness, fear, and (apparently) an agony of doubt, is hard to comprehend as a later Christian invention. It is entirely comprehensible as biography. It was, after all, failed Messiahs who ended up on crosses; the Jesus we have described throughout must have had to wrestle with the serious possibility that he might be totally deluded."

—N.T. Wright, *Jesus and the Victory of God*

Skull Place

Jesus was dragged away to face members of the Jewish ruling council, the Sanhedrin, and the high priest, Caiaphas. It's hard to tell exactly how the hearings were held. Parts of the description sound like a formal trial, while others sound like he had an informal discussion with the high priest. Either way, the authorities found Jesus guilty of blasphemy, accusing him of threatening to destroy the Temple. A religious accusation wouldn't help them with the governor, Pontius Pilate, so Jesus was handed over to the Romans on the charge that he claimed to be the king of the Jews and was therefore guilty of treason against Rome, a crime punishable by death.

The way the Gospels tell it, Pilate seems reluctant to have Jesus executed, while the Jewish authorities come across as almost bloodthirsty, a portrayal that has had many historians crying foul. Pilate was not at all known for his squeamishness when it came to shedding Jewish blood, they point out, and the accusations of Jewish complicity in the death of Jesus has helped to sustain a 2,000-year legacy of Christian anti-Semitism.

Pilate had already been in trouble with Rome for being too harsh in his conduct toward the Jews, and further complaints were likely to jeopardize his career (and, in fact, they later did). Pilate clearly saw Jesus as no threat to the state, but killing a popular leader during Passover was bound to stir up trouble. Pilate had no love for the Jewish authorities. His reluctance to have Jesus killed stems, it seems, not from any concern about Jesus, but out of political maneuvering and, perhaps, just plain spite.

As for Jewish involvement, the case is more complex. While the Gospel accounts were later used to implicate all Jews in the death of Jesus, that clearly could not be the case. Jesus was Jewish (this will still come as a shock to some folks, but there you go) and so were all of his followers. There were many people, such as Sanhedrin members Nicodemus and Joseph of Arimethea, who were not involved in the plot to get rid of Jesus. The Jewish historian Josephus, in a very controversial section of his *Antiquities of the Jews*, mentions that it was the accusation of "principal men among us" that led to Jesus' crucifixion, but this hardly fixes blame on even the entire population of Jerusalem, let alone the Jewish race as a whole. All evidence points to the Temple authorities, particularly the family of the high priest, in collusion with the Romans as the instigators of Jesus' death.

From the Source

"Now there was about this time Jesus, a wise man, *if it be lawful to call him a man,* for he was a doer of wonderful works, a teacher of such men as receive the truth with pleasure. He drew over to him both many of the Jews, and many of the Gentiles. *He was the Christ,* and when Pilate, at the suggestion of the principal men among us, had condemned him to the cross, those that loved him at the first did not forsake him; *for he appeared to them alive again the third day; as the divine prophets had foretold these and ten thousand other wonderful things concerning him.* And the tribe of Christians so named from him are not extinct at this day."

This passage comes from Josephus's *Antiquities of the Jews*. Several phrases are clearly additions by a later Christian editor (in italics). Below is one possible reconstruction of the passage without the added phrases.

"At this time there appeared Jesus, a wise man. For he was a doer of startling deeds, a teacher of people who receive the truth with pleasure. And he gained a following among many Jews and among many of Gentile origin. And when Pilate, because of an accusation made by the leading men among us, condemned him to the cross, those who had loved him previously did not cease to do so. And up until this very day the tribe of Christians (named after him) had not died out."

Roman crucifixion was bad enough, but, in order to speed up the process, it was frequently preceded by scourging, a vicious beating that often left the victim near death before he ever saw the cross. That helps to explain why Jesus had so much trouble carrying the cross beam to the site of execution, a rocky area outside the walls of Jerusalem with the very unpleasant name Golgotha, or Skull Place.

All the details of Jesus' crucifixion described in the Gospels are true to life. It was a brutal and humiliating way to die, designed to break a person before killing him. Some of the details differ in the various Gospel accounts, but the main outline of events is the same throughout, which gives us some confidence that they are based on eyewitness testimony. John's Gospel, in particular, claims to be the report of someone who was actually there.

Jesus died the same day, a fact that surprised Pilate. John Dominic Crossan alleges that Jesus' body would have been tossed into an open grave reserved for executed criminals and rebels, but since we know of at least one victim of crucifixion who made it into a tomb, there's no serious reason to doubt the Gospel accounts of a Jesus being buried in the same way. N. T. Wright has demonstrated that Jewish expectations of resurrection necessarily involved the transformation of the physical body, so the idea of a purely spiritual resurrection sounds like a contradiction in terms.

 In Depth

> In 1968, bulldozers in Israel unearthed a series of tombs that dated to the time of Jesus. Among the remains archaeologists discovered the skeletal remains of a young man in his mid- to late 20s named Yehohanan, son of Chaggol. What was fascinating about this man's bones is that they showed evidence of crucifixion. In fact, one of the nails used to secure his feet to the cross had bent when it was pounded in, so it and the chunk of wood in which it was stuck were buried with the man.
>
> It was the first time that physical evidence of crucifixion had ever been found, and it confirmed that the victims were frequently nailed rather than merely tied to the cross.

Finally, all of the Gospel accounts agree in portraying the followers of Jesus as utterly demoralized in the wake of Jesus' execution. That certainly makes sense. After all, as Wright correctly points out, only failed Messiahs end up on crosses. By all rights, the Jesus movement should have ended then and there. The fact that it didn't indicates that something extraordinary occurred.

And Then ...

Okay, here's the part where some folks start to get uncomfortable. Three days after his ignominious death, Jesus' followers claimed that they saw him, alive and well. Even more, they claimed that God had not simply resuscitated Jesus, but that he had resurrected him. This meant many things, but one above all else: God had vindicated Jesus.

Part of what makes the resurrection stories difficult to assess from a historical point of view is that Matthew, Luke, and John don't really try to give us a journalistic account of what happened in the aftermath of the crucifixion. That Jesus was suddenly alive and interacting with his followers is their plain assertion, but the scenes that they describe are loaded with theological language. That doesn't mean that they aren't accurate, or that Jesus wasn't really there. It just means that, for the early Christians, there is no separating the fact of the resurrection from the significance of the resurrection. This is a place where event and interpretation are irrecoverably fused.

For our purposes, what is most important is that they believed that Jesus had been raised from the dead. Their belief is what impelled them to share his story with others, often at great personal cost. Something about their experience with Jesus forced his early followers to regard his death not as an embarrassing fact to be covered up, but as the core of their proclamation.

Ultimately, some of the keenest questions about Jesus revolve around his significance as the founder of Christianity. To what degree did Jesus set out to establish a new religious community, no matter what its configuration or pedigree? In other words, did Jesus mean to found a church? How responsible is he for what came after his life, death, and alleged resurrection? How much of later Christian teaching began with him, and how much was a reflection of the implications of his life and death?

Christians hold that Jesus not only meant to establish the faith that claims his name, but that his living presence continues to accompany, teach, and lead those who follow him. Historians, not normally privy to the counsels of divinity, are forced to be much more circumspect in their assessment. From a historical perspective, the connection between Jesus and those who later claim to follow his teachings is more complex, as we will see in the chapters that follow.

The Least You Need to Know

- The New Testament is still our best source of historical information about Jesus.

- Jesus' baptism by John was the crucial turning point of his life.

- The heart of Jesus' message was the kingdom of God.

- Jesus' followers believed that he had come back from the dead as a triumphant Savior.

3

"First to the Jew ..."

In This Chapter

◆ The Spirit is coming!

◆ Peter and the apostles lay a firm foundation

◆ A cadre of Greek-speaking missionaries

◆ Old Camel-Knees takes over

The death of Jesus didn't stop his followers from continuing to teach the kingdom of God as they believed he had shown it to them. In fact, claiming that he had been raised from the dead and, hence, vindicated by God, they began to assert even more vigorously that Jesus had ushered in a spiritual kingdom, not the physical one the Jews thought an earthly Messiah would bring. God's kingdom is not just another empire based on violence and conquest, but is instead a new form of citizenship rooted in trusting Jesus and following his example in both life and death. You can imagine that this didn't sit well with the folks who had conspired to crucify Jesus in the first place: the Temple authorities and the Roman administrators.

The Great Turnaround

So your master has been raised from the dead and ascended to the right hand of God on high. Now what are you gonna do? If you're the disciples of Jesus, you huddle up in a room and try to figure out what just happened.

We Have Seen Him

As I pointed out in the last chapter, the resurrection accounts have the kind of confused, note-comparing, eyewitness flavor that one expects from people who have just participated in an event they can scarcely believe happened. Many of us, for example, watched the events of September 11, 2001, unfold right before our eyes, either because we were there or by television, and yet you may remember how confused and fragmented were most people's perceptions of that day, how long it took to get a clear picture of what had occurred, and how our emotions were on edge in the aftermath.

The followers of Jesus had just been through such an event. The words of a disciple named Cleopas on his way to Emmaus, talking to a stranger whom he doesn't yet realize is the risen Jesus, accurately describe the feeling: "Then our high priests and leaders betrayed him [Jesus], got him sentenced to death, and crucified him. And we had our hopes up that he was the One, the One about to deliver Israel. And it is now the third day since it happened. But now some of our women have completely confused us. Early this morning they were at the tomb and couldn't find his body. They came back with the story that they had seen a vision of angels who said he was alive. Some of our friends went off to the tomb to check and found it empty just as the women said, but they didn't see Jesus." (Luke 24:20–24)

You can almost hear the unspoken final sentence: "So, frankly, we're so emotionally exhausted that all we want to do right now is climb down a hole and pull it in after us."

The situation was particularly dire because Torah made it clear, as the apostle Paul would later point out, that anyone who was hung on a tree was cursed of God. Jesus was, by all rights, a failed Messiah, rejected by circumstances and by God alike. They said, "We had our hopes up that he was the One," but now all that was gone.

And then he shows up. However you might like to explain what occurred to all of these people, undoubtedly they came to believe that they had experienced the renewal of all of their hopes. God doesn't bring people back from the dead when they are cursed, right? Jesus' followers experienced his resurrection not merely as a wonderful miracle or the restoration of a beloved teacher, but as the validation of every aspect of his teaching. And those teachings had redefined the kingdom of God so that it centered not on the Temple, or even the Torah, but entirely on Jesus himself.

Pentecost

Some of the resurrection appearances took place in Galilee, others in Jerusalem. Either could have ended up as the center of Christian activity. The choice of Jerusalem, however it was made, put the followers of Jesus right at the heart of the opposition to their message. It also shifted them away from the agrarian towns and villages that had been Jesus' main arena and toward the urban jungle that was the heart of life in the Roman Empire. It was a fateful decision, as Christianity would not likely have ever developed beyond Galilee had they stayed there.

Fifty days after the Jewish festival of Passover, when Jesus was crucified, was the harvest feast known as *Shavuos* or Pentecost. Pentecost was also the memorial of the giving of the Mosaic Law at Mt. Sinai, an event accompanied by God's presence coming down on the mountain in fire and smoke, along with the sound of a loud horn being blown. Legends would later say that, when God intoned the Ten Commandments from the top of the mountain (just before Charlton Heston went up to get them in writing), God's voice was heard throughout the world in every language. Afterward, God's presence continued to dwell in the midst of Israel, occupying a large tent known as the Tabernacle. This tent was later replaced by the Temple. So you see that Pentecost represented the Torah and the Temple, God's divine word and God's divine presence. By these two signs, Israel was to be recognized as God's chosen people.

Word Knowledge

Shavuos is the Hebrew name for the harvest festival that takes place 50 days after Passover. Christians refer to it as Pentecost. Shavuos is the celebration of the end of the grain harvest, at which time a presentation of bread was made in the Temple, along with a commemoration of the giving of the Mosaic Law at Mt. Sinai following the escape from Egypt.

It shouldn't be hard to figure out where we're going. The Book of Acts describes how the disciples were gathered together in the upper room, supposedly the same room where the Last Supper had taken place, when Pentecost arrived. "Suddenly a sound like the blowing of a violent wind came from heaven and filled the whole house where they were sitting. They saw what seemed to be tongues of fire that separated and came to rest on each of them. All of them were filled with the Holy Spirit and began to speak in other tongues as the Spirit enabled them." (Acts 2:2–4)

What's important to note is that this Pentecost must have been almost immediately understood as a new Sinai. It was a realization that would color every bit of later Christian theologizing. For example, the idea of the Christian community as the living Temple of God finds its origins at least partly in this Pentecostal notion that the divine presence, the Holy Spirit, had come to dwell not in a tent or a temple, but in the followers of Christ as a unit.

Outside a crowd gathered to see what the commotion was, and this occasioned Peter's first sermon. The Book of Acts describes them as coming from just about every nation under the sun. Actually, it seems that they came from every nation where there was a Jewish community in the first century, and that explains a lot. In presenting the message about Jesus to them, Peter and the other disciples were already displaying the outwardly expansionistic character of Christianity.

Because the event carries so much symbolic baggage, some scholars have been suspicious. For example, they ask, how did the author know where all the folks in the audience that day came from? He gives quite a list, but how did he get that information? Did he take a survey after the event? The account in the Book of Acts has the feel of a story created to fulfill some expectation derived from Scripture. Others have pointed out, in Luke's defense, that just because an event carries great symbolic weight doesn't mean that it was made up. To the contrary, they contend, it seems just as likely that early Christians turned to scriptural language to interpret an actual event rather than creating an event to fit their preconceived expectations. Luke may be describing the event in biblical terms precisely because that's the way it was experienced and interpreted by those who were present that day.

   **In Depth**

> The Gospels tell us that Jesus was based out of the seaside town of Capernaum, home to several of his followers, including Peter. In fact, much of Jesus' ministry seems to have taken place in Peter's house. Here Jesus taught and performed miracles like the healing of the paralyzed man who was lowered through the roof (a story recounted in Mark 2:1–12). So it's not surprising that, for centuries, pilgrims making the journey to visit holy sites in Palestine include a stop at Capernaum to visit a church building operating out of the former home of the famous apostle.
>
> In 1968, archaeologists began excavating beneath the ruins of a Byzantine church that had been built in the fifth century. Below it they found the remains of another structure that had once been a private home. The largest room of the house had been converted sometime around the middle of the first century A.D. into a meeting space for Christian worship. Prayers scratched into the room's plaster walls by pilgrims (yes, Christian graffiti!) mention not only Jesus, but also Peter. The structure was expanded in the fourth century, and later an octagonal Byzantine church was built in such a way that it was centered over the original room.
>
> The Franciscans, an order of the Roman Catholic Church, have built a new church over the remains. The structure is elevated in pylons so that the ruins of Peter's house can still be seen.

Peter and the Twelve

In the immediate aftermath of Pentecost, the Book of Acts says that thousands were becoming disciples and that they "devoted themselves to the apostles' teaching and to the fellowship, to the breaking of bread and to prayer." (Acts 2:42) As the followers of Jesus (it's still too early to call them the Christian community) began to figure out their identity, it was the Twelve who were most significant. Let's look at each of them in turn:

Simon Peter   Heads up every list of the Twelve. His name, Peter, is the Greek equivalent of the Aramaic Kephas, both meaning "rock." This was a name Jesus gave him. Originally a Galilean fisherman from Bethsaida, Peter was living in Capernaum when Jesus called him.

Andrew   The brother of Simon Peter. According to the Gospels, he is the one who introduced Peter to Jesus.

James   A son of Zebedee and a Galilean fisherman. James was called with his younger brother, John. Together the two were nicknamed "sons of thunder" by Jesus, probably due to their fierce natures. James was later known as James the Greater, to distinguish him from other men named James.

John   The younger brother of James. John is frequently associated with Peter in the later history of the church. John, James, and Peter seem to have constituted an inner circle of Jesus' followers, accompanying Jesus into certain private moments.

Philip   From Bethsaida, and so part of the Galilean crowd of disciples. John's Gospel has Philip engaging in some dialogue with Jesus.

Bartholomew   Sometimes linked with the Nathaniel mentioned in John's Gospel.

Thomas   His name means "twin." In John's Gospel, he is also called Didymus, which is Greek for "twin." So he was Twin, also known as Twin. Later tradition in Syria identifies his name as Judas, which would make sense of the use of his nickname to distinguish him from the other Judases, particularly Iscariot.

James, son of Alphaeus   Known later as James the Less, to distinguish him from James the son of Zebedee.

Thaddeus   Probably the apostle named Judas in some of the Gospels, and so likely known as Thaddeus in order to distinguish him from Judas Iscariot.

Matthew   A former tax collector and purported author of the Gospel of the same name. He is sometimes identified with Levi son of Alphaeus.

Simon the Canaanite   Sometimes translated Simon the Zealot, which may indicate that he was associated with some of the more militant Jewish groups in Palestine.

Judas Iscariot   Known in all of the Gospels as "the one who betrayed [Jesus]." Iscariot may refer to his hometown or might be a reference to the sicarii, a group of assassins.

The picture of life in the earliest days of Christianity sometimes appears idyllic in the Book of Acts, and we know that it certainly could not have been all one long day at the beach. Since Luke was not himself an eyewitness to the events he records, he was dependent on the memories of those who had been. Whether the selectiveness with which he presents that early community is a result of his own editorial decisions or because of the selective memory of his sources is an open question. Consequently, it's difficult to know exactly how things were evolving at this early stage.

A few things are evident. One is that early Christianity involved instruction. It wasn't simply spiritual experience, though that must have formed part of it. The experience needed to be interpreted, and that's where the apostles came in. Second, early Christians were keeping Jesus' practice of table fellowship. Third, they continued to play some part in the Temple worship common to all Jews. Fourth, they continued to experience opposition from the Temple authorities because of their proclamation of Jesus.

What is truly amazing about this early period, perhaps just the first 5 to 10 years, is how fast Jesus' followers developed a distinctive set of beliefs and practices, most of which displayed an extraordinarily high view of Jesus and what scholars might call an advanced perspective of his significance. When the apostle Paul arrived in Jerusalem, perhaps in A.D. 37, he found a community that already had a unique body of theological convictions and worship practices centered on reflecting upon and interpreting Jesus. As we will see in later chapters, much of what Paul hands on to the churches that he establishes he received from this early tradition. All of that development took place in those first few short years.

Hebrews and Hellenists

As the early church in Jerusalem grew, it immediately drew in both native Palestinian Jews and Greek-speaking or Hellenist Jews. These Hellenists were either Jews born and raised outside of Palestine or Gentile converts to Judaism, known as proselytes, all of whom spoke Greek rather than Aramaic, the day-to-day language of Palestine; or Hebrew, the language of the Scriptures used in the synagogues.

The Seven

There was almost no welfare in the ancient world. At times, governments would distribute food as a way to buy loyalty or to calm the citizenry. Rome, for example, eventually gave away bread and olive oil free to its people. But in most cases, communities were responsible for taking care of their own. The most vulnerable in this society were orphans, the sick, and widows. The early church took responsibility for caring for those unable to care for themselves, particularly the widows.

A controversy arose between the Palestinian and Hellenist wings of the church when it appeared that the Hellenists were frequently overlooked in the daily distribution of food to widows. The apostles suggested that a body of men be created to oversee the food distribution. The seven men who were chosen all had Greek names and were therefore probably all Hellenists. The most prominent member of this group was named Stephen.

More than mere waiters, the Seven were the leaders of the Hellenist community and actively promoted their new faith in Jesus as the Messiah. The Book of Acts focuses specifically on Stephen as he debated in the Synagogue of the Freedmen, a religious gathering place for Hellenists from Cyrene and Alexandria in North Africa and from southern and western Asia Minor (modern-day Turkey). As a result of these debates, Stephen was accused of arguing that Jesus would destroy the Temple in Jerusalem and do away with the Law of Moses. He was seized and forced to offer a defense before the Jewish authorities and the high priest.

Stephen's speech took his inquisitors on a tour of the Pentateuch, the five books of Moses, detailing the history of God's promises to Israel and Israel's continued failure to follow the leaders that God sent, alluding to Joseph and Moses as predecessors of Jesus because they were rejected by their contemporaries. Stephen attacked the Temple itself, implying that with the coming of the Messiah it had become a form of idolatry comparable to Aaron's fashioning of a calf in the wilderness. Finally, possibly realizing that his fate was sealed, Stephen threw the accusation back at those present, charging them with failing to keep the very law they were using to judge him.

 In Depth

> Recently, some scholars have taken exception to the idea that there was such a division between the Hebrew and Hellenist members of the early Christian community. In particular, they question the notion that a rejection of the Temple was a special theological development of the Hellenists, and that the Hellenists were persecuted while the Hebrew followers of Jesus were left alone. They contend, in fact, that the persecution was directed at all of the believers.

Jesus himself had been charged with threatening to destroy the Temple. His followers had escaped his fate so far, perhaps partly by demonstrating continued participation in the Temple rites. Peter and John had healed a man while on their way to the Temple one day, and the early followers of Jesus could be found daily at Solomon's Porch in the Temple complex, asserting their newfound conviction that Jesus was Israel's Messiah. As long as their activities stayed within those boundaries, the Sanhedrin seemed willing to extend a certain tolerance to the disciples of the late Galilean rabbi. Stephen's argument that the Temple had been superseded by Jesus' death and resurrection took the new faith one step too far for the Temple authorities. Enraged, those present dragged Stephen out and stoned him to death. Then they turned their attention to those who agreed with him.

The Book of Acts tells us that the agent of this destruction was a certain Saul of Tarsus. We leave him now "breathing out murderous threats against the Lord's disciples" (Acts 8:1), but don't worry—Saul ended up playing a much bigger role in early Christianity than he had any idea he might. We'll tell that story in the next chapter.

The Scattering

Stephen's death unleashed the forces of repression against the church in Jerusalem. In particular, Saul targeted those Hellenists who agreed with Stephen's disregard for the Temple. He moved violently from house to house, searching for those who called themselves followers of "the Way," arresting and imprisoning them. The apostles, as representatives of the Hebrew wing of the church, seem to have been left alone, but the Hellenists were "scattered throughout the countryside of Judea and Samaria."

As Greek-speaking followers of Jesus moved out of Palestine and back into the wider diaspora community described in Chapter 1, there was already a significant network in place to provide them with both assistance and a base of potential converts. The synagogues offered a place to disseminate the Gospel to an audience already prepared to hear it, with a text of the Scriptures already translated into Greek and, therefore, understandable not only to native Jews, but also to those incapable of reading Hebrew. Still considered by most outsiders to be a sect of Judaism, the early church would benefit from the same legal protections accorded to the Jewish faith.

Most important, Jewish communities in the diaspora had gathered around themselves not only a group of Gentile proselytes, but also a large body of "God-fearers," Gentiles who were attracted to the Jewish faith but who were unwilling to be circumcised and uncomfortable adhering to the various food restrictions of the Mosaic law. It was among these "God-fearers" that the followers of Jesus would find the strongest response. More about them in the next chapter.

As the Hellenists fled for safety, they carried with them their own understanding of Jesus' message. What might have been contained within the bounds of Jerusalem and Judea instead shattered under Saul's hammer blows and was scattered around the Mediterranean coast and into Samaria, Egypt, Syria, and Asia Minor. While in Jerusalem the followers of "the Way" continued to wrestle with their place in Judaism, it was in the cities of the Roman Empire that Christianity was born.

Philip and the Eunuch

Following Stephen's death and the scattering of the Hellenists, the attention of the Book of Acts turns to Philip, another one of the Seven (not to be confused with the Philip who was one of the Twelve). His name is Greek, and he was selected by the Hellenists to be one of their representatives, which implies that he was a member of that wing of the church. Nevertheless, his activity in Samaria and the surrounding regions suggests that he may have been more attached to Palestine than to any of the diaspora communities. It's possible that he was originally from Caesarea Maritima on the coast of northern Palestine because that is where he eventually settled, but that's just speculation.

The heart of Philip's preaching took place in Samaria, the region between Judea and Galilee. It drew a quick response. His preaching was supposedly accompanied by the kinds of miracles attributed to Jesus: demons were cast out and the sick were healed. As a result, many of the Samaritans became followers of Jesus and were baptized. Among those converts was one Simon Magus, or Simon the Magician, whom we'll talk about more in Chapter 8.

The relationship between Jews and Samaritans had long been characterized by hostility. Jews viewed the Samaritans as ethnic and religious half-breeds who had attempted to hinder the rebuilding of the Temple after the Jews returned from Babylonian exile. The Samaritans adhered to the Mosaic Law as the Jews did, but they used a slightly different version of the Pentateuch. More important, as Jesus' encounter with the Samaritan woman in John's Gospel highlighted, the Jews insisted on worshipping God at the Temple in Jerusalem, while the Samaritans maintained a rival temple at Mt. Gerizim in Samaria. The Hasmonaeans destroyed it in 129 B.C.

As a consequence of this history, Jews tended to shy away from contact with Samaritans, a contempt that Jesus criticized in his famous parable of the Good Samaritan. Jesus' travels through the Samaritan region were unusual, as most Jews traveling from Galilee to Judea skirted around the edges of Samaria rather than traveling directly through it. John's Gospel, in particular, stresses Jesus' ministry among the Samaritans, and it may well have been on this foundation that Philip built.

In the wake of his successful mission to Samaria, Philip headed out to the road leading from Jerusalem along the coastal plains down to Gaza. Riding southward along the same road was a pilgrim in a chariot or wagon returning from Jerusalem, where he had been worshipping. The Book of Acts describes him as "an Ethiopian eunuch, a court official of the Candace, queen of the Ethiopians, in charge of her entire treasury."

Philip happened to overhear the eunuch reading (aloud, as all ancient readers did) from the book of the prophet Isaiah. Philip approached and asked if the eunuch understood what he was reading. The two struck up a conversation during which Philip presented Jesus as the Messiah. Under Philip's tutelage, the eunuch became a believer and was baptized. What happened to him after that, nobody knows. Christian tradition ascribes him a role in the eventual conversion of Ethiopia, though it wasn't until the fourth century that we know of Christians moving into that area. We'll talk more about that in Chapter 19. To Luke, writing the Book of Acts, it was another example of the expansion of the kingdom of God outside of the strictly Jewish context and into the wider, non-Jewish world.

 **In Depth**

Candace was a title, not a personal name, for the queen of Ethiopia, who at this time may have been Amanitere. The nation of Ethiopia here refers not to the modern nation-state, but to the kingdom of Meroë, which occupied the Upper Nile region south from Aswan to Khartoum where the Blue and White Nile rivers converge.

As for Philip, he ended up in the city of Azotus, on the coast directly west of Jerusalem. From there he continued preaching up through the coastal cities until he reached Caesarea Maritima, the military and administrative capitol of Palestine, where he remained. Twenty years later, he was still living in that city with his four unmarried daughters, "who had the gift of prophecy."

Meanwhile, the apostles in Jerusalem had heard of the response to Philip's preaching in Samaria. Peter and John were sent to investigate and discovered that, while the new Samaritan believers had been baptized "in the name of the Lord Jesus," they had yet to receive the Holy Spirit. The two apostles set about remedying that, laying hands on the Samaritans and praying for them, whereupon they received some visible or audible experience that confirmed to all present that the Holy Spirit had been poured out on them. This replication of the Pentecost experience certainly went a long way toward mitigating the inherited hostility between Jews and Samaritans, constituting the first major expansion of the Jesus movement outside of its Jewish boundaries.

Herod and the Church

At a time when the church was beginning to enjoy a brief moment of peace and security, a new threat emerged in the form of King Herod Agrippa I, appointed king of Judea by the emperor Claudius. Agrippa needed to maintain positive relations with the various factions in Jerusalem, particularly the Temple authorities represented by the Sadducee party. Sometime shortly after entering Jerusalem as its new king, Agrippa arrested James Zebedee, the brother of John and, with John and Peter, one of the three most important of the Twelve apostles appointed by Jesus himself.

The Book of Acts offers no explanation for why James Zebedee was singled out, nor does it offer any details of a possible trial. He simply writes that Herod Agrippa had "James … killed with the sword," a legal execution. "After he saw that it pleased the Jews," Acts continues, "he proceeded to arrest Peter also."

  In Depth

> James sure got around before his untimely death. Later legends say that he preached the Gospel in Spain prior to his execution. His remains were later transferred back to Spain, where they now reside, it is alleged, at Santiago de Compostela. Every year, tens of thousands of pilgrims from around the world walk the Way of St. James, one of the oldest and most significant pilgrimage routes in Christian history.

In the previous period of persecution under Saul of Tarsus, the apostles had been spared. What had changed that now made them targets? The answer is probably to be found in Peter's conversion of Cornelius and the Jerusalem church's support of that action. To the outside observer, it must have seemed that the followers of Jesus were abandoning the Mosaic Law and were teaching others to do the same. It would come as no surprise, then, that James the Just seems to have been overlooked in this affair. Despite being a prominent leader in the Jerusalem church, James the Just continued to honor the Temple and so would not have been seen as a threat.

Peter was locked away in one of the towers of the Antonia Fortress just north of the Temple in Jerusalem, guarded by four squads of soldiers—16 men! At night, he was shackled to two of his guards to guarantee that he would not escape. Peter was arrested during the Feast of Unleavened Bread, the days leading up to the Passover. Agrippa was waiting until after the Feast to have Peter executed.

The timing could not have been more ominous for the church. Jesus himself had been arrested and executed during the Feast of Unleavened bread perhaps a decade before. Unable to influence events and clearly out of options, the believers gathered in their house churches to pray.

Meanwhile, the night before he was to be executed (and so perhaps the night of Passover), Peter was awakened by a glowing individual who removed his shackles and led him out of his cell. In a trance, Peter followed his rescuer as they passed first one and then two sets of outer guards, and finally past the great iron door at the entrance to the fortress. Left alone in the night air, Peter suddenly came to his senses and ran to one of the house churches. He knocked on the door and waited as a servant girl named Rhoda asked who was at the door. When he responded, Rhoda (whose name means "Rose") was so surprised and elated that, in a truly comic moment, she ran back into the house to summon the gathered believers, leaving Peter still locked out on the street.

While Peter continued knocking on the door, the believers inside displayed incredulity at Rhoda's story, so certain were they that he would be executed in the morning. "You're out of your mind," some of them said. Others suggested that it might be Peter's angel. Finally someone rushed out and let him in. Knowing that he was still in danger, Peter asked that someone inform "James and the brothers" of his escape (by whom he meant James the Just, who we'll meet later in this chapter), and then left "and went to another place." Speculations abound as to Peter's destination; some say he went to Rome, others say Antioch. Antioch probably has the better claim, as we certainly see Peter there a couple of years later when he managed to antagonize Paul (more on that in the next chapter).

In the morning, Agrippa sent for his prisoner, only to find an empty cell and 16 sheepish guards. Enraged, he ordered the guards executed. It is not known how extensively he searched for Peter or if he attempted to harass any other members of the Jerusalem leadership, but shortly afterward he left Jerusalem for Caesarea.

Agrippa did not long outlive James. Perhaps two or three years later, he was in a dispute with the cities of Tyre and Sidon. To soften them up, he stopped shipments of grain to those cities. This seems to have had the desired effect, as they sent a delegation to Agrippa to regain the king's favor. At a festival being held in honor of the emperor Claudius, Agrippa rose at daybreak to speak to the assembled crowd dressed in a silver robe that flashed in the light of the rising sun. At the end of his speech, the delegation from Tyre and Sidon led the crowd in praising Agrippa. "The voice of a god," they shouted, "and not of a mortal!"

Seven years earlier, according to the Jewish historian Josephus, while still imprisoned by Tiberius on the isle of Capri, an owl had landed near Agrippa. One of his fellow prisoners told him that the owl signified good luck, and shortly afterward he was released from prison. The prisoner had warned Agrippa, however, that the next time he saw this owl, he would die five days later.

Standing before the crowd that day, basking in their adulation, Agrippa looked up and saw an owl. At that moment, an enormous pain struck him in his abdomen. Josephus tells us that he lingered for five days and then died. The story in Acts is even more brief, attributing Agrippa's sudden illness to "an angel of the Lord." In either case, Herod Agrippa I died suddenly in A.D. 44, at the age of 54.

James, the Lord's Brother

Regarding the church in Jerusalem, the second-century Christian historian Hegisippus wrote, "Control of the Church passed, together with the apostles, to James the Lord's brother, whom everyone from the Lord's time until our own has named 'the Just,' for there were many Jameses ...."

In terms of leadership and vision within the early Christian community, three names typically stand out. Two of them, Peter and Paul, are often discussed. The third, James, is a mystery even to most Christians. Yet he ranks right up with there with the other two.

Brother or Cousin?

Paul describes James as "the Lord's brother," as do several later Christian writers. This seems like a natural enough description, and isn't it nice that Jesus' kid brother followed him into the family business? Well, that's not quite the way many early Christians saw it.

As belief grew in the perpetual virginity of Mary, the possibility of her having a brood of kids after Jesus was out the window. Some Christian writers began to look for ways to explain how certain people in the Gospels were described as Jesus' brothers and sisters. Everyone believed in the virgin birth, which meant that James and Jesus couldn't be full blood brothers (they didn't have the same father), so there were only a couple of options left. First, some suggested that James was a son of Joseph from a previous marriage, in which case he and Jesus were stepbrothers. Others argued that the term *brother* is meant to be understood loosely as a close relation and really refers to Jesus' cousins. Finally, there were those who asserted that James was also the son of Mary by Joseph, and therefore Jesus' half-brother, but this became increasingly a minority view.

> **From the Source**
>
> "Isn't this the carpenter's son? Isn't his mother's name Mary, and aren't his brothers James, Joseph, Simon, and Judas? Aren't all his sisters with us? Where then did this man get all these things?"
>
> —Matthew 13:55–56 (there is a parallel passage in Mark 6:3)

Whatever James's genetic relationship to Jesus, they must have had a tight bond of some kind. While Jesus' family is portrayed as skeptical of him during his life, they are all present in the upper room at Pentecost. The turnaround could have been quite dramatic. The apocryphal Gospel of the Hebrews, one of those non–New Testament books I talked about in Chapter 2, records a possible post-resurrection appearance by Jesus to James.

From the Source

"And when the Lord had given the linen cloth to the servant of the priest, he went to James and appeared to him. For James had sworn that he would not eat bread from that hour in which he had drunk the cup of the Lord until he should see him risen from among them that sleep. And shortly thereafter the Lord said: Bring a table and bread! And immediately it added: he took the bread, blessed it and brake it and gave it to James the Just and said to him: My brother, eat thy bread, for the Son of man is risen from among them that sleep."

—*Gospel of the Hebrews,* quoted by Jerome

Bishop of Jerusalem

While the Twelve seem to be fully in charge early in the life of the Jerusalem community, there was clearly a shift over time. Whether James had a unique authority early on or not, he certainly did by the time Peter fled Jerusalem around A.D. 43 or 44. It may be too much to describe James, as later Christian writers did, as the bishop of Jerusalem in the way that bishops later were understood, but he did exercise significant authority in the Jewish Christianity of the mid–first century.

Our first inkling that James is more than he seems comes from Peter's comment that someone should send a message to James about his escape from prison and departure from Jerusalem. Five years later, Peter was back for the Council of Jerusalem (which we'll discuss in the following chapter). At that time, it was clear that James had assumed full authority of the church in Jerusalem and, in some sense, the right to decide the issue that caused the Council to convene. What had happened to the Twelve at this point, and where the members of that group had gone, is largely unknown. James's authority had something to do with his relationship with Jesus, since there was an understanding in later Christian writings that the bishopric of Jerusalem stayed within the ranks of Jesus' family members. As a matter of fact, James was later succeeded by Simon, either brother or cousin to Jesus.

Camel-Knees

Hegisippus, writing in the latter half of the second century, describes James like a high priest. He wore only linen and spent his days in prayer in the innermost chambers of the Temple, where only certain people were allowed to go. So often was he on his knees in prayer, Hegisippus recounts, that they were calloused over just like a camel's.

From the Source

"He drank no wine or other intoxicating liquor, nor did he eat flesh; no razor came upon his head; he did not anoint himself with oil, nor make use of the bath. He alone was permitted to enter the Holy Place: for he did not wear any woolen garment, but fine linen only. He alone, I say, was wont to go into the Temple: and he used to be found kneeling on his knees, begging forgiveness for the people so that the skin of his knees became horny like that of a camel's, by reason of his constantly bending the knee in adoration to God, and begging forgiveness for the people."

—Hegisippus

While this may be exaggerated (and then again, it may not), there is a definite nugget of truth to Hegisippus's description. James was intensely aware of the Temple and all that it meant to the Jews of Jerusalem, Christian or otherwise. It's possible that between the various persecutions, missionary outreaches, and James's leadership in Jerusalem, the tenor of Jewish Christianity in Jerusalem was decidedly unfriendly to those who would suggest that the Law of Moses was somehow defunct or that the Temple was meaningless. James presided over a church that had somehow made a certain degree of peace with reverencing both Jesus and the Temple.

For that reason, it was a form of Christianity that would soon come to a dead end, as we'll see in Chapter 5. While James was an important leader of the early church, his brand of Christian faith could not survive the calamity coming to Jerusalem.

End of the Road

After the conversion of Paul, which we'll see in the next chapter, The book of Acts really shifts away from following the larger Christian community and instead focuses on Paul. Jerusalem fades away except as it intersects with Paul's mission. The Jewish mission continued; however, more and more it seems to have become the prerogative of centers like Antioch. Eventually, the center of Jewish Christianity would find its strongest bastion in Asia Minor, far from the hills of Judea. Because the future of Christianity lies there, our story must follow.

The Least You Need to Know

- ◆ Pentecost set the church in motion.

- ◆ The early development of Christianity under the leadership of the Twelve was very swift.

- ◆ Hellenist believers took the Gospel outside of Palestine.

- ◆ James the Just was the leader of the Jerusalem church and those Jewish Christians who held to the Law of Moses.

4

"... and Also to the Gentile"

In␣This Chapter

- ◆ Come and dine, the master calleth …
- ◆ A bad boy sees the light
- ◆ Jesus' followers get a new name
- ◆ Paul gets to Rome the hard way

Jesus was a Jew, his earliest followers were Jewish, and it seems that it was assumed that if you wanted to follow Jesus, you should become a Jew as well. Non-Jews were welcome to come into the fellowship of the followers of Jesus, but they came the usual route: by being circumcised (if they were male) and keeping the Law of Moses.

If things had remained that way, odds are almost certain that the followers of Jesus would never have been anything more than another Jewish sect. But within just a couple of years, attempts were already being made to reach outside the Jewish community. What happened then is the subject of this chapter.

Peter Eats a Ferret

When *Gentiles* began to be attracted to the Christian faith is an impossible question to answer. It must have been very quickly, however. When describing the different people present at Pentecost, the Book of Acts mentions that the Romans who were there included not only Jewish residents of Rome, but also Roman Gentiles who had converted to Judaism. These were called *proselytes*. For all intents and purposes, however, they were living the same Jewish life as those born to Judaism. However, it is quite possible that these Gentile converts to Judaism who were now discovering Jesus were the first bridge to a predominantly Gentile Christian community, in which converts stepped right over the Jewish middleman and came straight to Jesus.

Word Knowledge

Gentile is the word that the Bible uses to describe non-Jews. The Greek word in the New Testament writings is *ethnoi*, meaning "nations, peoples" (it's where we get words like *ethnic* and *ethnicity*). So if it means "nation" why is it translated "Gentile"? Because when the Greek New Testament was translated into Latin, *ethnoi* was translated into the Latin word *gentilis*, which means "belonging to a tribe."

Proselytes are converts to a religious faith. Specifically, this Greek word was a way of referring to foreigners who decided to live in Israel, either living as Jews or abiding by certain basic laws as resident aliens. In the New Testament, proselytes are converts to Judaism.

In the meantime, there was still the Jewish church in Jerusalem to contend with. The mission to Antioch, which we'll describe in just a moment, was not the result of careful planning or forethought, but the result of spontaneous interaction between interested Gentiles and willing Jewish Christians. How would the Jerusalem Christians react to this? Something needed to happen to begin preparing the Jerusalem church and its leadership for what was coming.

Before the author of the Book of Acts even mentions Antioch and what is taking place there, he puts two men and two cultures on a collision course. The first is our old friend Peter, blissfully doing his apostolic work of encouraging and guiding the churches along the coast of Judaea. The other is Cornelius, a Roman centurion stationed in Caesarea Maritima, the provincial capital. Cornelius is described as a man who has come to believe in the Jewish God, but he hasn't become Jewish. He does, however, give money to the poor and pray regularly. One day, the Book of Acts tells us, Cornelius was confronted during his prayers by an angel who instructed him to send three men to retrieve Simon Peter and bring him back to Caesarea so that he could give Cornelius a message.

Peter, at the same time, was lounging around on the roof of his host's house by the sea. He fell into a trance, during which he saw the same vision three times. Each time, a big sheet was lowered from heaven like a giant picnic blanket. As it settled, Peter saw that it was full of all sorts of animals, all of them considered unclean by the Law of Moses and, therefore, unfit for consumption by a Jew. We're talking about critters like rabbits, pigs, owls, bats (someone tell Ozzy Osbourne), and, you guessed it, ferrets. A voice told Peter, "Peter, stand up. Kill and eat." Peter, being a good Jewish boy, demurred, claiming that he had never eaten anything unpure. To that the voice replied, "Don't call unpure what God has called pure." Just then, there was a knock at the door. It was Cornelius's men.

How long it took Peter to realize that the vision wasn't about animals but about people, we don't really know, but by the time he got back to Cornelius's house, he had figured it out. He pointed out to Cornelius that he was not supposed to be there, in a Gentile's house, but that God had shown him something different. Peter began to teach Cornelius and his extended household about Jesus, when suddenly the same thing happened to them that had happened to Peter and his friends at Pentecost. Faced with a situation in which these uncircumcised Gentiles had already received the Spirit of God, Peter saw no reason not to baptize them. Then all hell broke loose.

Peter had with him an entourage of Jewish Christians when he went to Cornelius's house, so news spread pretty quickly that he had not only visited the Gentiles and eaten with them, but had baptized them. The church leadership in Jerusalem summoned Peter back for a chat. He was forced to defend his actions before the assembled elders. Once Peter made his case, they were faced with the same fait accompli that had confronted Peter, and they (rather reluctantly, it seems clear) embraced the notion that God was reaching out to the Gentiles. Most probably saw it as an aberration, a fluke. They were in for a rude awakening.

The critical importance of this moment in the early history of the Christian movement can't be overstressed. For the author of the Book of Acts, probably a Gentile convert named Luke (author of the Gospel of Luke), the rest of the Gentile mission was viewed through the lens of Peter's experience with Cornelius. Not everyone was convinced, and there was a long fight over the status of uncircumcised followers of Jesus, but for the Gentile crowd, the matter had been settled by the intervention of the Holy Spirit.

From Saul to Paul

As strange as it sounds, the impact of the apostle Paul is sometimes overstated. He was not nearly the only person roaming around the Mediterranean in the first century planting Christian communities. He was, however, the only one from whom we have such an extensive body of literature. Paul's letters are the earliest Christian documents in existence. As such, they give us the best glimpse we can get into the emerging Christian community. While others had as much or more impact on the church in its earliest decades, Paul's impact has far outlasted all of the others. It is simply not possible today to imagine Christianity without him.

Saul of Tarsus

Paul's childhood is not recorded, but there's a lot we can deduce from what we do know. He was born a citizen of both Rome and the city of Tarsus in southern Asia Minor. Roman citizenship could be acquired several ways. In Paul's case, he inherited his citizenship from his father. It's possible that his father was captured and made a slave during one of the recent wars. Slaves of Roman households were usually granted citizenship when they were freed by their masters. If that was the case, Paul would have been born with the benefits of citizenship but without the obligations that came with the status of a freedman (check out Chapter 14 for more about what that meant). It's clear that he was given a marvelous education. By the time we meet him, he is fluent in Greek, Aramaic, and Hebrew, and possibly comfortable with Latin as well.

> ### Word to the Wise
>
> "Paul was a city person. The city breathes through his language. Jesus' parables of sowers and weeds, sharecroppers, and mud-roofed cottages call forth smells of manure and earth, and the Aramaic of the Palestinian villages often echoes in the Greek. When Paul constructs a metaphor of olive trees or gardens, on the other hand, the Greek is fluent and evokes schoolroom more than farm; he seems more at home with the clichés of Greek rhetoric, drawn from gymnasium, stadium, or workshop."
> —Wayne Meeks, *The First Urban Christians*

Paul was given two names as a child, one a Jewish name and another a Greek name attached to his citizenship. The Jewish name was Saul, the name of the first king of Israel and, given the state of the times, an intensely patriotic name to give to a son.

Paul's parents were apparently deeply attached to their Jewish roots and to their Jewish homeland. The Greek name, of course, was Paulus (shortened to Paul in English). The young Paul grew up with his feet in both worlds, Jewish and Gentile, but his Jewish heritage ruled him. While perfectly comfortable in the Greco-Roman world, Paul thought like a Jew. When it came time to pursue a course in life, there was little choice. Paul left Tarsus to study in Jerusalem.

I've described in Chapter 2 the various factions in Palestinian life during the early first century. Like his father, Paul became a Pharisee, a party that must have appealed to his zeal for his faith. Not above the use of violence, as we'll see, Paul's intense commitment to God expressed itself not outwardly against the Romans (as it did, say, with the Zealots). Instead, Paul longed for a pure Israel, a nation completely obedient to the will of God as expressed in the Torah. He would later describe himself as "circumcised on the eighth day, of the people of Israel, of the tribe of Benjamin, a Hebrew of Hebrews; in regard to the law, a Pharisee; as for zeal, persecuting the church; as for legalistic righteousness, faultless." This was a man proud of his heritage and determined to protect it.

Our first introduction to Paul, as we saw in the last chapter, was his participation in the mob lynching of Stephen. The Book of Acts describes members of the crowd laying their coats at Paul's feet, indicating that he was somehow complicit in Stephen's death. Once blood had been spilled, it seems that Paul was active everywhere in persecuting the followers of Jesus. In his own words, he later described how "intensely I persecuted the church of God and tried to destroy it." (Galatians 1:13) Once he had raided gatherings in Jerusalem, Paul set his sights on the city of Damascus.

Damascus

We wouldn't have known that Jewish followers of Jesus had made it as far as Damascus if Paul hadn't requested letters of authority to chase them down. Damascus is one of the oldest inhabited cities of which we know, its foundations going back as far as 10,000 B.C. Alexander the Great conquered it, and following his death, the Seleucids in Syria and the Ptolemies in Egypt fought back and forth for control of the city. Eventually, like most of the region, it came under Roman control. They, in turn, gave it to Aretas IV, the king of the Nabataeans (more about him in just a moment).

Sometime around A.D. 36, Saul of Tarsus set out for Damascus and a date with destiny. What might have been going through Paul's mind at the time is something we'd all like to know. What prepared him for the encounter that he claimed to have had on his way to Damascus? Or was he taken completely by surprise? One thing is for certain:

something extraordinary happened to turn the hunter of Jesus' followers into a follower himself.

The Book of Acts gives three different descriptions, all supposedly narrated by Paul, describing his encounter on the road to Damascus. In each case, he mentions that there were others with him, so it wasn't a solitary mission. Also in each case, he describes being blinded by a sudden light "from heaven" and hearing a voice asking, "Saul, Saul, why are you persecuting me?" Paul, terrified, asked in return, "Who are you, Lord?" to which the voice replied, "I am Jesus, whom you are persecuting." In the immediate aftermath of this vision, Paul found that he had gone blind. With the help of his companions, he made his way into Damascus.

In days, Paul was baptized by a Jewish Christian named Ananias. Supposedly, his blindness went away immediately, and he began to tell publicly in the synagogues what had happened to him. He probably sounded like a crazy person. The chronology gets a little confusing here. We know from Paul that he left Damascus for a while, heading out to the Nabataean Kingdom southeast of Judaea. The Nabataean king, Aretus IV (I told you he'd show up again), was having a really bad time with Herod Antipas. Aretus was already pretty unhappy with Herod for ditching Aretus's sister, to whom Herod was married, in order to marry his sister-in-law, Herodian. This was the incident that got John the Baptist beheaded. It also helped to provoke a war. By A.D. 36, the tension was ready to burst. It was a bad time to be a Jewish preacher going around telling everyone about the Jewish Messiah. At some point, Paul made his way back to Damascus, having gotten on Aretus's bad side somehow. In the end, the Christians in town had to lower him over the wall in a basket to get him out of town safely.

Paul set out for Jerusalem, now three years after his amazing change of heart. For obvious reasons, nobody in town wanted to touch him, but a Jewish Christian named Barnabas vouched for him, getting him in to see both James the Just and Simon Peter. In fact, Paul ended up staying with Peter for two weeks. Wouldn't you have liked to be a fly on the wall during those 14 days, to hear what kinds of discussions were going on?

Paul's visit to Jerusalem was cut short by threats from certain unnamed Jews, and the Jerusalem church packed him off to the one place he might be safe, his hometown of Tarsus. He remained there for 11 years, during which time we know nothing of his activities, except that he must have been active doing precisely the kind of evangelistic work that he was to do later. And that's where he was when a familiar face showed up at his front door one day.

 **In Depth**

> Barnabas means "son of encouragement." We don't know his first name, which means that it was probably something pretty common. A Jew originally from Cyprus, Barnabas comes across in the Book of Acts as perhaps the most generous person in the early church, financially and personally. We're introduced to him when he gives a large sum of money to the Christians in Jerusalem. His later involvement with Paul and his championing of the Gentile mission in its early days makes him an intriguing figure. We know that his travels continued after he and Paul split up, but his eventual fate is unknown.

The Gentiles Come In

The growth of Jewish communities in the diaspora was driven mostly by forced relocations and voluntary migrations from Palestine, but it is important to note the large number of Gentiles who were attracted to the Jewish faith as it established itself in the world. The pagan mythologies of the Roman world were losing their appeal for many. Numerous tombstone inscriptions attest to the futility felt by many people in the first century. There was little, if any, link between the character of the gods and the ethical behavior expected of their worshippers, and only a vague and indistinct promise of an afterlife. In contrast, Judaism offered its adherents a strong community that emphasized a sense of personal communion with a single, all-powerful deity whose own character formed the basis of ethical responsibility among his followers.

The difficulty came with the requirements of the Torah. The various food laws were seen as burdensome, especially as they had the inconvenient side effect of making it impossible to dine with fellow Gentiles. Then as now, many a social connection and business arrangement was made over the dinner table, and abiding by Jewish food laws made that difficult. Some found the general stigma of anti-Semitism to be too perilous to dare, preferring the kind of anonymous worship that their status allowed them.

By far the most offensive aspect of Torah, however, was the practice of *circumcision*.

 In Depth

> Women, who did not have to be circumcised as part of their conversion to Judaism, were more willing to make the leap and become Jewish.

 Word Knowledge

> **Circumcision** is the surgical removal of the foreskin from the end of the male genitalia. Yes, it's just about as bad as it sounds. In the Law of Moses, every Jewish boy was supposed to be circumcised on the eighth day after his birth.

To the average male in the Greco-Roman world, circumcision was akin to mutilation. So many of these so-called "God-fearers" found themselves on the fringes of two societies: not fully accepted as Jews because they would not become proselytes, and not entirely acceptable to their Gentile friends and family because they adhered to the Jewish God and his moral and ethical teachings. Less than Jews but more than just curious onlookers, the "God-fearers" were looking for a way to worship the Jewish God without becoming Jewish.

It is unknown precisely who the original missionaries to Antioch were, except that the Book of Acts describes them as diaspora Jews from Cyprus and Cyrene. It is likely that they were members of the same Synagogue of the Freedmen in Jerusalem where Stephen had spoken and in which he was killed. It seems very likely that one of the Seven, Nicholas of Antioch, was involved in this mission. He would have had the connections in the local community, but also as a Gentile convert, he would have had the motivation to begin reaching out across ethnic boundaries.

 In Depth

> Antioch-on-the-Orontes, built by Seleucus I in 300 B.C., was the third-largest city in the Roman world, a center of Hellenistic civilization and home to one of the largest diaspora communities in the empire. A cosmopolitan community, Antioch's population included Greeks, Syrians, Macedonians, and Jews, all thrown together in proximity. Its strategic location near the mouth of the Orontes River and on the road between Asia Minor and Egypt made it a prosperous commercial center.

The disciples of Jesus in Jerusalem and the surrounding region were known simply as "followers of the Way," a reference to their confidence in Jesus as, to quote John's Gospel, "the Way, the Truth, and the Life." As I've mentioned, this meant that, in practice, the followers of Jesus were viewed as another sect within Judaism. In the largely non-Jewish populations of the cities where diaspora Jews lived, however, nobody really bothered to make distinctions between different types of Judaism.

The introduction of Gentiles into the mix, especially Gentiles who had not been circumcised and did not observe the kosher food restrictions of the Law of Moses, really changed things. A new designation was needed to describe these non-Jewish Jews, who claimed to be the heirs of the Jewish covenant but also claimed that Jesus had set them free from the obligations of the Law. Since the difference between regular Jews and these other folks seemed to be Jesus the Christ, they were quickly dubbed (in Latin) *Christiani*, or Christians.

The Missionary Journeys

The Jerusalem church had heard about the doings in Antioch. They sent out trusty old Barnabas to check things out and report back. Barnabas was thrilled with what he found. In fact, he was so excited that he decided he needed some help to continue setting the Christian community in Antioch in order. Guess who he went looking for?

I don't know what Paul must have thought when Barnabas turned up on his front porch sometime around A.D. 41 or 42, but he seems to have accompanied the older man easily enough. Why Barnabas sought out Paul is an even more difficult question. Clearly, he knew where to find the former persecutor of the Christians, and just as clearly, he wanted Paul to be involved in what was happening in Antioch. Maybe their brief contact in Jerusalem a decade earlier had inspired Barnabas with the possibilities of a mission to the Gentiles. Paul had a way of doing that to people.

The Book of Acts says that the pair worked in Antioch for a year together before making a trip to see the church in Jerusalem. They came with money, a gift from the Antioch community to provide relief for a famine that had impacted the Jerusalem Christians. It was clearly an idea that stuck with Paul, and he would try the same thing again years later, though with a much frostier reception. After returning from their trip to Jerusalem, Paul and Barnabas set out on a larger journey, the first of Paul's three great missionary tours through Asia Minor and into Europe.

The Pauline Message

There's no need here to describe in detail Paul's journeys. The Book of Acts gives us at least a glimpse of his itinerary, though it does not exhaustively describe his travels. We learn about several important events only because Paul mentions them incidentally in his letters. Suffice it to say that first with Barnabas and then on his own, Paul launched out from Antioch repeatedly to establish new Christian communities in some of the most important cities of the eastern half of the Roman Empire.

His mission frequently came into conflict with others, both outside and inside the Christian community. Paul often faced resistance from the Jewish communities that he visited. In fact, despite being "apostle to the Gentiles," Paul usually began his work in the synagogues, moving out into the larger city only when his message was rejected. At the same time, Christians from Jerusalem and elsewhere, sharing the message exactly as Paul was, offered conflicting views of the Jesus story. Even within the communities that he founded, Paul was forced to repudiate and attempt to correct some practices and ideas, not always successfully.

In Depth _____

> There are actually some pretty comic moments in Paul's journeys. For example, after being forbidden "by the Spirit" to travel east in the heart of Asia Minor, Paul had a dream in which he saw a Greek man asking Paul to come over and preach his message in Greece. A short trip across the Dardanelles put Paul and his entourage in Greece, and a few days later they found themselves in the city of Philippi. Could Paul have been looking this whole time for that man he saw in his dream? Imagine his surprise when the person he meets next in the Book of Acts is not a man, but a woman. Lydia, a wealthy dealer in purple dyes (very important at the time), became Paul's first patron host in Greece and helped to found the church in Philippi. Dreams have a strange way of coming true.

Key to Paul's version of the Gospel was the conviction that Jesus had radically redefined the notion of the people of God. No longer based in the ethnic identity of the Jewish people, the church encompassed everyone who "called upon the name of the Lord." To that end, even cherished symbols such as circumcision were now moot. What mattered, Paul said, was a circumcision of the heart, not of the body. That involved the power of the Spirit of God taking up residence in the life of the Christian, joining him or her to Jesus in a mystical union that included all other Christians. While not denigrating the Law of Moses, Paul's teaching emptied the Law of continuing purpose in the life of the follower of Jesus. This was not a popular message with many of the Jewish Christians back in Jerusalem, which still constituted the mother church of the Jesus movement.

To Rome in Chains

In the hopes of alleviating some of the concern over his message, Paul returned to Jerusalem sometime around A.D. 57. As before with Barnabas, Paul came bearing a gift for the Jerusalem church. This time it was a collection of money from the various churches that he had founded in Asia Minor and Greece. Paul clearly had high hopes that the Jerusalem church would receive the gift of his congregations as a sign of their acceptance of his ministry. That doesn't seem to have been the reaction that he got.

Instead, Paul headed off to the Temple to engage in a ritual cleansing with a group of Jewish Christians. It was a move to mollify the crowds of Jewish Christians and others who had heard that he was teaching everywhere that Jews should abandon the Law of Moses. The plan went horribly awry when Paul was spotted in Temple and recognized. The rumor began to spread that he had brought a Gentile into the inner Temple courtyard, a big no-no. There was a riot (if you read the Book of Acts, you'll realize that happens a lot around Paul), and Paul ended up spending the next year or two in jail. When it looked like there was no other way out, he used his rights as a Roman citizen to appeal directly to Caesar. The Roman authorities put him on a boat and sent him off to Rome.

Shortly before his arrest, Paul had written the last letter of his that we have to the church that already existed in Rome. He described himself as eager to come and visit them. The intent of his visit was to find a new base of operations for his missionary enterprises. Asia Minor and Greece were getting too crowded, apparently. Paul was eager to carry the Jesus story farther afield. In fact, he had his eye on Spain as the next leg of his journey. Ironically, he did make it to Rome, only in chains. And that's where the Book of Acts leaves him, living in a rented house and teaching his Gospel to whomever would listen.

The Least You Need to Know

- ◆ Peter's encounter with Cornelius was the key moment in the beginning of the Gentile mission.

- ◆ The conversion of Saul of Tarsus to Paul the apostle changed the shape of Christianity for all time.

- ◆ The Gentile mission built on the diaspora Jewish communities.

- ◆ Paul ended up in Rome as a prisoner.

Chapter 5

The Passing of the Apostles

In This Chapter

◆ A tale of two burning cities

◆ Trouble comes in threes

◆ Despite death, Christianity experiences life and growth

◆ The last of the apostles dies

Standing atop the dismantled ruins of the Antonia Fortress by the side of the Temple Mount in Jerusalem, the Roman general and future emperor Titus watched as smoke and flame belched from the holiest of Jewish sanctuaries. The court surrounding the sacrificial altar ran red with the blood of unarmed civilians. Roman legionnaires, bored from a lengthy siege and furious at the city's stubborn resistance, slaughtered 6,000 women, children, and elderly who, sick with famine and terror, had fled to the Temple for safety from the Roman onslaught. It was August 10, A.D. 70. For the second time in its more than 2,000-year history, the City of Peace was crushed by war.

The fall of Jerusalem capped a four-year-long revolt in Palestine. Sixty thousand Roman soldiers were assembled to put down the insurrection. That many soldiers loose in an area as small as Palestine can do a lot of damage in a short amount of time. Some cities, such as Sepphoris, gave up without a fight. Other settlements, among them the Essene community at Qumran where the Dead Sea Scrolls were discovered, were annihilated.

The Beginning of the End

What effect the war had on Christians, particularly the Law-abiding followers of James, is hard to say. Many Christian communities in Palestine were disrupted or destroyed during the war. There are some indications that the leadership of the Jerusalem church and many of its members may have escaped, but this is not certain, and in any event, James was not among them if they did. In the years just prior to the destruction of Jerusalem, Christians had suffered the loss of three of their greatest names.

The Passing of James

James was the first to die. It was A.D. 62, just two years before the beginning of the Jewish revolt and eight years before Titus ended it with such brutality. The Roman governor, Festus, had died, and his replacement, Albinus, had yet to arrive. The new high priest, Ananus, took advantage of the power vacuum to arrest and try James and several others on bogus charges of "transgressing the law." It's much more likely that James was tried and executed because he had spoken out on behalf of poorer Pharisaical Jews (many of them Christians) who were suffering at the hands of the wealthy Sadducees represented by Ananus.

In Depth

> According to Hegesippus, James was buried "on the spot" where he died "by the Sanctuary," a reference to the Temple, "and his headstone is still there by the Sanctuary."

Josephus, who was later an eyewitness to the devastation at Jerusalem, reports that James was sentenced to be stoned to death. He continues, "Those of the inhabitants of the city who were considered the most fair-minded and were strict in the observance of the law were offended at this." Some of them complained to Herod Agrippa, who had appointed Ananus in the first place. Others met Albinus while he was en route to Jerusalem to complain about the high priest's actions. Killing James turned out to be a bad career move for Ananus; barely three months into the job, he was fired.

Those are the bare facts, but what was the impact on the Christian community in Jerusalem and beyond? Certainly, they must have been shocked and dismayed. Evidence suggests that the Jerusalem church didn't even select a successor for James until sometime after his death; perhaps not even until after the fall of Jerusalem.

The long-term consequences of James's death, combined with the later destruction of Jerusalem, were severe, if gradual. When James died, so did the form of Jewish Christianity that was observant of Torah (we talked about what this means back in Chapter 3). Without James to serve as a rallying point around which to regroup, many in the Palestinian Christian community must have moved out and melded with Hellenistic Jewish Christians in the diaspora. Others eventually lost their distinct identity as Christians and became in fact what they often must have appeared to be: just another sect of Judaism. Later Christian writers would refer to them as *Ebionites.*

Word Knowledge

The name **Ebionite** comes from a Hebrew word that means "poor ones." Like many group designations in early Christianity, it originally began as a reference to a characteristic trait rather than a specific sect. In this case, it may derive from the same teaching of Jesus on spiritual poverty that found its way into the Gospels. For example, in the Gospel of Matthew, Jesus says, "Blessed are the poor in spirit ..." (in the Gospel of Luke, he simply says, "Blessed are the poor ..."). Only later, after the fall of Jerusalem, did the term become associated with those Jewish Christians who still observed Torah.

The final nail in the coffin came later, in 132, when Simon bar Kokhba launched a second Jewish revolt against Rome. After three years of brutal fighting, Rome prevailed. The emperor Hadrian then attempted to stamp out Judaism once and for all. Torah observance, including circumcision, was outlawed. Jerusalem was renamed Aeolia Capitolinia and rebuilt as a pagan city with a statue of the god Jupiter erected where the Temple once stood. Jews were forbidden to enter the city. The leadership of the Christian church in Jerusalem, once Jewish Christian, now became Gentile.

The Passing of Peter and Paul

Six years before Jerusalem burned, Rome was devoured by fire. In July A.D. 64, flames broke out in one of the shops by the Circus Maximus. Like most cities at that time, Rome was basically a tinderbox, its shops and apartments built out of wood. The Great Fire of Rome burned for a week, and when it was finally extinguished, 3 of Rome's 14 districts had been turned to ash. Seven more were severely damaged. Barely a third of the city survived intact.

The emperor Nero immediately set about making plans for a new Rome, made in his own image. The people of Rome seem not to have shared his enthusiasm for the project, and ugly rumors started to circulate that perhaps the fire was more than a tragic accident. The Roman historian Tacitus tells us as much when he describes how Nero, in order to divert attention from himself, decided to frame "a class of men, loathed for their vices, whom the crowd styled Christians."

It took a while for people to get over their initial shock and for rumors to start getting around. Like everyone else, the Christian community in Rome certainly would have attempted to regroup in the immediate aftermath of the fire, and if later examples are any indication, they would have tried to assist their neighbors in attempting to put their lives back together. Who knows what brought the Christians to Nero's attention in the first place? Tacitus tells us that at first a small number of Christians were arraigned and interrogated. On the basis of their confession, "vast numbers" of Christians were arrested.

 In Depth

> In A.D. 68, the Roman Senate had had enough of Nero, and while he was absent from Rome, they replaced him. The Praetorian Guard, the emperor's personal military unit and the backbone of his power, was bribed to look the other way. Nero went into hiding and supposedly killed himself with the help of his secretary. But Nero was bigger than life, and many people (especially in the eastern part of the empire) refused to believe that he was actually dead and expected him to return. He was like King Arthur and Elvis rolled up in one. So prevalent was this belief that at least three imposters drew large followings by claiming to be Nero returned.
>
> Many Christian readers of the Revelation interpreted the "number of the beast," 666, as a veiled reference to Nero. By at least the end of the first century, some 30 years after his death, Nero became the template for the Antichrist, an evil counterpart to Jesus who will lead the world into destruction before the Second Coming of Jesus.

The point of Nero's witch hunt was not to find the "perpetrators" so much as it was to shake the suspicions that were focused on him. He needed a significant public event. Translation: the Christians weren't going to die quietly. The emperor devised "the utmost refinements of cruelty" to punish his victims. Tacitus describes Christians being sewn up in animal skins and thrown to ravenous dogs. This and other atrocities were on display at the Circus Maximus as public entertainment. Nero even opened his private gardens to the public, hoisting Christians up onto poles and setting them on fire as makeshift torches to light things up when the sun went down.

Nero's torments were brutal and apparently went on so long that average folks started to turn against the whole spectacle in disgust. The Christians were not beloved, certainly, but everyone could see that Nero was trying too hard. Despite the alleged crimes,

Tacitus writes, "there arose a sentiment of pity, due to the impression that they were being sacrificed not for the welfare of the state, but to the ferocity of a single man."

Somewhere in the midst of this slaughter, it seems, Peter and probably Paul were caught up in Nero's dragnet. What precisely happened to them is hard to say with any certainty. Despite the fact that less than 30 years later the church was rock-solid in its belief that both Peter and Paul died in Rome, as far as we know, there are no eyewitness accounts.

Paul, we know, had been sent to Rome as the result of his legal appeal. The Book of Acts leaves him there, around A.D. 62, having already been in the city for two years in a private residence. We have no idea whether he was tried before Nero or what the outcome of that trial might have been. Some have speculated that Paul was tried and released, and achieved his goal of making it all the way to Spain with the Gospel, only to be rearrested later. This second arrest would have brought him to Rome in time to die in the aftermath of the fire. More than likely, however, he met his end at the conclusion of his first trial sometime around A.D. 63. It is even possible, with some tragic irony, that Paul's trial before Nero is what alerted the emperor to the existence of the Christians in the first place.

Of Peter's death, we know even less. Tradition says that he came to Rome and remained with the Christian community there, though for how long we don't know. Paul's letter to the church in Rome written around A.D. 58, in which he greets more than two dozen people by name, never mentions Peter. It's too much to imagine that Paul would not have included Peter if he had known that he was in Rome, so this may indicate the earliest possible date for Peter to show up in Rome. As with Paul, we cannot know if he was present when Nero rounded up the Christians, but early Christian tradition holds this to be the case.

In Depth

All sorts of legends have grown up around Peter's death. One story has him fleeing from Rome to avoid being arrested by Nero's men when he sees Jesus walking the opposite direction—back into the city! Peter stops him and asks, in Latin, "Quo vadis?" meaning "Lord, where are you going?" Jesus supposedly replied, "I am going to Rome to be crucified." Peter turned around and followed his Lord back into the city, where he was arrested and crucified. Another tale, arguably the most famous, has it that, considering himself unworthy to die as Jesus did, Peter requested that he be crucified upside-down.

While they give us no truly reliable historical information about Peter's death, these stories do shine a light on how significant the fisherman-apostle became to Western Christians in later centuries.

Eastward to India

It's easy to get caught up in focusing entirely on the development of Christianity in Western Europe, but the truth is that, until the rise of Islam in the seventh century, the Christian world's center of gravity was in North Africa and the Middle East. Unfortunately, while Paul had Luke to write the history of his endeavors in the West, the story of those who planted Christianity in the regions where it flourished best will likely remain a mystery. Let's take a look, region by region, at how the Christian faith began making its way into the world throughout the first and into the second century A.D.

We've already seen how western Syria, particularly Antioch, became, for all intents and purposes, the headquarters for the mission to the Gentiles. Strangely, though, at the same time that the church in Antioch was sending out folks like Paul and Barnabas toward the west, we have little record of a mission being launched to the east.

It's not entirely difficult to understand. Eastern Syria was border country, where Rome rubbed up against its eastern neighbor, the Parthian Empire. The Parthians were the latest in a line of successors to what was once the Persian Empire. Parthia included all of modern-day Iran, plus bits and pieces of the surrounding nations, including parts of Syria and Afghanistan and what is now Pakistan. The Romans and the Parthians were not exactly the best of friends. Around 50 B.C., they began a series of conflicts that ended only around 200, when the Romans so battered the Parthian kings that they were overthrown by their own nobles. In 226, the Parthians were replaced by the Sassanids, who turned out to be a much tougher and more determined enemy.

In between Rome and Parthia were a string of small client-states like Osrhoene and Armenia. These little kingdoms served as buffers between the two empires, keeping them from coming into direct conflict. It was worth their while to keep the peace because a tremendous amount of trade moved through the region. In the first century, the ancient Silk Road ran from Antioch in western Syria through Edessa, the capital of Osrhoene, down the Tigris River to Baghdad, where it crossed Persia (Iran) and entered Afghanistan. From there it split into a northern route that ran all the way to Xian in China and a southern route that went to India.

Doubting Thomas

There is some evidence to back up speculation that Christian merchants traveling the Silk Road were the first to take the teachings of Jesus farther east. A more tantalizing possibility is the tradition that the apostle Thomas was responsible for spreading the Christian faith along the Silk Road as far east as India.

Antioch, Edessa, and Nisibis.

The Thomas tradition is difficult to prove historically, but it remains one of the strongest and best-attested hints about what happened to any of the apostles. The sources for this information come almost entirely from the end of the second century and later, but they are based on a much older set of traditions. They reveal a small but vibrant Christian community that populated the region from Edessa through Persia and perhaps as far as the Malabar Coast in southwestern India.

The Book of Acts of Thomas, written right around 200, is a fantastic romance typical of its time, and one of several apocryphal Acts that we know of from about the same period of time. Christian novels are hardly a new invention. There seems to have been quite a hunger for fictional literature starring well-known Christian heroes as well as lesser-known names associated with them (we'll meet Thecla, a supposed disciple of Paul, in Chapter 13).

The Book of Acts of Thomas relate how a recalcitrant Thomas Didymus was sold by Jesus as a slave to an agent of King Gundaphar of India. Thomas traveled to India, where he was commissioned by the king to build a palace for him. Thomas took the money and spent it on the poor. When Gundaphar called him to account, Thomas told the king that he was building him a mansion in heaven, a response that just got Thomas thrown in jail. But the king's brother died that night and saw Gundaphar's mansion in heaven. He came back long enough to tell his brother the good news, and Gundaphar promptly released his prisoner.

Later, Thomas moved on to another location, possibly Madras, where his radical asceticism caused all the highborn women, including the queen, to forswear sex with their husbands. Here's an understatement: this made the husbands, including the king, very unhappy. The king's soldiers hauled Thomas out to a nearby hill and speared him to death.

Okay, some of it sounds pretty crazy, and it's certainly a legendary telling of the tale, complete with Steven Spielberg–esque special effects. But we now know that there was, in fact, a King Gundaphar who lived in northwest India in the first century. He began his reign in A.D. 19 and lived for 40 or 45 years as the dominant ruler of an ethnically and religiously diverse country in a strategic part of the world during a time of political upheaval in the region. In other words, he was a big shot, and certainly a decent target for missionary endeavors.

There is also the testimony of the so-called Thomas Christians on the Malabar Coast, who hold that they were founded by Thomas when he arrived on their shores in A.D. 50 or 51 (right around the time Paul was writing his letter to the Corinthians). In A.D. 40, Roman sailors learned the secret of the monsoon winds that blow eastward toward India for half of the year and westward the other half. Travel time for ships going to

India took about three months, and soon vast ships ranging up to 300 tons were ply-ing the Arabian Sea. Christian missionaries could easily have made their way to the Malabar Coast in the first century.

Pantaenus

Thomas wasn't the only one making his way east. Around 180 or 190, the church in Alexandria sent Pantaenus to India. Pantaenus was born Jewish and studied Greek philosophy in Sicily before converting to Christianity and moving to Alexandria. There he was so highly regarded that he was asked to take over the fledgling cate-chetical school attached to the church. His students included men like Clement and Origen (whom we'll meet in greater detail in Chapter 15).

An Indian delegation visiting Alexandria had become very impressed with Pantaenus and invited him to visit them in India and continue discussions with their Hindu scholars. The church in Alexandria agreed and sent its star teacher away on a sabbati-cal. During his stay, Pantaenus claimed to have met Christians already living in India who possessed a copy of Matthew's Gospel in Hebrew (though, if true, it was likely in Syriac rather than Hebrew).

Back to Edessa

If Christianity made it to India that early, it certainly managed to find its way to eastern Syria. Late in the fourth century, a book called *The Doctrine of Addai* tells the legend of Abgar and Jesus (Eusebius, writing a bit earlier, tells much the same tale in his *Church History*). According to the story, King Abgar of Edessa wrote a letter to Jesus offering him protection and sanctuary, and requesting healing for an illness. Supposedly, Jesus wrote back declining the offer but promising to send one of his disciples to perform the healing. The *Doctrine* says that the apostle Thomas tasked Thaddeus (Addai in Syriac) with the job of healing Abgar. The actual letters written by Abgar and Jesus were supposedly kept in the church at Edessa in the fourth cen-tury, where they were a very popular object for pilgrims to see. There was a first-century King Abgar of Edessa, Abgar the Black, but there's no reason to believe that he actually corresponded with Jesus.

There was, however, another Abgar in the late second century. Abgar VIII began his reign in 177 as a client-king for Rome and ruled for 35 years. It was during that time, in 201, that the Chronicle of Edessa mentions that a devastating flood that hit the city happened to damage part of the church belonging to the Christians. The reference is almost an aside, but it demonstrates that there was an open Christian presence in Edessa in 201 that required a public worship building.

From the Source

"Departing thence, we arrived at Edessa in the Name of Christ our God, and, on our arrival, we straightway repaired to the church and memorial of Saint Thomas. There, according to custom, prayers were made and the other things that were customary in the holy places were done; we read also some things concerning Saint Thomas himself. The church there is very great, very beautiful and of new construction, well worthy to be the house of God, and as there was much that I desired to see, it was necessary for me to make a three days' stay there."

—*The Pilgrimage of Egeria* (late fourth century)

Two different figures mention Abgar VIII in terms that make it appear likely that he was at least nominally a Christian. Bardaisan, one of the most interesting and enigmatic of second-century Christians, was a member of high society in Edessa and might have grown up with the king. Himself a convert to Christianity, Bardaisan mentions that the king had put an end to a popular pagan ritual when he had come to Christian faith. Later, the Christian historian Julius Africanus met Abgar while traveling with the emperor Septimius Severus and refers to him as a holy man. He gives no details, but it seems unlikely that he would refer to a pagan king as holy. Combined, the two pieces of evidence suggest that Edessa, certainly by the late second century, had a visible Christian community and perhaps the support of the king.

Finally, there is the inscription of Abercius. The bishop of Hieropolis in Phrygia (where one of Philip's prophetic daughters was supposedly buried), Abercius had an inscription put on his tomb when he died near the end of the second century. The inscription describes the high point of Abercius's life, his trip to Rome around the middle of the second century. He mentions that, during his return trip, he ended up traveling east as far as Nisibis, a city near Edessa on the far side of the Euphrates River, and that everywhere he found fellow believers.

All this evidence points to a successful, if unorganized, Christian presence in eastern Syria, Persia, and even India no later than the end of the second century. It was an extremely diverse Christian presence, with all manner of different groups represented (as we'll see in Chapter 8). It was also a significant Christian community because it later became a site for education and the jumping-off point for missionary journeys as far east as China.

Egypt

Need to make some easy money? Here's what you do. First, invent a time machine. (Like I said—easy!) Then travel back to Egypt in the mid–first century A.D. and wait around for the first Christians to arrive. Finally, write a book telling everyone in the academic world how Christianity made it to the land of the Pyramids. Okay, maybe there won't be much money in it. But you'll never have to buy your own lunch at a Society for Biblical Literature meeting ever again.

We really don't have any solid idea when Christians first showed up in Egypt. There are traditions that young John Mark, the presumed author of the Gospel of Mark, was the first to establish a church in Egypt, but there's nothing to back that up at this point. In fact, the earliest hard evidence of a Christian presence comes from what appears to be a small fragment of a copy of the Gospel of John, dated to around 125.

 In Depth

> The Rylands Fragment is a triangular piece of a larger page, small enough to fit in the palm of your hand. It was discovered by C. H. Roberts among a larger collection of manuscript pieces that had been found in Egypt. What makes the fragment so significant is that it contains a portion of text from the Gospel of John. In fact, it appears to have been written sometime early in the second century, around 125 (although not all scholars agree). That makes it the oldest piece of any New Testament text ever discovered.

Christians certainly arrived in Egypt before the early second century. Alexandria was the third-largest city in the Roman Empire and had a huge diaspora community that would have been a prime target for early Christian missionaries. The Book of Acts alleges that there were Egyptian Jews (in all likelihood, from Alexandria) present in Jerusalem on the Day of Pentecost, and if so, it seems reasonable to imagine that they would have taken word back home with them.

The Book of Acts also introduces us to another one of those individuals about whom we know just enough to wish we knew more. Apollos is described as a native of Alexandria who "had been instructed in the way of the Lord." Paul's compatriots Priscilla and Aquila noticed Apollos preaching in the synagogue in Ephesus and recruited him. Eventually, Apollos ended up in Corinth, where he became especially popular—so much so that clashes between his followers and Paul's were part of what forced the elder apostle to write his first letter to the Corinthians. The important question, however, is whether Apollos learned about Jesus in Alexandria. If so, that would mean that Christianity had spread to Egypt by at least A.D. 45. But again, we can't be sure.

The Epistle of Barnabas

Alexandria was the intellectual capital of the Roman Empire, a place for experimentation and innovation in philosophy, literature, the arts, and religion. It was inevitable that Christians would make their presence known here at some point early on.

It is almost certain that *The Epistle of Barnabas*, an ancient Christian text, comes from Alexandria sometime during the end of the first century or the beginning of the second. This theological essay—for that's what it really is—gives us a glimpse into the kind of Christianity that may have been knocking around in Egypt during those crucial early decades.

Word Knowledge

An **allegory** is a story in which certain concrete characters or places are representative of something beyond themselves. The story is not intended to be taken literally, but figuratively, as a means of pointing to a deeper truth.

Due in large part to the work of Jewish scholars in Alexandria, above all a fellow named Philo, a system was already in place for reading the Hebrew Scriptures *allegorically*, in the Greek manner. Christians in Alexandria were quick to adopt this system. *The Epistle of Barnabas* provides an example of this kind of thinking.

Barnabas is forceful in its insistence that ethnic Israel has completely missed the boat with regard to God's intentions. By reading the Torah literally rather than "spiritually" (that is, allegorically), they have fallen into idolatry and disobedience. In their place, he claims, Christians have become the new Israel, heir to all the promises of Abraham and God's covenant.

Through his allegorical reading of the Hebrew Scriptures, the author of *Barnabas* is able to find Jesus behind every nook and crevice. For example, the book of Genesis recounts a story about Abraham circumcising himself and the members of his household as a marker of the covenant he has made with God. The number of those who are circumcised is 318, which in Greek is written IHT. As *Barnabas* points out, the *IH* are the first two letters of the name Jesus (a common way of writing his name, as we'll see in Chapter 10), while the *T* resembles the cross. So here, *Barnabas* claims, is Jesus and his cross right in the middle of the story of Abraham's covenant making.

That probably sounds pretty hokey to some of us, and some of the allegorical readings can strain the imagination. Nevertheless, it was the predominant way of reading religious texts in intellectual circles in late antiquity. Christians in Alexandria would excel at the task, and this made them a very congenial community for the birth and growth of gnostic attempts to fuse Greek philosophy, apocalyptic religion, and the Jesus story into a new kind of faith (as we'll see in Chapter 8). Down the road a few centuries, the allegorical style of the Alexandrians would clash with the more literal style of folks in Antioch, a family feud that contributed to the eventual break between the eastern and western parts of the church. But we're getting ahead of ourselves.

Rome and the West

As in Egypt, the name of the person who brought Christianity to Rome is lost to the mists of time. Roman Jews as well as Gentile converts to Judaism were present at Pentecost, so it is possible that some of these folks returned to the Eternal City with more than a slide show and tourist trinkets from their pilgrimage to Jerusalem.

Paul's letter to the Roman Christians details a community that is fairly well rooted in the city. It's also, apparently, divided between Jews and Gentiles. The last part of Paul's letter offers greetings to more than two dozen folks who were part of the Christian community there. What makes it so interesting is that so many of the people that he greets are women and men who have been active in spreading the message of Jesus in other parts of the empire, primarily Palestine, Syria, and Asia Minor, though it may be that Paul is just greeting the folks that he already knows. He mentions several who worked with him personally, for example.

Priscilla and Aquila

The first hints of a Christian presence in Rome are ambiguous. The Roman historian Suetonius, writing some 70 years after the event, mentions in passing that the emperor Claudius expelled the Jews from Rome in A.D. 49. The reason? Apparently, they "constantly made disturbances at the instigation of Chrestus." Now, it has long been assumed that Chrestus is just a garbled form of *Christus* or *Christ*, and that Suetonius has captured a snapshot of the Jewish community at war with itself over Jesus. Modern scholars are less certain about that identification, noting that Chrestus was an actual name, and not an uncommon one, at that. Also, Suetonius correctly identified Christians by name when writing about Nero, so why would he get it wrong elsewhere?

What still makes the story tantalizing is when you read Suetonius's remark next to the Book of Acts when it first introduces Priscilla and Aquila, a married couple who became close friends and co-workers with Paul. The apostle met Priscilla (whom he addresses in one letter by the more intimate diminutive "Prisca") and her husband during his first visit to Corinth, possibly because they were also in the tent-making trade. They had recently arrived in Corinth, we are told, after having been expelled from Rome by Claudius's decree. Here we have two very strong, very energetic Christians who had, until just months before they met Paul, been living in Rome.

So there are two questions to ask. First, were they already Christians when Paul met them? The Book of Acts doesn't give any indication that they were Paul's converts, so let's tentatively say yes, they were already Christians. Second, did they become Christians while living in Rome? If so, that pushes the arrival of Christianity in Rome to at least A.D. 48, and probably much earlier. That doesn't tell us if Suetonius's mysterious Chrestus riots were really a fight over Jesus, but it indicates the possibility.

We know that Priscilla and Aquila did eventually return to Rome. Paul mentions them by name at the end of his letter to the church in Rome. Scholars typically date that letter to anywhere from late A.D. 57 to 59. By this time, Claudius had died and Nero had lifted the ban and allowed the Jews to return to Rome. We can reasonably assume that many Jewish Christians, like Priscilla and Aquila, made their way back home.

I Clement

Things are pretty quiet until very late in the first century. The next thing we hear from Christians in Rome is in the form of a letter. The *First Epistle of Clement* was addressed to the church in Corinth from the church in Rome. Apparently, some folks in Corinth had gotten out of hand and removed all of their leaders from office. The Romans were writing to address the matter and express their concern. Whoever actually wrote the letter never signed it, but tradition ascribes it to a fellow named Clement. It was thought that this was the same Clement mentioned by Paul in his letter to the Romans, but the only reason for thinking that is because of the similarity in names.

The Shepherd of Hermas

Some books just have a way of resonating with their readers. *The Shepherd of Hermas* was so popular in the second century that many Christians regarded it as sacred text. While it was not ultimately recognized as part of the New Testament, it remained a highly regarded book.

The Shepherd relates several visions or dreams given to a guy named Hermas (bet you didn't see that coming), as well as the means to interpret and understand them. The visions that he received were usually visits by angels or divine messengers, the most important of which shows up as a shepherd, hence the title. Hermas was a Christian living in Rome sometime in the first half of the second century. He was a freedman, meaning that at some point he had been a slave but was now his own man. As such, he was a member of one of the lower classes of Roman society.

What troubles Hermas is the question of sin, particularly sins committed after one has become a Christian and been baptized. The church taught that certain sins, the daily kind of struggles that people face, could be forgiven. But the biggies, those huge cover-of-the-supermarket-tabloid kinds of sins like murder and adultery, were very difficult to recover from, if it's possible at all.

The visions actually begin when Hermas is confronted by a vision of his former owner, a woman named Rhoda, who reminds him of a moment when, while holding a towel for her after her bath, he happened to look at her naked body and felt a moment of desire. Ultimately, the answer is yes, forgiveness for such grievous sins is possible after one has been baptized, but only once and only if one repents right away.

Hermas is also frustrated about the relationship between the rich and poor in the Christian community. He describes the mutual obligations that the two groups have for each other. The rich are to supply the poor's need, while the poor are to pray for the rich. As one of the economically less fortunate class, Hermas is particularly sensitive to the place of the poor in the church.

The Cities of Asia

I've saved Asia Minor for last because it is one of the most fruitful areas of Christian growth in the late first and early second century. The region is also important as the field of activity for many of the apostolic figures that we have met, including Paul and Peter, but also one that we haven't gotten to know too well, and that's John. We'll get to him in a minute.

We are familiar now with Paul's journeys through Asia Minor, his activities on the southern coast around his hometown of Tarsus, and his later ministry in Ephesus in western Asia Minor. The Book of Acts tells us in its description of Paul's journey that he was forbidden "by the Spirit" to turn east into the interior of Asia Minor. Instead Paul turned west into Greece, and it seems that he never got around to evangelizing Bithynia, Pontus, or Cappadocia, the regions of northern and eastern Asia Minor (you can find a map of these regions in Chapter 8). Here's where the mystery begins. The first letter of Peter, written sometime in the A.D. 60s, is addressed to "God's elect, strangers in the world, scattered throughout Pontus, Galatia, Cappadocia, Asia, and Bithynia."

Okay, so if Paul didn't go to Pontus, Cappadocia, and Bithynia, who did? You should know the answer by now, so let's all say it together: "We don't know for sure." What we do know is that Asia Minor was home to some of the largest and wealthiest diaspora Jewish communities in the empire. We saw how Paul usually began his evangelistic attempts at synagogues, and how much trouble the Jewish communities could cause him when they resented his message. Those same communities were the target of other missionary efforts as well.

Many of Paul's associates were actively spreading the message, and some of them may have headed east and north. We know from Paul's letter to the Corinthians that there were folks in Corinth who called themselves followers of Peter, and others who were especially set on Apollos, possibly because they had been converted by one or the other. And we also know that Paul frequently mentions in his letters "false apostles." Some of these were probably sent out by James and the church in Jerusalem. Antioch was also a sending church, and Barnabas may have been active in the region as well. What is interesting, if Peter's letter is any indication, is that there are already enough Christians present in these areas to merit a letter.

In the next chapter, we'll meet Pliny the Younger, who in 112 was governor of Bithynia and Pontus. While traveling through the same regions to which Peter addresses his letter, some 60 years after the fact, he discovered strong Christian communities. In the process of his interrogations, he even found people who claimed to have left the Christian faith some 20 years before. So all signs point to a very vibrant Christian community forming in northern Asia Minor well before the end of the first century, and perhaps as early as the A.D. 50s.

The Revelation, written near the end of the first century during Domitian's persecution of the church, indicates that the writer had oversight for communities in the seven cities to which the work is addressed. All seven cities are in the western end of Asia Minor, grouped together in a fairly close chain. Whether these are the only cities that the writer has authority to speak to is unknown.

From the Source

"For in Asia [western Asia Minor] also great lights have fallen asleep, which shall rise again on the day of the Lord's coming, when he shall come with glory from heaven, and shall seek out all the saints. Among these are Philip, one of the twelve apostles, who fell asleep in Hierapolis; and his two aged virgin daughters, and another daughter, who lived in the Holy Spirit and now rests at Ephesus; and, moreover, John, who was both a witness and a teacher, who reclined upon the bosom of the Lord, and, being a priest, wore the sacerdotal plate. He fell asleep at Ephesus. And Polycarp in Smyrna, who was a bishop and martyr; and Thraseas, bishop and martyr from Eumenia, who fell asleep in Smyrna. Why need I mention the bishop and martyr Sagaris who fell asleep in Laodicea, or the blessed Papirius, or Melito, the Eunuch who lived altogether in the Holy Spirit, and who lies in Sardis, awaiting the episcopate from heaven, when he shall rise from the dead?"

—Polycrates, bishop of Ephesus (late second century), quoted in Eusebius's *Church History*

The End of the Beginning

In his letter to the Galatians, Paul describes James the Just, Peter, and John as "pillars" of the church. We've seen what happened to James and Peter, not to mention Paul himself. But what about John? What happened to the last of the apostles?

John is frequently associated with Peter in the New Testament. The two are sent out together by the Jerusalem church, for example, to confirm and receive the Samaritans who began converting to Christianity in response to Philip's preaching. But if the Book of Acts provides us skimpy coverage of Peter or James, it gives us even less of a glimpse into the life of John. Past his involvement with the Jerusalem church and being regarded as a pillar of the community by Paul, nothing more is known for certain.

This is a pity because he might be responsible for one of the most intriguing yet enigmatic texts in the whole New Testament. John's Gospel is certainly named for the younger son of Zebedee, but whether he wrote it is an open question. Like the other three New Testament Gospels, John's Gospel is unsigned and, therefore, anonymous in the strictest sense. But whereas the Synoptic Gospels seem to gather together several traditions and stories from many eyewitnesses, John's Gospel appears to be based entirely on one person's perspective, that of the Beloved Disciple. This seemingly singular vision makes John's Gospel unique.

The external evidence is extraordinarily unified in saying that the author of John's Gospel is John son of Zebedee and one of the Twelve. Many scholars now disagree based on questions about the content of the Gospel. And there is a complication that makes identifying the author a little more difficult. It may very well have been John, just not the same John that we're talking about. You see (wait for it), there may have been more than one John running around Asia Minor.

The confusion comes from a Christian writer named Papias, who wrote a five-volume work sometime around the early to mid–second century. In that series, which no longer exists except for a few brief quotations, Papias mentions meeting people who would tell him about the testimony of the elders who knew Jesus and the apostles. In the process, he mentions first the apostle John and then an "Elder John," as if the two were different men. Eusebius, who preserves this passage for us, himself points out the discrepancy.

Along with the Gospel attributed to John, there are three letters (1, 2, and 3 John) and the ever-popular Apocalypse or The Revelation (not Revelations, thank you very much). Scholars differ not only on who exactly wrote all of these documents, but whether the same person wrote them all.

From the Source

"And again, on any occasion when a person came (in my way) who had been a follower of the Elders, I would inquire about the discourses of the elders—what was said by Andrew, or by Peter, or by Philip, or by Thomas or James, or by John or Matthew or any other of the Lord's disciples, and what Aristion and the Elder John, the disciples of the Lord, say. For I did not think that I could get so much profit from the contents of books as from the utterances of a living and abiding voice."

—Papias of Hierapolis (mid–second century)

Tradition says that John lived until the time of Trajan, who began his reign in A.D. 98. There was a tomb in Ephesus known as John's final resting place. In fact, if Eusebius is right, there were two tombs, both known as John's resting place. The upside of this is that you've got twice the chance that one of them is actually the apostle John. John's passing, whenever and however it occurred, is important less for its immediate impact than for its symbolic value. It represents the end of that generation that could claim to have been an eyewitness to the life and words of Jesus. Although they were never infallible and frequently seem to have been ignored, while they lived they were the living voice of the written texts that had begun to circulate: what Justin Martyr later called "the memoirs of the apostles." When they were gone, all that was left were the words on the page.

The Least You Need to Know

- The burnings of Rome and Jerusalem marked significant turning points for the early church.

- The church lost three of its most vocal and significant leaders almost at once.

- The Christian faith spread in every direction, including many places where no record exists.

- The death of John (both of them?) marked the end of the generation of eye-witnesses to Jesus.

Part 2

Conflict and Crisis

No family is without its difficulties. There are always external pressures and internal squabbles. Both increased in intensity and frequency as the Christian movement edged its way into the second century. The consequence, at the end of the century, was a Christianity that was tighter, more disciplined, and, in many ways, more regimented.

This part focuses on the external pressures and internal arguments that shaped the emerging Christian community, and the ways that Christianity developed in response to those conditions. On one hand, Christians were forced to answer the hostile perceptions and attacks of those outside of their religion, and we'll see the extremes to which they went to do so. At the same time, serious debates were taking place over what constituted core Christian teachings.

Chapter 6

Haters of Humanity

In This Chapter

◆ Hey, there's a psycho living next door!

◆ A reasoned plea for Christians to convert to paganism

◆ Christians get the late-night comedy treatment

◆ Here comes da judge

◆ Be nice to them and they'll be nice to you

So far, we've been pretty exclusively interested in how Christians saw themselves and told their own story. But as it began to leave behind its exclusively Jewish character and attract more Greeks and Romans, it was inevitable that the new faith would attract the attention of the larger public. Their reactions to Christianity would do much to shape how this new religion developed over time.

Contempt

In his account of Nero's persecution of the Christians in Rome in A.D. 64, the Roman historian Tacitus mentions that Christians were arrested "not so much on the count of arson as for hatred of the human race." Christians are repeatedly described in the earliest sources as members of a "superstition," a term used to describe religious groups that were considered dangerous to society. Suetonius, a contemporary of Tacitus who also tags Christianity as a superstition, groups Christians into the same class of people as charioteers and (gulp!) mimes, two of the lowest forms of life in the Roman social world. Both men wrote their historical works in the earliest years of the second century (Tacitus around 110 and Suetonius perhaps a decade later), just as Christianity was beginning to capitalize on a period of quiet growth. They were far from the last to hold Christians in contempt.

You have to realize how small a group the early Christians were. Most historians put the number of Christians at the beginning of the second century at around 50,000 (although sociologist Rodney Stark has suggested less than 10,000). That doesn't sound too shabby until you realize that the population of the Roman Empire was somewhere between 50 million and 60 million people. Using the most generous estimates, Christians still numbered fewer than 1 out of every 1,000 people. Even when you take into account the fact that this relative handful of people was clustered in cities like Rome, Antioch, and Ephesus, giving them a higher profile than they might have otherwise had, most people in the empire had never heard of Christians, and even fewer actually had experience with them. In such an atmosphere, it is easy to see how rumors and innuendo would have spread quickly. Common wisdom about Christians was based more on tabloid-type stories than on any hard evidence or experience.

From later writers, we get a sense of what kind of stories were told about Christians. Christians tended to withdraw from involvement in public life, referred to each other as "brother" and "sister," and ate the flesh and blood of their God at their "love feasts." These facts were spun off into all sorts of stories. Two accusations, in particular, seem to have been widespread. First, Christian gatherings were thought to be wild sexual orgies. Second, it was suggested that human flesh was eaten as part of the ritual meal.

From the Source

"A young baby is covered over with flour, the object being to deceive the unwary. It is then served before the person to be admitted into the rites. The recruit is urged to inflict blows upon it—they appear to be harmless because of the covering of flour. Thus the baby is killed with wounds that remain unseen and concealed. It is the blood of this infant—I shudder to mention it—it is this blood that they lick with thirsty lips; these are the limbs they distribute eagerly; this is the victim by which they seal their covenant ...."

—Marcus Cornelius Fronto, second-century tutor to emperor Marcus Aurelius, quoted by the third-century apologist Minucius Felix

It's easy to simply dismiss these rumors with a roll of the eyes. Yet there *were* some strange versions of Christianity running around during this period. Clement of Alexandria (whom we'll meet in Chapter 15) mentions a group of gnostic Christians called Carpocratians who turned the worship gathering into a sexual free-for-all. Justin Martyr (he shows up in the next chapter) was quick to try to distinguish his own branch of Christianity from groups that engaged in these practices. With such small numbers, it would be easy for one or two groups of Christians to taint the reputation of all the rest. The vast majority in the Roman Empire would have had no way to distinguish between one kind of Christian and another.

Also, it's hard to know whether Clement or Justin was familiar with these groups themselves or whether they were simply reacting to rumors. Stories about sexual perversity and cannibalism are stock rumors that seem to be applied to just about any small or secret religious group in the ancient world. Christians themselves would later say similar things about groups with whom they disagreed—even more so after Christianity became a legal religion. Similar stories were bandied around about Jews during the Middle Ages.

Whether there was any truth to these rumors or not, the fact remains that these kinds of stories were circulating in the social atmosphere just as the numbers and spread of Christians began to grow. That they colored the perceptions of non-Christians is undoubted. How would you like to suspect you had an adulterous cannibal as a next-door neighbor? Since so much of the early persecution of Christians was driven by local sentiments, rumors and suspicion played a significant role in the experience of Christians in the second century.

 **In Depth**

If you think that stories of sexual perversity and human sacrifice are things of the past, consider the kinds of stories that frequently appear in the American media about secret Satanic cults and the allegedly bizarre practices of Wiccans.

Celsus

The first truly significant critique of the Christian faith from a pagan perspective was written, probably in 177, by a fellow named Celsus. We don't know very much about him. He was probably a resident of either Rome or (more likely) Alexandria. Definitely an educated fellow, Celsus seems to have been acquainted with at least some Christian writings, including at least some of the Gospels. He had some firsthand experience with Christians and speaks from an abundance of knowledge and study.

Celsus authored a book called *The True Word*. It doesn't seem to have made a very big impact when it was published, and it no longer exists. However, about 80 years after he first wrote it, Celsus's critique was answered by the Alexandrian teacher Origen (who takes up a good chunk of Chapter 15, for good reason), who devoted a massive eight-volume book to refuting Celsus's arguments. The great thing is that Origen quotes verbatim from Celsus so often, at such length, and with such an ordered approach that it is possible to reconstruct not only the charges that Celsus makes, but in most cases, even his exact words. As a result, scholars believe that they can reconstruct at least 75 percent of the original text of *The True Word*, and it's possible to guess at more.

Celsus divides his book in two. In the first half, he presents arguments against Christianity as if he were a Jew. For Celsus, as for most of his non-Christian contemporaries, whatever was ancient was true. Those religions that were rooted in the past had a claim to authority that new and innovative faiths did not. Celsus understands that Christians claimed to be the true heirs to the legacy of Judaism. This is a preposterous claim, he argues, because Jewish communities still exist—in fact, they thrive—yet Christians have separated themselves from the Jews. By adopting a Jewish stance in the opening half of his book, Celsus was not only debating specific points of belief, but he was also shaming Christians with the notion that they were abandoning the very heritage that they claimed to embody.

The Jewish arguments against Jesus included a ridiculing of the notion of the virgin birth. Celsus, surely echoing what he had heard from some Jewish source, claims that Mary was impregnated by a Roman soldier named Pantera. She was thrown out by her husband and headed to Egypt, where she raised her son. Here Celsus says that Jesus, living in Egypt, learned how to do magic and became a sorcerer, which was the source of the miracles attributed to him. Magic was outlawed in the Roman Empire, so this was a real indictment of Jesus and of Christians by association. There is some indication that charges of using magic were sometimes leveled against Christians, so Celsus isn't just making this up.

In addition to being a low-rent wizard, Jesus wasn't even all that successful. His own countryman killed him off, and then his handful of followers concocted this story about resurrection that isn't any different from other legends about gods coming back from the dead. In fact, the story of Jesus' resurrection isn't anywhere near as exciting or awe inspiring as those other myths, so why bother with him?

It's when Celsus shifts away from the Jewish persona and begins to attack Christianity from his own pagan philosophical point of view that he really gets revved up. Not a pure philosopher by any means, Celsus seems to be more eclectic. He has imbibed deeply of the common Platonism that characterized the general mood of the second century, but beyond that he doesn't have a precise philosophical viewpoint. He's more pragmatic, interested in defending society as it exists against Jews and Christians generally.

From the Source

"Everywhere they speak in their writings of the tree of life and of resurrection of the flesh by the tree—I imagine because their master was nailed to a cross and was a carpenter by trade. So that if he had happened to be thrown off a cliff, or pushed into a pit, or suffocated by strangling, or if he had been a cobbler or stonemason or blacksmith, there would have been a cliff of life above the heavens, or a pit of resurrection, or a rope of immortality, or a blessed stone, or an iron of love, or a holy hide of leather. Wouldn't an old woman who sings a story to lull a little child to sleep have been ashamed to whisper such tales as these?"

—Celsus, *The True Word* (quoted by Origen, *Against Celsus*)

The Jews and the Christians are really just derivative anyway; there isn't anything unique in what they say, he claims. Everything worthwhile they could find in almost any of the wisdom of the ancients. The Jews split off from the Egyptians, and now the Christians are splitting off from the Jews. None of them have any original ideas about God or the universe.

The Christians themselves can't seem to stick together. There is a main body—the "great Church," as Celsus puts it—and then there are all of these various splinter groups like the gnostics and the Marcionites (we'll see them in Chapter 8). In any event, the Christian message is so ludicrous that it really appeals only to the ignorant masses. Every other group in the world has standards for its members, but the Christians actually *brag* about how stupid and sinful are the folks to whom they appeal.

At last, after demonstrating to his own satisfaction how every Christian teaching is really just a perversion, offshoot, or misunderstanding of a superior philosophical teaching, Celsus makes his final pitch. He appeals to Christians to put aside their newfangled religion, which does nothing but cause them to withdraw from public life and isolate themselves from the greatness of Greco-Roman society. This may be, ultimately, the core of what bothers Celsus about Christianity. To his way of thinking, the empire is in a difficult time. It needs all the help it can get from its citizens, but instead of participating in public life the way they should, the Christians are off constructing some kind of silly counterculture.

Unlike so many others who attacked Christianity, Celsus really does try to avoid taking too many cheap shots. Celsus was a reasonable man. While he certainly looked down on the Christians, he also attempted to persuade them to see the foolishness of their ways and return to the company of decent society.

Lucian of Samosata

Lucian of Samosata was cut from an entirely different mold. Sharp witted and droll, Lucian's satire was as biting as Celsus's arguments. If Celsus berated Christians for their faith, Lucian simply held them up to ridicule and scorn.

Born in eastern Turkey on the banks of the northern end of the Euphrates River, Lucian was originally apprenticed to be a sculptor. Instead, he left to study rhetoric, a field for which he had a particular gift. Lucian traveled broadly, looking for opportunities to exercise his considerable comedic talent. The fact that so many of his essays, speeches, and writings still exist demonstrates how popular he became.

Lucian also happened to preserve one of the earliest references to Christianity by a pagan author. It comes from his work *The Passing of Peregrinus*, written shortly after 165. Peregrinus Proteus came from a lousy family. He and his father fought constantly, until one day dear old dad died. The fact that Peregrinus's hands were around his neck at the time may have had something to do with it. Peregrinus felt it wise to get out of town immediately. It was the start of a beautiful career. After careening around the empire for a while, he ended up in Palestine, where he connected with a Jewish Christian community. They so thoroughly embraced Peregrinus that he became a leader in the church, authoring commentaries and eventually getting arrested for his faith. Christians swarmed to support him in his imprisonment, and Peregrinus found himself flush with both goodwill and money.

It was all too good to last. Eventually, Peregrinus managed to run afoul of the Christians' strict dietary restrictions, perhaps by eating food offered to idols. Whether as a result of his expulsion from the community or because of a longstanding weariness with Christians, Peregrinus took up the Cynic philosophy, something that had been of interest to him prior to his Christian conversion. Eventually, he established a school in Athens. After a first blush of success, things began to unravel for him. Desperate to recapture his celebrity, he announced that he would burn himself to death on a pyre at the conclusion of the Olympic Games in 165, and that's exactly what he did. He definitely went out in a blaze of glory.

Lucian seems to have been present at the event and clearly couldn't wait to give his take on the whole affair. Lucian's focus is on Peregrinus, whom he saw as a grand-standing egomaniac desperate for the adulation of the crowd. What's important for our purposes, however, is that Lucian took the opportunity to paint a picture of Christians as naïve simpletons easily duped by a con artist, and this portrayal seems to have found a receptive audience. As the second-century equivalent of a modern comedian, Lucian spoke for the regular guy on the street, people who had neither the education nor the inclination to assess Christianity philosophically. The Christians were strange. They believed weird things, and that made them objects of derision. Christians were under threat legally and assailed intellectually, but the greatest challenge must have come from people like Lucian, who simply dismissed Christianity with a roll of the eyes.

From the Source

"You see, these misguided creatures start with the general conviction that they are immortal for all time, which explains the contempt of death and voluntary self-devotion which are so common among them; and then it was impressed on them by their original lawgiver that they are all brothers, from the moment that they are converted, and deny the gods of Greece, and worship that crucified sage, and live after his laws. All this they take quite on trust, with the result that they despise all worldly goods alike, regarding them merely as common property. Now an adroit, unscrupulous fellow, who has seen the world, has only to get among these simple souls, and his fortune is pretty soon made; he plays with them."

—Lucian of Samosata, *The Death of Peregrinus*

Coercion

Celsus and Lucian express the attitude of the elites of Roman society toward early Christianity. Their contempt for the Christian faith could make life difficult for the young church, but it wasn't inherently fatal. Government officials, on the other hand, were empowered to act on society's rejection of the early Christians. Christianity was classified as an illegal religion in the Roman Empire, a status perhaps stemming from Nero's assault on Christians in Rome. There is additional evidence of a period of persecution toward the end of the first century under the reign of the emperor Domitian, which was remembered in Asia Minor as being severe.

Despite these brief run-ins with the law, almost all Christian persecution through the second century was prompted by local events and controlled by local personalities. Provincial governors and other military and government officials appointed by the emperor were more often than not left to referee these occasional outbreaks of violence against Christians. One such example is Paul's experience when a Jewish riot was broken up by the Roman army. Paul actually found a certain degree of sympathy from the governors Felix and Festus, and King Herod Agrippa II.

Pliny the Younger

Pliny the Younger was born to the elitist circles of the Roman Empire. His uncle, Pliny the Elder, was described in later centuries as a "renaissance man," having been at various times a naturalist, soldier, historian, politician, and naval commander, a friend of emperors and wealthy, to boot. Upon his death in A.D. 79, his entire estate became the property of his namesake.

 In Depth

> Both Plinys had the distinction of being present in A.D. 79 when Mt. Vesuvius erupted and destroyed Pompeii and Herculaneum. Pliny the Elder was admiral of a fleet of Roman ships based in Misenum, which he hurriedly led across the Bay of Naples to help evacuate people stranded on the beach as they tried to escape the fumes and falling ash. Trapped on the shore by the increasingly thick ash, Pliny, who was old and in poor health already, fell ill and died. At the time, his friends and nephew thought that the fumes had poisoned him, but none of the people with him were affected. It's more likely that he died of heart attack due to the stress and physical exertion.
>
> Pliny the Younger, left behind in Misenum, made observations of the eruption and the tsunami waves that followed until the falling ash forced him and his mother to evacuate. He was the first person ever to record the appearance of an eruption column, the towering pillar of ash that rises out of a volcanic eruption. To this day, eruptions that result in these belching clouds and heavy ash fall are known as Plinian eruptions.

The younger Pliny utilized his late uncle's wealth and connections to follow in his footsteps. He advanced in his career as a government official, steadily working his way up the ladder toward a governorship, usually the pinnacle of a career in civil service. Sometime around 110, he was appointed by the emperor Trajan to be the new governor for the province Bithynia-Pontus, on the northern coast of Asia Minor. It was there, while traveling through the province and attending to its governance, that in 112 he encountered Christians.

Pliny and the Christians

It seems pretty clear that Pliny had heard of Christians before. Perhaps he had heard some of the rumors I've mentioned about what Christians got up to in their worship gatherings. He points out, for instance, that upon questioning, he discovered that the Christians ate "food of an ordinary, harmless kind," possibly suggesting that he expected something different and more lurid. At the same time, Pliny's experience with Christians seems to have been entirely through secondhand accounts and rumors.

We don't know which city Pliny was in when the problem with the Christians arose. He was approached by some of the local citizens. The suggestion has been made that it might have been butchers or others involved in the sale of meat that had been offered to idols. Apparently, business had been down considerably because of the activity of Christians. The delegation lodged complaints against a number of people who Pliny had brought in for questioning. At the same time, uncertain of the process for dealing with Christians, Pliny wrote a letter to Trajan seeking the emperor's guidance. His letter and Trajan's response open a valuable door onto the state of Christianity early in the second century.

The nub of Pliny's query to the emperor had to do with the actual nature of the offense. Was Christianity illegal because of certain crimes associated with its practice, or was being a Christian itself a crime? And should he execute anyone who had been associated with this "superstition," or if someone recanted should they be allowed to go free? Did age matter, or were old and young to be punished alike?

Reading Pliny's letter is sort of like watching *Star Wars* from the Imperial point of view, with Pliny playing the role of a mild-mannered Darth Vader. Those accused of being Christians were brought to him to answer the charges. "Are you a Christian?" he would ask. When they responded in the affirmative, he would remind them that they faced execution for the crime of being a Christian, and then ask a second and even a third time. If they persisted in their confession of faith, Pliny had them taken away for execution. As he put it, "I had no doubt that, whatever the nature of their creed, stubbornness and inflexible obstinacy surely deserve to be punished."

As so often happens, the first group of accusations suddenly became a flood. An anonymous pamphlet began circulating with a list of names of people who were or had been Christians. Pliny, upon investigating, discovered that some of those listed had once been Christian but had left the faith, in some cases as much as 20 years before. It was pretty clear to Pliny that some of the locals were using this opportunity to get back at people they disliked. While he was resolute in his condemnation of those who persisted in claiming to be Christians, he was equally unwilling to become involved in local disputes, and his instructions from Trajan reinforce this view.

 In Depth _____

> Some people will say anything to keep their head attached to their neck. Many of the people who were brought to him accused of being Christians were willing to recant in order to avoid execution. But how can you be sure? What does it take to separate real Christians from the falsely accused?
>
> Pliny's solution was to erect statues to several of the most important Roman deities in his headquarters. The accused was invited to offer a small sacrifice of grain and wine to the gods, a very common practice at the time. They were also instructed to curse Christ by name, "none of which those who are really Christians, it is said, can be forced to do." Those who did went free. Those who didn't, didn't. Pliny didn't invent this religious test, but he may have been the first to use it on Christians. He wouldn't be the last.

Pliny's role as governor was both to enforce the laws outlawing Christianity and to keep the locals from dragging him into a witch hunt. Trajan instituted his own version of a "don't ask, don't tell" policy, where it was okay to investigate if someone was accused of being a Christian, but Roman officials shouldn't go out of their way to hunt down Christians. This pattern held for several decades, effectively sparing Christians from systematic, empire-wide persecution until the reign of Decius in 251 (see Chapter 16 for more about that).

Esteem

We shouldn't get the idea that Christianity was entirely discounted by the Roman elite. There are several instances of Roman writers expressing admiration for Christianity, or at least aspects of the religion. It's true that Christians were probably concentrated in the lower social classes, the kinds of people who didn't write books, but it is also true that many in even the highest levels of Roman society found the Christian faith attractive.

One of the first features of Christianity that attracted outside admiration was the self-control exhibited by Christians, particularly with regard to sex. While sexual mores in the Roman Empire were lax even by today's standards, some believed strongly in the need for sexual renunciation of some kind. We'll talk more about this in later chapters, but here it's enough to say that some found Christian sexual ethics to be worthy of comment.

The person who immediately comes to mind in this regard is Galen. A native of Asia Minor, Galen became the foremost medical practitioner of his day. His medical texts were standard reading well into the Middle Ages, and even today he is revered as one of the founding fathers of medicine. Active throughout the second half of the second century and in proximity to the imperial court in Rome, Galen had reason to comment on Christians that he encountered.

From the Source

"Most people are unable to follow any demonstrative argument consecutively; hence they need parables, and benefit from them … just as now we see the people called Christians drawing their faith from parables and miracles, and yet sometimes acting in the same way as those who philosophize. For their contempt of death, and of what comes after death, is patent to us every day, and likewise their restraint in cohabitation. For they include not only men but also women who refrain from cohabiting all their lives; and they also number individuals who, in self-discipline and self-control in matters of food and drink, and in their keen pursuit of justice, have attained a pitch not inferior to that of genuine philosophers."

—Galen, *Summary of Plato's Republic*

While he was not entirely impressed with the way that Christians depended more on faith than on reason, Galen remarked favorably on their philosophical lifestyle. Despite their less refined approach to life, Christians appeared to face both death and sexual renunciation with equal enthusiasm. In the next chapter, we'll talk more about the Christian attitude toward death as it was displayed publicly in martyrdom, and in Chapter 12 we'll talk about Christian attitudes toward marriage and sex. While Galen had little interest in Christianity as a faith, its ability to produce individuals whose lives aimed for the same ideals of self-mastery as those of the philosophical schools clearly impressed him.

The other virtue that made an impression on those who encountered Christians was their generosity and support for one another. Tertullian of Carthage (we'll see him in Chapter 9) reported the reactions of non-Christians to the Christian practice of keeping a common purse for the sake of charitable giving and support. "'See,' they say, 'how they love one another'; for they themselves hate one another; 'and how they are ready to die for one another'; for they will be more ready to kill one another." We see the practice of financial support all through the New Testament writings, both examples and the teaching that motivated them. This commitment to the care of others continued, as we'll see in Chapter 14. What's important for the moment is to recognize that this kind of mutual care was unusual enough for outsiders to take note of.

More than a century after Tertullian, the emperor Julian tried to revive paganism in an empire grown increasingly Christian. His first efforts were focused on getting priests in the pagan temples to follow the Christians' lead and extend support to the needy. In his frustration, he paid the Christians a backhanded compliment by pointing out how extensive they were in their care for the poor, but also how it had been helpful to their efforts to share their message.

From the Source

> "Atheism [Christianity] has been specially advanced through the loving service rendered to strangers, and through their care for the burial of the dead. It is a scandal that there is not a single Jew who is a beggar and that the godless Galilaeans care not only for their own poor but for ours as well; while those who belong to us look in vain for the help that we should render them."
> —Julian

Julian's reaction was probably typical of most of the Roman elite as they began to encounter Christianity: a mixture of disgust and fascination. For the lower classes, Christians were both attractive and repulsive. It's interesting to see how quickly a community could turn against the presence of Christians in their midst, as Pliny the Younger discovered. The more important question was how Christians would respond to these reactions to their teaching and their communities. That is the subject of our next chapter.

The Least You Need to Know

- Christians were the subject of all sorts of rumors.
- Celsus offered the first reasonable critique of Christian beliefs.
- Lucian exemplified the more cynical approach to Christianity, ridiculing rather than engaging.
- Pliny the Younger was the first of many Roman government officials to have to decide how to deal with Christians.
- Both their life of self-discipline and their charitable works softened the Christians' image and opened opportunities for them to share their message.

7

Martyrs and Apologists

In This Chapter

- ◆ They're just dying to tell you about Jesus
- ◆ Super Christians
- ◆ The pen is mightier than the martyr
- ◆ The first Christian philosopher

In the previous chapter, we saw the hostile response the early Christians often received as their message and way of life became known to their neighbors. In the face of these challenges, early Christians stumbled upon two different responses. On one hand, some Christians simply stood firm in their convictions and allowed their willingness to suffer rather than turn aside to be their answer to the rumors and charges. Other Christians attempted to reason with non-Christians, principally by writing literature both explaining Christian beliefs and attacking pagan cultural assumptions.

Martyrdom

For the average non-Christian resident of the Roman Empire, there wasn't much more dramatic than watching Christian *martyrs* in action. Tertullian of Carthage (whom we'll meet in Chapter 9), one of many Christians who

Word Knowledge

Martyr comes from a Greek word that means "witness." Early on, however, the word became exclusively associated with those whose witness led to their deaths.

were so impressed by the poise and courage of the martyrs that they joined the church themselves, coined the phrase "the blood of martyrs is the seed [of the church]." The more of us you kill, he crowed in his *Apology*, the more attractive you make our faith. As we'll see, Christian martyrs were not simply fatalists unwilling to bend to the whims of the state. They were convinced that by standing firm to their deaths, they were demonstrating before a watching world the power of Jesus and the truth of his message.

The Jewish Martyrs

Christian attitudes about martyrdom were rooted in the stories of Jews who were killed for remaining true to their faith under the reign of the Seleucids. The so-called Maccabean Martyrs even had their own cult, or special observance, among Christians beginning in the fourth century. They included Eleazar, who refused to eat pork when he was ordered to on pain of death. When approached by friends who urged him to at least pretend to eat the forbidden meat, Eleazer's concern was for the example he would set for younger men. "Therefore, by manfully giving up my life now," he told his judges, "I will prove myself worthy of my old age, and I will leave to the young a noble example of how to die willingly and generously for the revered and holy laws." That was a sentiment that the early Christians could embrace.

Eleazar wasn't the only Jewish martyr revered by the early Christians. In one famous story, an unnamed Jewish mother is forced to watch as her seven sons are tortured and executed one by one. The entire time, she keeps encouraging them to put their faith in God and their adherence to the Law of Moses ahead of their own lives. Eventually, the mother is killed as well. The story is compelling in part because the youngest of the sons claims that, by dying, he and his brothers are helping to free the Jewish nation from its sins. Again, this was an idea very much in line with Christian thinking. After all, hadn't Jesus himself died for the sins of humanity?

Martyrdom in the New Testament

Whatever Jewish antecedents there might be, for the Christian, the model of all martyrs was Jesus himself. The Revelation of John, a text inordinately concerned with martyrdom, describes Jesus as "the faithful witness." 1 Timothy 6:13 claims that Jesus "made the good confession" in front of Pontius Pilate. The goal of every martyr was to imitate that "good confession."

Other biblical figures lost their lives because of the confession of their faith. Stephen was widely regarded as the first martyr, dying in the earliest days of the Christian community, as described in Acts 7. Both Peter and Paul died for the crime of being Christian. While no one recorded their actual deaths, fictional accounts based on the traditions of the Roman church circulated early in the second century.

As I've already mentioned, The Revelation of John focuses a great deal of attention on the prospect of suffering for the faith. The author describes himself as "your brother and companion in the suffering and kingdom and patient endurance that are ours in Jesus." To the church in Smyrna is told, "Be faithful, even to the point of death, and I will give you the crown of life," and Christians in the city of Pergamum are reminded of "Antipas, my faithful witness, who was put to death in your city." Beneath the altar in heaven that he sees in his visions, the author describes those who have been killed "because of the word of God and the testimony they had maintained," crying out for justice. The entire Revelation throbs with intensity, exhorting the listener to press in closer to the heart of faith in order to face the severe challenges soon to come.

The Heroic Martyrs

Accounts and descriptions of martyrdom from the first century are often sketchy, at best, and genuine persecution of Christian communities was rare, if only because there were so few of them at the time. The second century is another matter entirely. So important did martyrdom become that reports of the events surrounding the deaths of Christians circulated throughout the churches. Often these reports were given by actual eyewitnesses or derived from official court records describing the trials. These are called the "acts of the martyrs." Descriptions of the actual deaths of the martyrs were known as passions or passion accounts. Then there are letters and other writings from second-century Christians describing how martyrs were received.

For example, there are the letters of Ignatius of Antioch, whom we will meet more fully in Chapter 9. One of the most significant Christians of his day and a leader in the Christian community in Antioch, he was arrested and condemned to die in Rome. Writing ahead to the Christians in Rome, Ignatius begs them not to do anything to prevent his coming death. He is fully prepared to die, claiming that because of his sufferings "at last I am beginning to be a disciple."

From the Source

> "I am writing to all the churches and am insisting to everyone that I die for God of my own free will—unless you hinder me. I implore you: do not be unseasonably kind to me. Let me be food for the wild beasts, through whom I can reach God. I am God's wheat, and I am being ground by the teeth of the wild beasts, so that I may prove to be pure bread."
>
> —Ignatius of Antioch, *Letter to the Romans*

No account exists for Ignatius's death, but there is one for his friend and colleague Polycarp, the bishop of the city of Smyrna in Asia Minor. Again, we'll get to know him better in Chapter 9. The record of Polycarp's death is actually the first of the passion accounts that exists. As such, it was the model for many of the accounts that followed.

In *The Martyrdom of Polycarp*, we find the 86-year-old bishop being hunted down after members of his congregation have been killed. At the urging of his church, Polycarp retreats to a home in the country, but he is discovered there and willingly turns himself in. After a dramatic showdown before the magistrate, Polycarp is condemned to be burned. The fire, however, doesn't burn him, so finally someone is sent up to stab him to death.

From the Source

> "But when the magistrate persisted and said, 'Swear the oath, and I will release you; revile Christ,' Polycarp replied, 'For eighty-six years I have been his servant, and he has done me no wrong. How can I blaspheme my King who saved me?'"
>
> — *The Martyrdom of Polycarp*

Around 177, persecution of the churches in Lyons and Vienne became severe. Dozens of Christians were taken into custody, tortured extravagantly, and finally killed. Among them, the most famous became Blandina, a slave girl about whom "the heathens themselves confessed that never among them did woman endure so many and such terrible tortures."

At the beginning of the third century, in 203, we get perhaps the most compelling passion account. *The Martyrdom of Perpetua and Felicity* describes the deaths of Vibia Perpetua, a 22-year-old Roman matron in Carthage, and a slave girl named Felicity, along with their companions Revocatus, Saturninus, and Saturus. What is most remarkable about this passion account is that it contains portions of a journal kept by Perpetua herself during her captivity, and thus gives us not only our first definitively female Christian voice, but also a first-person insight into the experience of the martyrs.

The Spirituality of Martyrdom

Martyrs were the public-relations shock troops of the early church. They were in combat against darkness and demonic powers represented by the authorities who condemned them for their faith. Athletic language abounds in the descriptions of the martyrs. There is no better example than that of Perpetua. In one of the dreams she records, Perpetua is brought out into the arena to wrestle with a very large, very powerful Egyptian. She herself is oiled up, having transformed into the body of a man (we'll get into this in the next chapter), and fights with the Egyptian, eventually prevailing and receiving the branch of victory from the judge. Perpetua understood this to mean "that I should fight, not with beasts but against the devil; but I knew that mine was the victory."

Athletic terms were used to describe the sufferings of the martyrs in Lyons. Blandina "in bout after bout had defeated her adversary," eventually winning her way to victory "through conflict." In fact, all of her companions were described as "noble athletes" who "endured many contests and gained great victories."

From the Source

"Nobody indeed willingly suffers, since both panic and danger are inevitably to be faced; and yet the man who complained about battle fights with all his strength and rejoices when he conquers in battle, because he attains both glory and booty. Our battle is that we are summoned before tribunals, to fight there for the truth at the risk of our lives. But to obtain that for which one has struggled is a victory, a victory that carries with it both the glory, of pleasing God, and the spoil, which is eternal life."
—Tertullian, *Apology*

The Strength of the Martyrs

Throughout the descriptions of martyrdom there is the repeated note that the martyr does not suffer alone. In fact, what makes a martyr a martyr is precisely that at the moment of suffering, he or she takes on the very presence of Jesus. *The Martyrdom of Polycarp* points to this when it describes the Christians who suffered prior to Polycarp's death. They were beaten and abused, often very severely, but they did not seem to feel it. The author of the text notes that "at the very hour when they were being tortured," it was clear that they were "absent from the flesh," or, more to the point, that Jesus himself "was standing by and conversing with them."

A similar experience shows up in *The Martyrdom of Perpetua and Felicity*. Felicity is near to giving birth, a condition that will prevent her from accompanying her fellows into the arena. Eventually she does give birth but begins complaining about the pain of labor. Some of the prison attendants give her a hard time, telling her that if she thinks labor is painful, she's really going to suffer when they throw her to the beasts in the arena. Felicity's response: "I myself now suffer that which I suffer, but in the arena someone else shall be in me to suffer for me, because I am to suffer for him." She fully expected that, because she was prepared to suffer for Jesus, Jesus would be with her to suffer for her.

Her cellmate Perpetua demonstrates some of this transference in the arena. At one point, she is forced to face off against a mad cow that tramples her. Making her way back to where her fellow Christians are standing, she keeps asking, "When are they going to throw us to the cow?" She seems startled when her companions tell her that she already has been, and doesn't believe them until she sees the cuts and bruises on her body and her torn clothes. She is almost unaware of her suffering, "so much [is] she in the Spirit and in ecstasy."

Martyrs and the Spirit

Martyrdom was meaningful because it was an act of the Holy Spirit. The Spirit was present in the martyrs to make Jesus visible. Blandina, secured to a post in the arena, though she was to all outward appearances "a small, weak, despised woman," was able to "put on Christ, the great invincible champion." *The Martyrdom of Polycarp* also suggests that Polycarp's death was an imitation of Christ's.

From the Source

"Those were the days when Christians really were faithful, when the noble martyrdoms were taking place, when after conducting the martyrs' bodies to the cemetery we returned to meet together, and the entire church was present without being afraid, and the catechumens were being catechized during the very time of the martyrdom and while people were dying who had confessed the truth unto death .... Then we knew and saw wonderful and miraculous signs. Then there were true believers, few in number but faithful, treading the straight and narrow way that leads to life. But now when we have become many, out of the multitude that profess piety there are extremely few who are attaining to the election of God and to blessedness."

—Origen, *Homily on Jeremiah*

Because the martyrs were so close to the Spirit, it was assumed that they would be gifted with prophetic insights. Ignatius, for example, is nicknamed "God-Bearer" and alludes to certain revelations given to him. Polycarp, while hiding from the authorities, dreams that his pillow is on fire and concludes that he will be burned to death. Perpetua and her fellow martyr Saturus both describe prophetic dreams and visions that they have.

Martyrs were considered to be so close to Jesus that they were able to offer forgiveness of sins to others. This became a problem later, when so many who had recanted their faith under threat of persecution attempted to get back into the church after things were safe by receiving absolution from the martyrs. We'll see the conflict this caused more clearly in Chapter 16.

The Martyr and Salvation

The martyr herself could expect to find herself immediately by Jesus' side in heaven. Dying for Christ was akin to a second baptism in the minds of Christians. For those who had not yet received water baptism, martyrdom could take its place. For those Christians who had committed sins like adultery or murder and thus invalidated their baptism, martyrdom offered a second chance at receiving the grace of God. In Tertullian's words, martyrdom "makes actual a washing which has not been received" and also "gives back one that has been lost."

From the Source

"We have indeed a second washing, it too a single one, that of blood, of which our Lord said, I have a baptism to be baptized with, when he had already been baptized. For he had come by water and blood, as John has written, so as to be baptized with water and glorified with blood. Likewise, so as to give us our vocation by water and our election by blood, he sent forth these two baptisms from out of the wound of his pierced side [John's Gospel says that when Jesus' side was pierced with a spear, blood and water flowed out of the wound], because those who had faith in his blood were to be washed in water, and those who had washed in water would need also to be washed in blood. This is the baptism which makes actual a washing which has not been received, and gives back again one that has been lost."

—Tertullian, *On Baptism*

By the time of Polycarp's death, there was already a willingness among Christians to revere the martyrs. We see several instances where authors express grief that the bodies of the martyrs are desecrated and then destroyed. Those physical remains that could be collected were. There was a practice in Roman society of holding feasts on the birthdays of significant family members who had passed away. Christians picked up on this practice to commemorate the martyrs. Instead of their birthday, however, Christians celebrated the day of a martyr's death, when they were born into immortality. Because of their exalted state, Christians asked martyrs, whom they believed to be alive in the presence of God, to pray for them.

Apologists

While the martyrs were infuriating the authorities, the *apologists* were trying to mollify them. Where the martyrs were unreasonable, the apologists sought to rationally present the Christian faith in terms that their audiences could understand. That doesn't mean that the apologists were above talking tough. They frequently pointed out the hypocrisy and injustice in Roman society and in Roman attitudes toward Christians. But the mere fact that they wrote for non-Christians indicates that they believed that some dialogue was not only possible, but also positive.

Defense Against the Jews

Right from the start, the Christian message was in contention with the larger Jewish world from which it emerged. Beginning with Jesus himself, Christians offered a distinct reading of the Hebrew Scriptures that differed from what most Jews would accept. Very early on in the life of the church, there is evidence of *testimonia*, collections of texts from the Hebrew Scriptures that were regarded as supportive of the Christian claim that Jesus was the Messiah. In his Letter to the Romans, the apostle Paul was already addressing the questions raised by the continued existence of the Jews and their rejection of Jesus as Messiah. Our friend Celsus from the last chapter had made quite an issue of the fact that the Christians were attempting to redefine the meaning of the Jewish story in the face of the Jews themselves.

> **Word Knowledge**
>
> **Apologist** is a word derived from the Greek *apologia*, which means "to make a defense or to explain." 1 Peter 3 encourages Christians to always be ready to give an apologia for their faith. An apology, then, is not a way of saying sorry so much as it is an explanation for something.

There seem to have been two kinds of apologetics against Judaism. On the one hand, there were books like the Letter to the Hebrews in the New Testament or the Letter of Barnabas (remember this from Chapter 5?) that form a kind of defensive apologetic. In other words, they dealt with the Christian take on Jewish arguments against Jesus, but primarily for a Christian audience. They were trying to inoculate Christians against Jewish thinking.

On the other hand, there were books written with a Jewish audience at least partially in mind. Justin Martyr's *Dialogue with Trypho* (we'll meet Justin in just a moment) is the best known of a series of literary dialogues written to pit Christians and Jews against one another in a one-on-one debate. Some of these texts may record actual debates, though most are highly edited and some are just out-and-out fictional. Whatever their source, they were intended to provide a public example of Christians taking apart the Jewish argument and demonstrating that, in fact, Jesus was the Messiah.

Defense Against the Greeks and Romans

While dialogue between Christians and Jews began right from the start, dialogue with the Greco-Roman world evolved over time. Rather than beginning with a projected goal in mind, apologists writing for the larger society were faced with a series of unfolding concerns. At first, the issues facing the church were more matters of mere survival as an almost microscopic minority in the culture. As Christians began drawing more attention to themselves, they were forced to answer the charges leveled against them both by popular rumor and by the political authorities. Finally, it became necessary to offer a philosophical defense of Christianity.

Already in the New Testament writings there are hints of a need to be circumspect with regard to outsiders. Christianity was not at all well known, and it wasn't difficult to get mobs of people angry about what they didn't understand. In those cases where Christians seemed to be making headway early on, there was even more danger that a backlash could result in disaster.

The apologetical writers include Quadrates (whose apology is lost) and Aristides, Justin Martyr (whom we'll meet next), and his student Tatian (more about him in Chapter 8). Later writers like Tertullian and Melito of Sardis also produced apologies. And then there is the amazing *Letter to Diognetus*, which is officially anonymous but which many scholars would love to recognize as the supposedly lost apology of Quadrates.

In the previous chapter, we heard about the rumors and the arguments offered against Christianity by its "cultured despisers." I won't rehearse those again in detail now. As a reminder, however, remember that because of their secrecy and withdrawal from society, Christians were subject to all sorts of bizarre rumors and innuendos, and their appeal to many in the lower class seemed to prove that the Christian message was rubbish. More important, critics accused the Christians of endangering society by refusing to pay due homage to the gods and encouraging others to stop as well. Last of all, there were the philosophical objections leveled by people like Celsus.

From the Source

"For Christians are not distinguished from the rest of humanity by country, language or custom. For nowhere do they live in cities of their own, nor do they speak some unusual dialect, nor do they practice an eccentric way of life. This teaching of theirs has not been discovered by the thought and reflection of ingenious people, nor do they promote any human doctrine, as some do. But while they live in both Greek and barbarian cities, as each one's lot was cast, and follow the local customs in dress and food and other aspects of life, at the same time they demonstrate the remarkable and admittedly unusual character of their own citizenship. They live in their own countries, but only as nonresidents; they participate in everything as citizens, and endure everything as foreigners. Every foreign country is their fatherland, and every fatherland is foreign …. In a word, what the soul is to the body, Christians are to the world."

—*The Letter to Diognetus*, author unknown (late second century)

Christian apologists wrote initially to dispel many of the rumors, asserting forcefully that they were innocent of the many crimes, legal and moral, being attributed to them. In fact, they argued, how can we be hated for the very moral failings exhibited by the pagan gods worshipped by the masses who swallow these rumors? Tertullian, in particular, rails against the injustice of Christians being attacked and executed simply for the name.

On the philosophical concerns, Christian writers were on even stronger ground. Many of them were extraordinarily well educated for their day and quite capable of making the intellectual case for their faith. They were also helped by the fact that Hellenistic Jews like Philo of Alexandria had already done a great deal of the heavy lifting philosophically, reimagining Jewish beliefs and practices through a philosophical lens. Philo's Logos theology, for example, would be of great service to Justin Martyr. The Christians also benefited from the fact that the philosophers tended to discount the worship of pagan gods. Christians were able to pit the pagan philosophers against the pagan masses, arguing that it was ridiculous to accuse Christians of being atheists (because they had no images for their god), when philosophers like Socrates were guilty of the exact same thing.

Ultimately, the primary contribution of the apologists was to provide language for Christians to describe themselves in ways that highlighted both their similarities and their genuine differences from the culture at large. The vast amount of apologetical literature published during the second century demonstrates that their efforts were not ignored. Nobody ever said that the writings of the apologists is the seed of the church, but the literature that they created and the foundations that they laid for more substantive writing in the third and fourth centuries contributed greatly to the growth and development of a form of Christianity that could survive in the Greco-Roman world.

Justin Martyr

I suppose that with a last name like Martyr, you would have to know that things weren't going to end pretty, wouldn't you? No, Martyr wasn't really Justin's last name, but there's a reason that the most important of the early Christian apologists was so closely associated with martyrdom that it literally ended up as part of his name. As both an apologist and a martyr, Justin serves as the perfect case study in how Christians negotiated these two extremes in the second century. We'll end this chapter by briefly looking at his life and legacy.

Justin's Life and Death

Justin was a seeker. In his own description of himself, he talks about how he traveled all over the world looking for a philosophy that made sense to him. Eventually, while sitting on a beach one day, he met an old man who turned him on to the writings of the Hebrew prophets. Through that man's influence, and persuaded by the examples of the martyrs that he saw, Justin eventually became a Christian.

At some point he moved to Rome, where he opened up a school. In fact, as a Christian teacher, he continued to wear the robe of a philosopher, testimony to his belief that Christianity was the realization of everything that the philosophers had been striving to reach. In 165, he and several of his students were accused of being Christians. They were tried before Rusticus, the city prefect, and beheaded.

Justin's Philosophy

Justin wrote and published several works, the most famous of which are the *First and Second Apologies* and his *Dialogue with Trypho*. In these works, Justin argued favorably for the many points of contact that he found between Christianity and pagan philosophy. For example, he latched on to the philosophers' assertion that there was a supreme deity above all things on which all things depend as evidence of the same monotheism that Christianity embodied. How did Justin explain these similarities? Like many others, Justin believed that the Greek philosophers had at some point encountered the teachings of Moses and the Hebrew prophets, but that wasn't all. More important, Justin adopted the Greek belief in the Logos. The Logos means both "word" and "rationality" or "reason" in Greek. The philosophers used this word to describe the rational principle at work in the universe.

From the Source

"We have been taught that Christ is the first-born of God, and we have declared above that He is the Word (Logos) of whom every race of men were partakers; and those who lived reasonably are Christians, even though they have been thought atheists; as, among the Greeks, Socrates and Heraclitus, and men like them; and among the barbarians, Abraham, and Ananias, and Azarias, and Misael, and Elias, and many others whose actions and names we now decline to recount, because we know it would be tedious. So that even they who lived before Christ, and lived without reason, were wicked and hostile to Christ, and slew those who lived reasonably."

—Justin Martyr, *First Apology*

Since John's Gospel had claimed that the Logos became a human being in Jesus, Justin argued that the very reasonable nature of the universe, the capacity for reason that had inspired the philosophers, was the founder of the Christian faith. Thus the philosophers like Plato and Socrates were, in a sense, pre-Christians, in that they knew Jesus as the Logos, although only partially. With this piece of reasoning, Justin was able to embrace whatever was good in the philosophers as Christian truth. Christians would not need to be afraid of classical culture, but rather could adopt it and build on it.

The Least You Need to Know

- ◆ Martyrdom was the principal reaction to the attacks of the Roman state.

- ◆ The martyrs were regarded as special witnesses of the life and power of the Gospel.

- ◆ The apologists offered an intellectual explanation for the Christian message, as well as a defense of the Christian community itself.

- ◆ Justin Martyr epitomized both tendencies in the second century, being both an apologist and a martyr.

Chapter 8

Identity Crisis

In This Chapter

- ◆ The pressure is on inside the Christian community
- ◆ A group of teachers try to wed Christianity and Plato
- ◆ It's cool to be a virgin
- ◆ Out of central Turkey comes a new prophetic voice
- ◆ Marcion makes our Bibles lighter by taking out everything Jewish

We've seen how the perceptions of outsiders challenged Christians to find ways of bearing witness to their faith. At the same time, Christians were struggling with pressures inside of their communities. The new faith was still struggling to define itself. Even the apostles had not been able to maintain total unanimity. In their absence, and without any other authority to look to, Christian communities began to split along more expansive fault lines. The problems were as old as Paul's letter to the Corinthians, only larger and more daunting.

The Neighborhood Just Isn't the Same Anymore

The middle years of the second century, roughly 130 to 180, were a period of identity crisis for the Christian faith. Jesus and his earliest disciples were Jewish, and the vast majority of those who embraced the Christian faith in the first century were either themselves Jewish or those who had some familiarity with Jewish life and worship, such as the Gentile "God-fearers" we met in Chapter 4. For quite a long time, it was unclear if Christianity would ever be anything more than another sect of Judaism.

All of that began to change in the second century. The Christian faith began to appeal to a broader population as a kind of philosophy. Seekers began to discover Christianity without coming through the Jewish route. Several of the apologists we saw in Chapter 7 fall into this category. These new generations of Christians had grown up less with Moses and David than with Homer and Plato, and they began asking how the Jesus story made sense of their own heritage. If, as the earliest disciples of Jesus argued, the story of Moses and David had come to completion in Jesus, was it possible that the culture of Homer and Plato had as well? Again, we've seen these questions at work in the arguments of the apologists. Some Christians, however, took things further and even began to ask whether Jesus could best be understood outside of the Jewish context altogether.

Know-It-Alls

One of the movements that emerged out of this trend is known to us today as gnosticism. The *gnostics*, so called because they claimed to have special knowledge about God, were never a single, monolithic group. Instead, gnosticism was a set of related ideas about the nature of God, humanity, and the world that interpreted the story of Jesus in light of Greek philosophy, particularly that of Plato. Defining gnosticism precisely is a slippery business because there is so much variation in the different schools of gnostic thought. However, it is possible to get at least a bare-bones idea of what the gnostic teachers were saying. Ultimately, here are the basic assertions on which gnosticism rests.

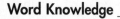

Word Knowledge

The **gnostics** got their name from the Greek word *gnosis*, which means "knowledge." Literally, they are "ones who know."

First, the Jewish God who created the world is not the same being as the Father of Jesus Christ. Picking up on the writings of the philosopher Plato, the gnostics argued that the true God was a perfect being who could not possibly have anything to do with physical matter, which is inherently unstable and corrupt. Plato had suggested that, instead, a lesser being called the Maker had crafted the world out of this eternally existing matter. Because the Maker was less than perfect, it was unable to fashion a perfect world, and thus the world is a mess.

In Depth

Until recently, almost everything that scholars knew about Christian gnostics they had to learn from the works of mainstream Christians who opposed gnosticism. There were very few sources of information written directly by the gnostics.

All of that changed in 1946. A pair of Egyptian peasant-farmers, digging for fertilizer near the city of Nag Hammadi, discovered an earthen jar. Inside, sealed away for centuries, were 12 leather-bound books and parts of a thirteenth. Altogether, they contained 45 never-before-seen texts, most of them of gnostic origin. It was a fantastic treasure trove, which included works like the now-famous Gospel of Thomas. (If you're interested in finding out more about the Nag Hammadi library, you might check out *The Complete Idiot's Guide to the Gnostic Gospels*, by yours truly.)

The gnostics took this story one step further. They argued that, in fact, something had gone wrong in the perfect heavenly place where God exists. Out of this catastrophe, the Jewish God (their version of the Maker) came into being, and it was he who made this material universe. In the process, some aspect of the true God became trapped in the material world. These "sparks of the divine" now reside in the spirits of at least some human beings. Still with me so far?

For those who possess this divine spirit, the physical world is a mirage that keeps them trapped and unable to return to the heavenly realm where they may reunite with God. While Plato's Maker was a fairly benign fellow, the gnostic Creator is often portrayed as either insane or evil, and often both. He and his angelic hordes attempt to thwart all attempts by those who are "spiritual" to escape this world and return to God. The Creator's principal weapon is deception. He and his minions try to keep those who are spiritual from realizing what they truly are. This world, then, is a prison that uses ignorance for chains.

All is not lost, however. For Christian gnostics, this is where Jesus comes in. He enters our world on a sort of rescue mission, behind enemy lines, sent by his Father God to bring a word of truth to those souls that long to be free. For the gnostics, true salvation was not found in forgiveness from the guilt of sins. Consequently, the crucifixion had little, if any, place in their theology. Instead, Jesus came to provide enlightenment.

To those who would hear, he teaches the knowledge (gnosis) that will allow his followers to escape from the present age and be set free to return to God.

Simon the Magician

So who were these Christian gnostics? Well, in every heresy hunter's handbook, public enemy number one was a near-legendary fellow named Simon Magus, or Simon the Magician. Simon makes a rather dramatic debut in the pages of the Acts of the Apostles, where he tries to purchase the power of the Holy Spirit from Peter. Peter sends Simon packing with the kind of salty language you would expect from a Galilean fisherman. As far as the New Testament is concerned, that's the last we hear of Simon the Magician.

From the Source

> "Now for some time a man named Simon had practiced sorcery in the city and amazed all the people of Samaria. He boasted that he was someone great, and all the people, both high and low, gave him their attention and exclaimed, 'This man is the divine power known as the Great Power.' They followed him because he had amazed them for a long time with his magic."
>
> —Acts of the Apostles 8:9–11

It's an odd sort of story, one that cries out for a sequel. As a matter of fact, late in the second century, the author of the Acts of Peter gives us exactly that, describing a fictional showdown between Peter and Simon in Rome years after their first encounter. The two go head to head in a signs-and-wonders showdown that ends when Simon, attempting to fly, crashes into the middle of the Roman Forum. Is it too much to say that he went out with a bang?

According to the later critics of gnosticism, Simon claimed to be the Great Power, or God. More than that, he also claimed that in the eternal past he had had a companion named Thought. Somehow, through the trickery of some angelic spirits, Thought had become trapped in the material world, where she was forced to live one life after another through reincarnation. Eventually, she ended up as a prostitute named Helen, living in the coastal city of Tyre. That is where God, who had come into the world as Simon, discovered her and rescued her.

It's really a rather romantic story, after a fashion. More important, it foreshadows some of the later gnostic assertions that human beings are spiritually feminine and are, like Helen, waiting to be rescued by a masculine spirit. Some of Simon's successors added other elements to the gnostic puzzle, including the idea that Jesus did not have a real body but only appeared to have one. Still, it wasn't any of Simon's followers who kicked the development of gnosticism into high gear. Instead, the city of Alexandria in Egypt became a living laboratory for gnostic thinking.

Basilides

Alexandria was the place to be in the early second century if you had any kind of philosophical interests. The city, created by Alexander the Great and home of the Great Library, was a hotbed of intellectual speculation. It was in Alexandria that young Basilides began piecing together the first coherently Christian form of gnosticism.

A native of the city, Basilides was also a prolific writer. We know, for example, that he penned a 24-volume set of commentaries on the Gospels at a time when such resources were not widely available. It is also believed that he wrote a number of songs, which would have been used as teaching aids to communicate his views to the masses. All in all, he was a very busy boy.

From the Source

"Wherefore he [Jesus] did not himself suffer death, but Simon, a certain man of Cyrene, being compelled, bore the cross in his stead; so that this latter being transfigured by him, that he might be thought to be Jesus, was crucified, through ignorance and error, while Jesus himself received the form of Simon, and, standing by, laughed at them."

—Irenaeus, *Against Heresies* (describing Basilides' teaching about the crucifixion)

It isn't easy to reconstruct exactly what Basilides was teaching, but a couple of ideas come through. He was no fan of the material world, considering its opposition to the spiritual life. He believed that Jesus was the Cosmic Redeemer sent to show humanity how to break free from its material prison. The crucifixion was meaningless. In fact, Basilides did not even believe that Jesus was crucified at all, but that he escaped while another man was executed in his place.

Most of the ideas that Basilides used to create his philosophy were readily available to him in Alexandria. What made his system of thought unique was that, for the first time, it was based entirely around Jesus of Nazareth. It was the first real Christian form of gnosticism, and it laid the groundwork for one of the more brilliant minds in second-century Christianity, Valentinus.

Valentinus

Even his detractors had a hard time criticizing Valentinus's intellect. Following in the footsteps of his older contemporary, Basilides, Valentinus pursued the goal of creating a truly Hellenistic form of Christianity, reimagined through the lens of Plato's philosophy.

What made Valentinian gnosticism so powerful was its subtlety. Valentinus and his followers were able to remain within the larger Christian community long after other gnostic groups had either voluntarily split or been forced out. Valentinus taught from the same sacred texts as mainstream Christians and utilized many of the same worship practices; only in private gatherings were Valentinians instructed in the hidden or secret meanings to all of these practices.

Because of this circumspect behavior, Valentinus was able not only to remain in the larger Christian community, but to aspire to leadership. Apparently, when elections were held to determine the next bishop of Rome (we'll talk about hierarchies and the evolution of the bishop as the leader of the church in the next chapter) after the death of Hyginus around 143, Valentinus was nominated to take his place and reportedly lost by only a handful of votes. Later, it seems, he either broke with the Roman church or was expelled. There is evidence that he left Rome for Cyprus or possibly returned to Alexandria and died around 160. With him, the golden age of Christian gnosticism came to a close. While their teachings would continue to have influence for decades (in some cases, centuries) to come, Christian gnostics were never again as creative or as productive as they were during the middle years of the second century.

Asexual Healing

Not everyone was as passionate as the gnostics about melding Christianity with Greek philosophy. For those later known as *Encratites*, the answer to the brokenness of human living was to bring human desire completely under control. Encratites specifically targeted sex as the enemy of spirituality. They believed that genuine Christianity required celibacy. Encratites were very conscious of the power of sex to distract a person from God. In fact, they saw it as a form of spiritual adultery.

Like the gnostics, the Encratites were not a specific group, but rather people influenced by a particular way of looking at the world. Both groups viewed the physical world as dangerous to the soul, and both made powerful appeals to lead lives of self-control, but that's where the similarities end. If the gnostics turned away from the world because it was a meaningless deception, the Encratites withdrew from the world because they realized how very real and powerful it was.

Word Knowledge _____

Encratites was a term for Christians who refused to marry or engage in sexual relations, out of a belief that sexuality itself was evil. The word comes from the Greek *enkrateia*, which means "continence" or "self-control."

An ascetic way of living was not alien to Christianity in any form. Throughout Jewish history there are stories of prayer and fasting, and Christians certainly had Jesus and, later, Paul as compelling models for radical self-control. The Encratites were fairly typical of highly committed Christians. What set them apart was the theology underlying their rejection of marriage.

The first person to describe it for us is Tatian. A native Assyrian (modern Iraq), Tatian traveled to Rome, where he encountered Christianity for the first time. He became a student of Justin Martyr (whom we met in the last chapter), eventually opening his own small school. At some point, Tatian may even have studied with Valentinus as well. Eventually, he returned to his homeland and died around 185.

Tatian was one angry guy, and it showed up in his writing. One work, in particular, *Address to the Greeks,* is a contemptuous dismissal of all things Greek. Tatian is unsparing in his rejection of the very philosophy that the gnostics were embracing. The heart of the Hellenistic project was to make Greek culture the measuring stick for everyone and everything else. Tatian was having none of it. They call us barbarians, Tatian writes in the opening lines of his screed, but what do they have that they didn't steal from the rest of us? Far from fawning over the Hellenistic culture of the day, Tatian mocked the inferiority of the Greek philosophers when their teachings were compared to Christian doctrine.

Tatian developed the view that, in the Fall, Adam and Eve had lost their special connection with God and had replaced it with something far less meaningful—namely, their marriage. For Tatian, sexual union was the cheap door prize that kept human beings from being united with God through the Holy Spirit. It was either be married to a husband or wife or be married to God. Tatian saw no other possibility.

Tatian's views were spread in a unique manner. He created a harmony of the four New Testament Gospels, weaving the different narratives together into a single story. He used this opportunity to make some alterations to the scriptural texts as well, heightening any language that stressed his point about the need for absolute sexual self-control. This harmony, the *Diatesseron*, became the most popular version of the Bible in Syria for the next two centuries.

Word Knowledge

Diatesseron literally means "through the four." It was an attempt by Tatian to create a single, harmonized version of the Jesus story by weaving together the four New Testament Gospels, Matthew, Mark, Luke, and John. In the process, Tatian smoothed over some of the differences in those four narratives. He also edited key passages in the Gospels that dealt with sex and celibacy in the Christian life so that they would better support his Encratite views. The *Diatesseron* was the most popular version of the New Testament in Syria for two centuries.

The challenge posed by the Encratites was the way that they dissolved almost all typical social relationships, such as marriage and family, and replaced them with a kind of universal kinship of the Spirit. Mainstream Christians were constantly in the process of negotiating the tension between the often radical demands of Jesus' teachings and the limitations that came with gender, family relationships, and social standing. The Encratites threatened to unravel the natural tapestry that held homes and churches together, and replace it with a radical commitment of the whole self to the Holy Spirit. The ideal could be attractive, but for many Christians it was like walking a tightrope without a net—the net, in this case, being that web of social and family relationships that exists to catch us when we fall. For most Christians, Jesus' command to love neighbor was exercised in family life and through friendships and business relationships. Bishops and priests watching the emergence of encratism were concerned for the weaker members of their churches. Tatian threatened to make Christianity a faith for zealots only.

The New Prophecy Movement

Asia Minor (modern-day Turkey) was, we will see again and again, a center of gravity for Christianity. Conservative stalwarts and innovators alike emerged from that region to challenge the growing Christian community with ancient traditions and new insights. One movement that grew out of Phrygia in central Asia Minor would pose a serious challenge particularly to the bishops and priests in the mainstream church.

Montanus was originally a priest of Cybele, a manifestation of Earth Goddess worship popular in Phrygia, but he converted to Christianity sometime around 155. At some point prior to 170, he encountered the Gospel of John, with its assurances from Jesus that he would send his disciples "another *Paraclete* ... the Spirit of truth" to be their companion as they followed in Jesus' footsteps. Montanus was convinced that he was possessed by the Holy Spirit and thus had become the Paraclete promised by Jesus. By this, he didn't simply mean that he was a tool of the Spirit, as some prophets described themselves. Rather, he believed that he *was* the Spirit in human form, in much the same manner that Jesus was the Word of God incarnate.

Word Knowledge

Translated variously as "advocate," "comforter," and "counselor," the **Paraclete** (from the Greek word *paracletos*, which literally means "one called alongside") describes the role of the Holy Spirit in the lives of Jesus' followers. As such, it appears exclusively in the Gospel of John.

Somewhere along the line, Montanus picked up two followers, Priscilla and Maximilla, who accompanied him in his travels and claimed to be extensions of the Spirit as well. From what we can gather, it seems that Montanus, Priscilla, and Maximilla taught that there are three stages or periods of God's activity in the world, which correspond to the Christian experience of God as Father, Son, and Holy Spirit. So the first period is the age of the Father, which was the history of the Jews and their relationship to God; followed by the age of the Son, which refers to Jesus; and finally the age of the Spirit, when the Kingdom of God would come into being. Its capital, the New Jerusalem, would be Montanus's hometown, Pepuza.

Because they were the Spirit incarnate, the prophecies of Montanus and his two lady friends essentially superseded the writings of the apostles. In fact, given that the new age of the Spirit was dawning through their activity, there was a sense in which Montanus superseded Jesus himself. And that's the line that the rest of the Christian community would not cross.

That's not to say that Montanism was immediately or wholeheartedly rejected. A passion for the prophetic, combined with anticipation of the end of the age and the Montanists' rigid focus on strict holiness, were all welcome qualities, and many early Christians embraced Montanism, some for a time and others for good. (In the next chapter we'll meet the most famous convert to Montanism.)

Still, as more people became acquainted with what Montanus was actually teaching, they began to distance themselves from the New Prophecy movement. Montanism remains as a reminder of the apocalyptic passions that still swirled beneath the sometimes conventional exterior of mainstream Christianity.

Marcion

You can see some of the currents that were floating around within Christian communities in the second century. It may be an oversimplification, but this last movement in the early Christian community tied several of these tendencies together in one package.

Asia Minor (modern Turkey)

Marcion was born with a silver spoon in his mouth, to a wealthy family in Sinope, a city in northern Turkey. His family was heavily involved in shipping, and Marcion himself seems to have inherited some of his family's skill at business. It's possible that his father was a bishop as well.

Sometime around 142, Marcion arrived in Rome. He made quite a splash when he showed up, handing church leaders a gift of 200,000 *sesterces*, a huge sum of money. In no time, Marcion was teaching in the church and involved in leadership. You'll recall, by the way, that Valentinus was in Rome at this same time. At some point, somebody got uneasy with what Marcion was teaching, and in 144 he was expelled from the church. The church even went so far as to return his money to him.

 Word Knowledge _____

A **sesterce** is one fourth of a denarius, which was a typical day's pay for a laborer in the Roman Empire.

So what got them all so riled up? The core of Marcion's teaching was a complete rejection of anything Jewish. He was convinced that the God of the Jews—warlike, tribal, and jealous—could not possibly be the same being as the Father of Jesus. Marcion argued that Jesus simply appeared, fully grown and ready to do business.

In order to reinforce his views, Marcion began to put together his own Bible. He got rid of the entire Old Testament and tossed out all of the Gospels except Luke. In his mind, Paul was the only apostle who understood that embracing Jesus meant rejecting Judaism, so Paul's letters made it into the collection. Even at that, both Paul and Luke were heavily edited to remove any references to the Old Testament. Luke's stories about the birth of Jesus also ended up on the cutting-room floor. By the time Marcion was done, there wasn't a whole lot left.

Since he had his own Bible, Marcion decided he should have his own church to preach it in. The Marcionite churches spread rapidly, based around the same structure of bishops, priests, and deacons that formed the basis of the mainstream churches. (I'll describe this in more detail in the next two chapters.) Only 10 years after Marcion's expulsion, Justin Martyr could write that Marcion's followers included people from every nation.

A list of those who wrote books attacking Marcionism reads like a who's who of mainstream Christianity. It didn't work that well. In some places, particularly in the region of eastern Syria and beyond, Marcionism was the dominant form of Christianity for a time. While its expansion burned out by the middle of the third century, individual Marcionite communities continued to exist for centuries longer.

Marcion's challenge to mainstream Christianity was profound. As we'll see in Chapter 10, Christians were forced to respond to Marcion's rejection of the faith's Jewish roots and to decide, once and for all, which texts were authoritative and which were not. Marcion did a great deal to speed up the creation of what we now refer to as the New Testament.

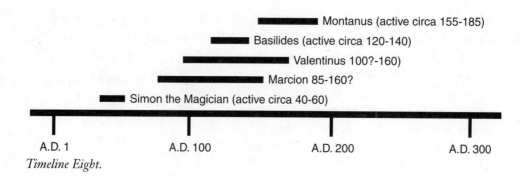

Montanus (active circa 155-185)

Basilides (active circa 120-140)

Valentinus 100?-160)

Marcion 85-160?

Simon the Magician (active circa 40-60)

| A.D. 1 | A.D. 100 | A.D. 200 | A.D. 300 |

Timeline Eight.

The Least You Need to Know

◆ Christianity in the second century began to move away from its Jewish roots in significant ways.

◆ The Gnostics began interpreting Jesus through the lens of Greek philosophy.

◆ Tatian and the Encratites argued for a celibate church.

◆ The New Prophecy movement stirred up the continuing desire among Christians for ecstatic spirituality.

◆ Marcion created a rival church that rejected all Jewish links to Christianity.

9

Architects of Orthodoxy

In This Chapter

- ◆ A dead man walking
- ◆ The disciple of John
- ◆ The heresy hunter
- ◆ The founder of Latin theology

The various groups that we've just seen looked to the Jesus story for answers to some of the pressing questions of the second century. Within the mainstream church, their solutions were not persuasive. It took time, however, for the leaders of the Christian communities to work their way toward their own answer to these philosophical challenges. By the end of the second century, the fluid diversity of Christianity in the late first and early second centuries had begun to narrow as the boundaries of the Christian faith became more clearly defined. In the next chapter, we'll look at how the orthodox consensus evolved, but before that, let's meet some of the guys who were instrumental in bringing it about.

Ignatius of Antioch

Some early Christian figures, like Paul and Peter, developed a reputation over many years. Paul's letters, for instance, were written over the span of a decade or more. Later Christian leaders, like Tertullian (see later in this chapter) and Origen (whom we'll meet in Chapter 15), operated for years, their influence guaranteed by the breadth of their literary output.

Ignatius, by distinction, flashes across the sky like a brightly lit meteor. We know only what we can learn of him from a series of seven letters that he wrote over the course of a couple of weeks sometime in 107 or 108 while on his way to Rome to die in the Coliseum. Yet those brief letters offer us an incomparable window into the life and practice of one of the earliest Christian communities.

Ignatius was bishop of Antioch. As we saw in Chapter 4, Antioch was the first Christian community to actively reach out to Gentiles as part of its mission. It was the first place that the followers of Jesus were called "Christians." It was a base of operations for several important figures in the early church, including Peter and Paul. And many scholars believe that Antioch is the place where Matthew's Gospel was written. So all in all, it was a pretty significant place by Christian standards.

Ignatius himself was born around the middle of the first century. The rumor was that he had been appointed bishop of Antioch by the apostle Peter, but that is likely a later invention. More likely is the possibility that he was a hearer or student of the apostle John. That might explain his close connection with another fellow we'll meet in just a moment, Polycarp of Smyrna.

Sometime during the reign of the emperor Trajan (98–117), the church in Antioch faced some kind of difficulty. It may have been some form of outside persecution, but comments that Ignatius makes suggest that there were some internal disagreements as well. Somehow, in the midst of this struggle, Ignatius was arrested and accused of being a Christian. Found guilty, he was being transported to Rome, where he was to be thrown to the animals in the Coliseum as entertainment for the masses.

Under the escort of a unit of Roman guards whom he described as "ten leopards … whose treatment of me grows harsher the kinder I am to them," Ignatius had his death march turned into a triumphal procession. As he traveled, several churches in Asia Minor rushed to send representatives to meet him along the way. This network of Christian leaders demonstrates how closely connected the early Christian communities were. Through these brief consultations, Ignatius was able to get a glimpse of what was happening in the various Christian communities. These insights then informed the letters he wrote to the congregations that sent emissaries to him.

In his letters, Ignatius is quick to strengthen the position of the hierarchy of the churches, the bishop, the presbyters, and the deacons. A *bishop* (sometimes translated "overseer") is a position of leadership in the Christian community. The Greek word is *episkopos*, from which we get words like *Episcopal*. While the development of this office is a matter of great debate, it's clear that by the middle of the second century, bishops have attained dominance as the highest authorities in the Christian community.

Presbyters are also mentioned in the New Testament, where the word is usually translated "elder" or "elders." At first, this office seems to have been synonymous with the bishop. Over time, and certainly by the beginning of the second century, the bishop appears to have become the first among the presbyters. Eventually, the presbyters would be seen as the agents of the bishop, appointed by him as his helpers. The word *priest* is derived from *presbyter*, and that's how most presbyters are referred to today.

Deacon comes from the Greek *diakonos*, which means "to serve." Possibly based on the Seven led by Stephen in the Book of Acts, deacons were the officers of the Christian community responsible for providing relief for the poor and indigent, visiting the sick and those who had been arrested, and assisting the elders of the church at the worship gatherings.

Ignatius's letter to the Christians in Smyrna is typical, as he writes, "Follow the bishop as Jesus Christ followed the Father." To the church in Ephesus he advises, "It is right for you to set your minds in harmony with the bishop." One of Ignatius's key concerns was that the Christian communities should unite around the teaching and authority of the bishops. We'll see in the next chapter how this emphasis on the leadership of the bishops became a key component of the emerging orthodox consensus in the early church.

Numerous scholars have pointed out the value of this kind of organization when faced with state-sanctioned persecution, and Ignatius was surely aware of the unifying effects of singular leadership. At the same time, his primary concern is with the state of the interior of the church. Certain kinds of teachings were making the rounds of the Christian communities, and Ignatius wanted to warn them not to listen.

Principal among these teachings is what theologians call *docetism*. It's the belief that Jesus didn't actually have a flesh-and-blood body, but only appeared like he did, and it caused Ignatius no end of fits. He was dead set against it as contrary to the very heart

Word Knowledge

Docetism comes from the Greek word *dokeo*, which means "to seem, to appear." It was the idea that Jesus did not have an actual body, but only appeared to. The most immediate implication of this teaching was that Jesus had not actually suffered and died on the cross.

of the reality of Jesus because, he believed, it invalidated the life, death, and sacrifice of Jesus. He went so far as to describe the docetist teachers in one letter as "atheists" and "wicked offshoots that bear deadly fruit." Docetist views later characterized some of the groups that we examined in the last chapter, including the Marcionites and the gnostics, so it's easy to see why these groups provoked such a visceral response from the orthodox crowd.

In opposition to the docetists, Ignatius several times asserts the historical reality of Jesus by reciting several important moments or events in his life. We'll look more closely at this idea in the next chapter when we talk about the development of the creeds, but here it's enough to notice that Ignatius is clearly drawing on a preexisting confession of some kind, but also modifying it to emphasize that docetism is incompatible with the Jesus story. He writes, "Be deaf, therefore, whenever anyone speaks to you apart from Jesus Christ, who was of the family of David, who was the son of Mary; who really was born, who both ate and drank; who really was persecuted under Pontius Pilate, who really was crucified and died while those in heaven and on earth and under the earth looked on; who, moreover, really was raised from the dead when his Father raised him up. In the same way his Father will likewise also raise up in Christ Jesus us who believe in him. Apart from him we have no true life."

As we'll see in the following chapter, this short summary of the important moments in the life of Jesus closely resembles others that were being used throughout the second century.

Polycarp of Smyrna

In the middle of his march to Rome, Ignatius and his guards stopped in Smyrna, one of the most important cities in Asia Minor. There he was hosted by the church and their bishop, Polycarp. It's possible that they both knew each other already and might have had a common mentor in the apostle John. After leaving to continue his journey, Ignatius wrote a warm and encouraging letter to Polycarp, addressing his fellow bishop as both a friend and a confidante.

Polycarp carried a tremendous amount of moral authority with the churches in Asia Minor. Irenaeus of Lyons (who is next on our dance card) said that Polycarp was a disciple of the apostle John. We've already talked about the potential confusion surrounding the identity of this John, whether he was the apostle or another disciple of Jesus known later as "the Elder." The consistent claim of those writers in the second century is that Polycarp's mentor was, in fact, the apostle John, and that this connection made him a living witness to the teachings of the apostles and, therefore, of Jesus.

Years after Ignatius's death, in 154, Polycarp traveled to Rome to meet with bishop Anicetus. The Christians in Asia Minor celebrated the resurrection of Jesus annually on the Jewish Passover. Christians through-out the rest of the empire either didn't observe an annual celebration or did so on the Sunday immediately following Passover. Believe it or not, this caused quite a bit of friction, both then and later. Polycarp was meeting with Anicetus to try to put an end to the dispute. While it appears that the two were unable to find a solution, they did demonstrate great respect for each other, a fact that Irenaeus pointed to when the same issue flared up again several years afterward.

From the Source

"And Polycarp himself, when Marcion once met him and said, 'Do you know us?,' replied, 'I know the first born of Satan.'"

—Eusebius of Caesarea, *Church History*

Shortly after his return from Rome, Polycarp was arrested, tried for being a Christian, and dramatically executed. (We looked at some of the account of his martyrdom in Chapter 7.) The account of his death is the first example of the acts of martyrdom, as well as the first evidence we have of Christians holding feasts to honor a martyr on the anniversary of his or her death.

Polycarp wrote one letter. The church at Philippi had requested copies of the letters of Ignatius, which Polycarp sent along with a cover letter of his own. It is a solid let-ter, comprised largely of quotes or allusions to scriptural texts. It is clearly the work of a pastor, a man charged with watching over the congregation. His concerns are sincere and echo many of the themes in Ignatius's letters. Still, Polycarp's principal importance to the emerging orthodox consensus was his role as a living connection to the authority of the apostle John and his impact on the generation of leaders that solidified orthodoxy in the latter half of the second century. Chief among these was Irenaeus of Lyons.

Irenaeus of Lyons

Of the four men profiled in this chapter, Irenaeus may have had the longest and most far-reaching impact. Still highly regarded in both the Western and Eastern halves of the Christian world, the bishop of Lugdunum in the province of Gaul (modern-day Lyons in France) was the critical theological voice defining the orthodox consensus. His five-volume *Against Heresies*, which set out to expose and refute what he regarded as the illicit activities and aberrant teachings of gnostic Christians (some of whom had been involved with members of his own congregation), became one of the most important theological tracts of the second century.

Irenaeus refers to Polycarp as "that blessed and apostolic presbyter" under whose ministry he sat at a young age. Polycarp clearly had an enormous impact on young Irenaeus, who frequently turned to him and his legendary relationship with the apostle John in his later writings to demonstrate the strength of the tradition within the mainstream of the church.

Born probably in Smyrna, Irenaeus eventually studied in Rome before becoming a presbyter and being sent to Lugdunum, the most important city in the northern provinces of the empire due to its strategic location in the Rhone River valley. He went as part of the mission with Bishop Pothinus to found a Christian community in this city of 50,000. Many of the Christians who formed that initial community were also from Asia Minor, which grated on the nerves of the native Gauls. Sometime in 177 or 178, this combination of xenophobia and religious intolerance boiled over. For unknown reasons, a mob attacked the Christian community, taking almost 50 into custody. We saw in Chapter 7 that all of them were executed; some, including Bishop Pothinus and the famous Blandina, died in the arena.

Irenaeus was not actually in town when everything went crazy. He was in Rome delivering a letter to the bishop there about the growth of Montanism in the church in Lyons. He returned to find his bishop dead, along with several other leaders in the Christian community and most of the people in hiding. In the wake of Pothinus's death, Irenaeus was chosen to be the new bishop of Lyons. It must have taken incredible nerve.

As bishop, Irenaeus was deeply troubled by the growing influence of several of the groups we looked at in the last chapter. In particular, he was infuriated by the conduct of a particular gnostic teacher named Mark, who, Irenaeus alleged, was using his claims to have a higher spiritual understanding as a way to get women in the church to sleep with him. Irenaeus was familiar with many of the gnostic writings and teachers from his time in Rome, but its intrusion into his own congregation motivated him to write against it.

The Refutation and Overthrow of Falsely-Called Knowledge, or, as it is generally known, *Against Heresies*, is Irenaeus's claim to fame. In five volumes, he surveys the teachings of the various schools of gnostic thought (including Marcion, for good measure) and then sets about demolishing them. In contrast to the secret knowledge and individualistic enlightenment of the gnostics, Irenaeus argues, God has given us his divine revelation openly in the four Gospels, the rule of faith, and the apostolic succession of the bishops. We're going to get into all three of those in the next chapter, so I won't try to tackle it now except to note the Irenaeus doesn't have much patience for speculation for its own sake. The kind of creative, almost playful theologizing of the gnostics drives him nuts. His preeminent concern stems from his role as a pastor, and that is the spiritual well-being of the Christians in the community that he leads. As I say, more about this in the next chapter.

Nearly everything else that Irenaeus had written, which was quite a bit, appeared to be lost until 1904. An Armenian copy of another of Irenaeus's works was discovered. *The Demonstration of the Apostolic Preaching* really doesn't seem to be much to look at right away, but that can be deceiving. *The Demonstration* is really intended to be Irenaeus's expansive summary of the essential message taught by the apostles. In the next chapter, we'll talk about how mainstream Christians used both in their worship and in their polemics, or short summary statements of the Gospel. *The Demonstration* is basically a lengthy version of one of these confessional statements designed to orient candidates for baptism.

Irenaeus's eventual fate is unknown. Much later, tradition had it that he was martyred, but there's no evidence to suggest that. He simply fades into history, dying sometime just after the end of the second century.

Tertullian of Carthage

I have to confess up front that of all the characters who were active during the second century—and there were some real live ones—for sheer entertainment value, Tertullian is hands down my favorite. Bitingly sarcastic with a razor-sharp mind, Tertullian was his own man from start to finish. Widely read for his day, his knowledge combined with a caustic wit to produce a triumphant Christian rhetoric at a time when being publicly Christian could be very bad for one's health.

Much of what we thought we knew about Tertullian has been questioned in recent years. His biography is a bit hazier now, but certain elements still stand out. Born sometime in the middle of the second century, Tertullian was a native of Carthage, a city in North Africa (modern-day Tunisia). Once

From the Source

"If the Tiber rises too high for the walls, or the Nile too low for the fields, if the heavens do not open, or the earth does, if there is famine, if there is plague, instantly the howl is, 'The Christians to the lion!' Really? All of them? To one lion?"

—Tertullian, *Apology*

Rome's greatest rival, the city was destroyed in 146 B.C. at the end of the Punic Wars. Julius Caesar reestablished the city, and by Tertullian's time, it was one of the most important cultural centers in the empire. His father may have been a Roman centurion, and Tertullian clearly was given a first-rate education. His later training appears to have been in law, a field that required a great deal of skill at public speaking.

His conversion to Christianity likely took place sometime in 197 or 198, when he was in his 40s. We don't know the precise circumstances, but it seems to have been a sudden and dramatic event. Given his sensitivity to the power of the martyrs to attract new converts, it's probable that they had an effect on Tertullian as well.

Tertullian was the first of the early Christian writers to write in Latin. As such, he is sometimes called the father of Latin theology. His thoughts on the condition of the human soul and the nature of God were foundational for the development of Christian theology in the West. He was instrumental in the evolution of the doctrine of original sin, for example, and he is the one who used the word *trinitas*, or Trinity, to describe the doctrine of God as Father, Son, and Holy Spirit.

At the same time, Tertullian's uncompromising attitude could lead him to some dark conclusions. He is, as we'll see in Chapter 13, the source for some of the worst condemnation of women. He had little use for philosophy, especially when it seemed to be behind the speculations of the gnostics and the followers of Marcion, and his words on the subject were dismissive of speculative knowledge and discovery. The Christian already knew everything that he or she needed to know, he argued. And because Tertullian remained so influential on later Western thinkers in the church, his less uplifting thoughts became the foundation for later attitudes toward women, heretics, and the relationship between faith and reason. As Walter Wagner acerbically observed, "Tertullian embarrasses Christians."

From the Source

"What indeed has Athens to do with Jerusalem? What agreement is there between the Academy and the Church? What between heretics and Christians? Our instruction comes from 'the porch of Solomon,' who had himself taught that 'the Lord should be sought in simplicity of heart.' Away with all attempts to produce a mottled Christianity of Stoic, Platonic, and dialectic composition! We want no curious disputation after possessing Christ Jesus, no inquisition after enjoying the gospel! With our faith, we desire no further belief. For this is our palmary faith, that there is nothing which we ought to believe besides."

—Tertullian, *The Prescription Against Heretics*

After years of putting his pen at the service of the church, fed up with what he saw as an increasingly lax Christian community, Tertullian abandoned the mainstream church and joined up with the Montanists. Later tradition suggests that even the Montanists disappointed him, and in the end he had his own small group known as Tertullianists. If accurate, it indicates a sad end to a remarkable life.

His defection to Montanism colored how Tertullian was received by later Christian writers, but it couldn't obscure his native genius or the attractiveness of his style. Cyprian of Carthage, whom will we will meet in Chapter 16, was a huge fan of his. He would frequently ask his secretary for one of Tertullian's works with the phrase, "Hand me the master."

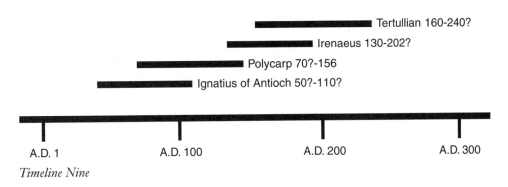

Timeline Nine

The Least You Need to Know

◆ Ignatius gives us a glimpse of the church at a very early and formative stage.

◆ Polycarp is most important as a symbol of apostolic succession.

◆ Irenaeus is our most important source of information about gnostics in the second century.

◆ Tertullian was the father of Latin theology and the most important theologian for the later development of Western Christianity.

10

Canon, Creed, and Church

In This Chapter

- ◆ Piecing together the Bible
- ◆ Meet the Fourfold Gospel
- ◆ Now repeat after me …
- ◆ Pass it on

In Chapter 8, we learned about the diverse viewpoints that were developing in the early church as it wrestled with life after the deaths of the apostles and their immediate successors. Diversity in the Christian community was by no means new, and neither was controversy, but as distance grew between the time of Jesus and the apostles, it became increasingly unclear where genuine authority could be found.

By the end of the second century, a consensus had formed about what ought to constitute a sound Christian faith. This consensus was like a three-legged stool. It rested on a recognized set of authoritative sacred writings, a clear summary statement of what Christians believe, and a strong emphasis on a broad-based tradition transmitted through the bishops. In each case, the issue at stake was authority.

Canon

The ancient world tended to respect living voices over written accounts. This is almost completely the opposite of modern attitudes, which tend to privilege documents over eyewitnesses and oral history. Slowly, the number of people who had known Jesus or who had sat at the feet of the early disciples began to dwindle. In their place, written accounts, letters, and theological tracts had begun to be distributed.

It's important to point out that the arguments over which texts ought to make up what came to be called the New Testament had nothing to do with the spiritual value of reading books other than the canonical writings. The best example of this is *The Shepherd of Hermas.* Highly regarded by a host of orthodox Christian writers, *Hermas* was ultimately not included in the canon. Nevertheless, it remained on everyone's recommended reading list. The question was not whether Hermas contained good or sound teaching, but whether it represented apostolic teaching, which it did not. As the Muratorian Fragment put it, *The Shepherd of Hermas* "ought indeed to be read; but it cannot be read publicly to the people in church either among the Prophets, whose number is complete, or among the Apostles, for it is after their time."

 In Depth

The Muratorian Fragment is a list of recognized writings written sometime around 170, which makes it perhaps the oldest list of the New Testament to come out of the orthodox consensus. The anonymous author put together a list of all the writings that were used in the church that he was a part of. They included four Gospels, the last two of which are Luke and John (the first two are unknown due to the loss of the first part of the Fragment). They also included the Book of Acts and 13 letters of Paul (not including the Letter to the Hebrews). The letter of Jude and two of the letters of John are included as well. Both of Peter's letters and the Letter of James are not on the list, either. The Revelation of John, however, is.

Some writings that might be new to you are on the list. The Wisdom of Solomon, a collection of wisdom literature that is still recognized as canonical by Roman Catholics and Eastern Orthodox Christians, but not by Protestants. A Revelation of Peter is mentioned, although the author points out that some protested its use in church. Two pseudonymous letters of Paul, to the Alexandrians and to the Laodiceans, are also mentioned and noted as rejected. Finally, *The Shepherd of Hermas* is highly regarded, but not to be read in the churches.

Determining which of these documents should be read in the churches—in other words, which should stand in for the living presence and word of the apostles—was a tricky task that provoked a great deal of controversy and conflict. Many of the writings that were produced in the late first century and throughout the second century would be named for one of the apostles or someone else of authority in the early church as a way of using that person's reputation as a cover for the teachings in the text. Paul himself ran into some of these *pseudonymous* writings early on in his career (see 2 Thessalonians 2). Identifying an authoritative *canon* of Christian writings was a key task occupying the Christian community throughout the second century.

> ### Word Knowledge
>
> A **canon** was originally a ruler or measuring stick. In literary terms, it refers to a list of writings that are considered essential and foundational for a given culture, subject, or group. They are the literature against which everything else is measured. A text that belongs to a canon is called canonical.
>
> **Pseudonymous** writings were forgeries, documents written by someone different from the person they were attributed to.

The Old Testament

The earliest followers of Jesus were immersed in the Hebrew Scriptures. In that, they were just following Jesus, who found his identity and purpose in those prophecies. As they marched out into the world to share the Jesus story, it was the Hebrew Scriptures, in the form of the Septuagint, that the apostles took along. They believed that they alone had found the true meaning of those texts in Jesus.

Anti-Semitism is not a Christian invention. It was waiting for the Jewish followers of Jesus when they started traveling the empire. Gentile converts brought a lot of their own religious, philosophical, and cultural baggage with them when they came into the church. Paul spent much of his time putting out the fires started by well-meaning but, in his mind, misguided Christians on both sides of the Jewish/Gentile divide.

A lot of folks in the empire, Jews and Gentiles alike, had come to have real difficulty with the God of the Hebrew Scriptures. Some of them found their way into gnostic groups that subverted the meaning of the texts and presented the Creator-God of the Jews as a demon. Others tried to remain within the church but redefined the relationship between the Jesus story and what was coming to be known as the Old Testament.

Like the gnostics, they believed that there could be no relationship between the God of the Old Testament and the Father of Jesus of Nazareth. For these folks, Marcion was a hero.

As we saw in Chapter 8, Marcion put together his own canon of scriptural texts. In fact, as far as we know, Marcion is the first person to assemble an authoritative list of New Testament texts. Using only a trimmed-down version of Luke's Gospel and the Book of Acts and an equally edited set of Paul's letters, Marcion set out on his own. His Marcionite church became a serious rival to the mainstream Christian community. Believing that Marcion's version of the New Testament was flawed, Christians in the second century began to grope their way toward their own version.

One of the first things they did, however, was assert forcefully their embrace of the Old Testament. Early Christians argued that Christian faith was always a fulfillment of the Jewish story, not some disconnected thing that fell out of the blue. Holding on to the Old Testament became a bright-line distinction between mainstream Christians and others.

Paul's Letters

It's almost certain that the first Christian documents gathered together in one collection were Paul's letters. The process may have started while Paul was still alive. We know that Paul himself directed the church at Colosse to share the letter he sent them with the church at Laodicea, and vice versa, so copies were already being exchanged between churches. Paul probably kept copies of his letters as well, so his own associates may have assembled the ultimate collection. Churches in centrally located cities like Ephesus did a great deal to reach out to the region around them and start new Christian communities. The relationship between these mother and daughter churches would certainly have included the sharing of religious texts.

Word Knowledge

A **codex** is the earliest form of the modern book. It is a series of pages stacked and bound together at one edge, and often given a cover. While technically any book is a codex, the term tends to be reserved for handwritten works dating from the first century up until the dawn of printing in the late Middle Ages.

The early collection of Paul's letters may also explain why early Christians were so fond of the *codex* as the form, as opposed to the scroll, for publishing their writings. In the first and early second centuries, scrolls were still by far the medium of choice for important texts, so the Christians' choice of the codex is highly unusual and unexpected. The construction of a codex required more skills than the assembly of a scroll, making it an unlikely choice for a brand new, very small religious group whom we would expect to adopt technology that was already available. Basically, in a world of PCs, the Christians decided for some reason to start using Macintoshes.

 In Depth _____

> Who actually compiled Paul's letters together into one collection? Several theories exist. My favorite theory, however unlikely it might be, credits the collection of the Pauline literature to a runaway slave named Onesimus.
>
> Onesimus belonged to one of Paul's converts near Ephesus in Asia Minor, a fellow named Philemon. Apparently, Onesimus ran away from his master and somehow ended up finding Paul, who converted the young slave to Christianity. Paul then sent Onesimus back to his master along with a letter asking Philemon to receive him back not as a slave but as a brother in Christ.
>
> That's all the New Testament tells us about Onesimus. However, there is an intriguing possibility. When Ignatius of Antioch wrote his letters to thank the various churches that met with him on his journey to Rome, one letter is written to the church at Ephesus and its aging bishop. The bishop's name? Onesimus.
>
> Could the elderly leader of the Ephesian church be the same Onesimus that we knew as a fugitive slave? Onesimus was a common name at the time, so it's hard to say, but some evidence suggests that Paul's letters were first assembled in Ephesus. And who, besides Onesimus, would have had both access to Paul's private letter and the motive for including it? Sure, it's a longshot, but it's fun to speculate.

The Christian adoption of the codex was swift and almost complete. While scrolls were still produced and used, the majority of early Christian literary remains come from codices. Many theories have been put forth to explain this, but none of them is entirely satisfactory. The most likely reason is that codices provided an easy way to transport and use multiple documents. Since Paul's letters are the only collection of documents early Christians were likely to have been carting around with them and using in such fashion, and the only documents that had enough authority to cause such a shift in the use of technology, they may have sparked this phenomenon.

Alongside the Pauline collection was a collection of the Gospels. These are the documents that got the most circulation and that were considered most important in the life of the church, so we'll turn to them next.

The Fourfold Gospel

It took time for the Gospels to be produced, reproduced, and distributed. The first evidence that we have of the canonical Gospels starts to come in at the end of the first century and early second century. By the middle of the second century, the Roman Christian Justin Martyr can talk about "the memoirs of the apostles," a transparent reference to the Gospels, though how many and which ones is less certain.

There is some evidence that sometime early in the second century, the Gospels were bound together into a single volume. This is very sketchy, but it explains some of the later assumptions about there being only four Gospels. The inclusion of more than one Gospel text was bound to cause some head scratching. Modern scholars often point to contradictions or inconsistencies between the Gospels, as if the early Christians didn't see the same things. They must have been aware, since their critics, like Celsus, were quick to point out the apparent conflicts among the various accounts. Some have suggested that part of the motivation behind Tatian's Diatesseron was to demonstrate that the four Gospels were not at odds with each other, but, with the initial exception of Syria, the early church seems not to have embraced the idea of creating a single harmonious Gospel account. Somehow a difference of details doesn't seem to have caused them many sleepless nights.

The origin and development of the canonical Gospels has been a source of tremendous debate and investigation by historians and biblical scholars. Let's take a minute or two to run through some of their explanations for how we got the Gospels that we have before we move on.

From the Source

"But it is not possible that the Gospels can be either more or fewer in number than they are. For since there are four zones of the world in which we live, and four principal winds, while the church has been scattered throughout the world, and since the 'pillar and ground' of the church is the Gospel and the spirit of life, it is fitting that she should have four pillars, breathing incorruption on every side, and vivifying human afresh. From this fact, it is evident that the Logos, the Maker of all, he that sits on the cherubim and holds all things together, when he was manifested to humanity, gave us the gospel under four forms but bound together by one spirit."

—Irenaeus of Lyons, *Against Heresies*

Gospel Structure

So what's going on with these Gospels, anyway? Well, if you read them, the first thing you may notice is that three of the gospels—Matthew, Mark, and Luke—are remarkably different from the last one, John. The first three seem to be more like biography, with a focus on events, while John's Gospel spends a lot of time with Jesus making long speeches. Because of their similar focus, scholars refer to Matthew, Mark, and Luke collectively as the Synoptic Gospels.

You might also notice that the Synoptics tend to cover the same basic stories. In fact, their content and even their structure shows a great deal of overlap, so much so that you might be tempted to think that at least one of them is copying from the others. If so, you're in good company. Most scholars agree that there is some dependence between the Synoptics, though they differ on which is dependent on which and to what degree. The dominant theory is that Mark's Gospel was written first, and that Matthew and Luke utilized Mark as part of their own writing process. This is called *Markan priority*, meaning that Mark came first. A smaller group of scholars hold to a view of *Matthean priority*, seeing Matthew as the first Gospel and Mark as a kind of summary version. For purposes of our discussion, we'll assume Markan priority.

> **Word Knowledge**
>
> **Markan priority** is the theory that Mark's Gospel was written first and was used by Matthew and Luke to compose their own Gospels.
>
> **Matthean priority,** which had been the dominant theory for most of Christian history, is the belief that Matthew's Gospel is the source for the common elements in the Synoptics.

It doesn't stop there, however. A lot of stuff that Matthew and Luke have in common doesn't show up in Mark. These tend primarily to be sayings of Jesus, such as the parable of the man who builds his house on rock (from Matthew 7:21–27 and Luke 6:46–49) or the Beatitudes (found in Matthew 5:3–12 and Luke 6:20–23). If these sayings don't come from Mark, then where did Matthew and Luke get them? New Testament scholars have suggested the possibility of a second common source. The word for *source* in German (most of this theorizing was done by German scholars) is *quelle*. Scholars simply refer to it as Q for short. Finally, there are parts of Matthew and Luke that are unique to each of them, often referred to as M and L for short.

Gospel Intents

So much for the mechanics, but what does all of that mean? It means the Gospel writers were working with the traditions and stories about the life and ministry of Jesus to craft their own narratives. In other words, each writer has a purpose for doing what he's doing. They aren't just regurgitating the party line; each of the Gospels has a particular view of Jesus and his significance, and they mold and shape the traditions to bring out what they see in him.

 In Depth

> The existence of Q and what exactly it may have looked like is very controversial. Some scholars, particularly those associated with the Jesus Seminar, have built their entire theories around the existence of Q as a written document that existed and was used early in the Christian community. Several attempts have been made to reconstruct this hypothetical document from the material found in the New Testament Gospels. Some scholars have even attempted to show that Q evolved over time and have tried to peel back the layers of this development. Those who champion the existence of Q are especially likely to support the use of the Gospel of Thomas, since Thomas as a collection of sayings looks very similar to what they imagine Q would look like.
>
> As I say, these attempts are controversial. A growing body of scholars has questioned the assumption that Q was a written document, preferring instead to cite oral tradition as the source of the Q material. Other historians doubt whether Q existed at all. They point to the fact that no such document has ever been discovered, even in fragmentary form, and that no early Christian writer ever refers to it.

For example, Matthew's Gospel is cleverly crafted so that Jesus' teachings are broken into five sections. The first of these sections is the famous Sermon on the Mount. Now, it may not immediately mean much to you and me, but a first- or second-century Jew hearing about a man who goes up on a mountain to deliver God's word will hear echoes of Moses, especially if you happen to be waiting for a new Exodus (remember what we talked about in Chapter 1?). So it seems that Matthew has sculpted the Jesus story in such a way that he gives the impression of Jesus as a kind of new Moses, which indeed is one of the early Christian claims about Jesus. Mark and Luke similarly arrange their telling of Jesus' story to make theological claims about Jesus.

We should stop here and mention John's Gospel again. Because it is so different from the Synoptics, historians tend not to rely too heavily on John for information about the life of Jesus. John omits many important moments mentioned in the Synoptics. Where they locate the center of Jesus' ministry in towns and villages of Galilee, John puts the action in Jerusalem and Judea. In the Synoptics, Jesus' ministry could conceivably have lasted as little as a year before his death. John's Gospel gives the impression that it was more like three years. In the Synoptics, Jesus celebrates the Passover meal with his disciples and dies the next day, while John has him celebrate the meal the day before and then die on Passover. The confrontational wisdom and action-driven message of the Jesus of the Synoptics is replaced in John by a mystical Jesus who talks endlessly about himself and the significance of his life.

At the same time, studies have demonstrated that John's Gospel shows a remarkable knowledge about the geography of Palestine and the layout of cities like Jerusalem, much more so than that displayed by the Synoptics. Some scholars even speculate that the source of John's Gospel (who may not have been its writer) was a native of Jerusalem. To put it bluntly, he seems to know the place like the back of his hand. So we have this paradox, where John's Gospel seems very reliable about the setting in which Jesus operated, but seems utterly independent of the Synoptics in terms of the story that he tells.

Scholars may never get it all worked out. You might think of John's Gospel as *Jesus: The Musical*. In a musical, things can be going along just the way you would expect, when suddenly the lights dim, the spotlight comes on, and one of the characters suddenly starts singing. The songs are there not as literal dialogue, but as a way of revealing the truth at the heart of the character. Perhaps that's what John is doing with Jesus: letting him stop at key moments to offer a kind of poetic commentary on himself.

Gospel Origins

Two more questions to consider: when were the Gospels written and by whom? Regarding the dates, there is very little evidence in the Gospels themselves to give us any clues. The range of ages that scholars have suggested runs the gamut from as early as the A.D. 40s all the way up into the early second century. In the Synoptics, Jesus describes the destruction of Jerusalem, which fell to the Romans in A.D. 70 (we saw that in Chapter 5), so if you don't believe in the possibility of predictive prophecy, you'll almost certainly have to date the Gospels after A.D. 70. Questions about dates also hinge on how quickly scholars believe that certain theological ideas about Jesus developed. Generally, the majority of historians date Mark to between A.D. 60 and 70, with Matthew and Luke between A.D. 80 and 90, and John shortly afterward.

As for who wrote them, of course, we keep referring to them by their titles, but none of the Gospels' writers includes a claim of authorship in the text, so authorship is primarily determined by a critical reading of Christian tradition. For some time, it has been believed that the Gospels circulated anonymously (that is, without titles) until sometime early in the second century. All four canonical Gospels seem to be known by name no later than 140, so that would appear to be the cutoff date.

Some scholars, however, have objected to this idea of anonymous circulation. They argue that that's simply not how books were distributed in the ancient world. Once you had at least two different Gospels being read in the same church, which had to have happened much earlier than the second century, there would have to have been some way of distinguishing them. They also point out that, when later Christian writers began to refer to the Gospels by name, everybody gets the names right. In other words, you don't have cases of someone quoting Luke's Gospel but calling it, say, Fred's Gospel. The titles were clearly not being assigned randomly or regionally, as with some of the apocryphal writings. Everyone knows the names of the New Testament Gospels, which is hard to explain if they had been circulating without attribution.

Creed

It wasn't enough just to settle on a selected list of authoritative texts. The Valentinians, for example, were perfectly happy to use the same Gospels and letters of Paul that everyone else used. Yet they kept coming up with ideas that didn't fit into the emerging orthodox consensus. Irenaeus accused them of weaving "ropes of sand" by adapting scriptural texts to their own teachings. Beyond just a set of texts, then, Christian communities were finding that there had to be some agreement on essentially what those texts were trying to say. What are the bedrock basics that make Christians Christian? What does the Jesus story really mean?

Up until now, I have used the word *canon* as if it meant the authoritative list of books in the New Testament because that's what the word means today. That wasn't always the case. Prior to the ascension of Constantine (whom we'll meet in Chapter 17), during the period of early Christian development, the word *canon* referred not to the texts, but to their content. In other words, prior to the lengthy process of identifying which books should be read in church, there was already a general agreement about the core elements of Christian belief. The confessional content of Christian faith within the mainstream Christian community acted as a kind of quality-control mechanism for the reading of the texts.

> **Word Knowledge**
>
> **Creed** comes from the Latin word *credo*, meaning "I believe." It's a confession of belief.

More important, the canon served as a sign—the word *symbol* is often used—for the Christian to use as part of an initiation into the Christian faith. Think of the way new citizens to the United States recite the Pledge of Allegiance at their swearing-in ceremony. Another way to think of it is like wedding vows. The *creeds*, which were the final form that these confessions took, were recited as part of one's baptism. They describe exactly what the Christian was promising him- or herself to.

Confessions

The process of creedal development actually began in the daily life of the individual Christian communities at their earliest stages, especially with the mother church in Jerusalem. Jesus' earliest followers needed language to express their convictions and the truth that they believed they had found in Jesus. To do this, over time they created a body of confessions that could be used as part of the community gatherings for worship. Some of this confessional material was adapted from the Hebrew Scriptures or from other Jewish forms of confession and worship. Some of it was, if you will, home grown. This material was then handed on in the form of tradition to churches that formed later.

Initially, these ritual confessions were probably variations of invoking the name of Jesus. The two central ritual acts of the church (we'll get into this in Chapter 11), the Eucharist and baptism, were certainly bound up with ritual forms "calling upon the name of the Lord." These usually involved invoking the name of Jesus in relation to God—for example, Thomas's cry from John's Gospel, "My Lord and my God," or Peter's exclamation in Matthew's Gospel, "You are the Christ, the Son of the Living God." Paul uses an Aramaic expression, something that must go back to the earliest days of the church. The word is *maranatha*, meaning "Come, Lord."

What each of these three examples have in common is the notion of Jesus as the Lord. In Greek, the word is *Kyrios*, which the Septuagint used as the equivalent for the Hebrew name for God. At the same time, for residents of the Roman Empire, there was only one Lord, one Kyrios, and that was the emperor. So you can see how Christian confessions were loaded with danger. On the one hand, they equated Jesus with God. On the other hand, they describe Jesus in language reserved for the Roman emperor. The first got them in trouble with the Jews. The second earned them the suspicion of the imperial authorities.

The Rule of Faith

Over time, the various confessions condensed into a specific narrative structure. A passage in 1 Timothy contains one of these early storied confessions: "Beyond all question, the mystery of godliness is great: He appeared in a body, was vindicated by the Spirit, was seen by angels, was preached among the nations, was believed on in the world, was taken up in glory." (1 Timothy 3:16) As you can see, we've gone beyond simple confessional statements and happened upon a more complex statement of belief. There were several different names for this narrative confession (*canon* being one of them), but the one that stuck was the *rule of faith*.

Word Knowledge

Rule of faith comes from the Latin words *regula fidei*. It's one of several phrases used to indicate a core body of teaching that summarizes the essential truths of the Jesus story as it was perceived by the mainstream church beginning at least at the beginning of the second century.

As with the simpler confessional statements, the primary use of the rule of faith was in baptism. Irenaeus mentions "the rule of the truth which he [the Christian] received by means of baptism ...." Hippolytus, a Roman presbyter and writer, describes how the Christian was baptized three times, each time after being asked to affirm faith in the Father, Son, and Holy Spirit. The Roman baptismal creed is familiar to many Christians today as the Apostles' Creed.

From the Source

The Apostles' Creed

I believe in God the Father, Almighty, Maker of heaven and earth:

And in Jesus Christ, his only begotten Son, our Lord:

Who was conceived by the Holy Spirit, born of the Virgin Mary:

Suffered under Pontius Pilate; was crucified, dead and buried: He descended into hell:

The third day he rose again from the dead:

He ascended into heaven, and sits at the right hand of God the Father Almighty:

From thence he shall come to judge the living and the dead:

I believe in the Holy Spirit:

I believe in the holy catholic church:

the communion of saints:

The forgiveness of sins:

The resurrection of the body:

And the life everlasting.

Amen.

The Christian Confession

Now that we've seen what the rule is and what it consisted of, let's take a moment to sketch out what Christians believed to be the non-negotiable core of their faith.

When we examine the various versions of the rule, the first thing to notice is that there is a commitment to the idea of one God, but that this one God is worshipped as Father, Son, and Holy Spirit. It's hard to know when this Trinitarian emphasis came about, but it appears to have been quite early. Some scholars see a contradiction between the idea of baptizing in the name of Father, Son, and Holy Spirit, as commanded by Jesus at the end of Matthew's Gospel, and the practice of baptizing "in the name of Jesus," as we see described in the Acts.

The difference is more apparent than real, however, since it was precisely the willingness to speak of Jesus in the place of God that was so unique about early Christianity. The difficulty of adding another name to that confession later, combined with the emphasis on the Holy Spirit in Paul's teaching, suggests that the Spirit was also regarded in the same manner as Jesus and could not have been an afterthought.

Sacramental Religion

There is also a sure interest in the actual life of Jesus of Nazareth. Modern scholars are not the first people to care about the "historical Jesus." Early Christians rooted their hopes and faith in the belief that these events actually occurred. It is this confidence in concrete historical events that causes such problems between mainstream Christians and the Christian gnostics, for whom the historical reality of Jesus was much less important than the spiritual impact of the stories about him.

Two specific events are usually mentioned in the life of Jesus. The first is his virgin birth to Mary. The second is his death under the authority of Pontius Pilate. Already at the beginning of the second century, Ignatius tells us that Jesus' birth and his death are the *principal elements* of the message about him that must be proclaimed, suggesting that he had something like the rule of faith in mind.

Irenaeus asserted the critical importance of the *incarnation* for Christians, arguing that Jesus had *recapitulated* the human experience. When Mel Gibson's controversial *The Passion*

Word Knowledge

Incarnation literally means "in flesh." It's a theological term for the idea that God became a human being in Jesus of Nazareth. **Recapitulation** means "to sum up or summarize." Theologically, the idea that Jesus recapitulated human experience is the notion that he lived every aspect of human life and, in so doing, made human existence holy.

of the Christ was released, one of the promotional posters carried this caption: "Dying was his reason for living." Irenaeus might have countered that it was just as accurate to say that living was his reason for dying. The early Christian writers demonstrate a keen holistic sense of the life and death of Jesus. Neither was explainable without the other.

By implication, then, Christianity would be a *sacramental* faith. It asserted that all of life and all of material existence was open to God. There was nothing that was base or meaningless about existence, no place that God couldn't or wouldn't go. We'll see in the next chapter how the most important act of Christian worship, the Eucharist, embodies precisely this notion.

Word Knowledge

Sacrament is often called a visible sign of an inward grace. The idea is that physical acts, rituals, and elements can carry the love and mercy of God and make it available to people in their day-to-day existence. In early Christianity, baptism and Eucharist were two ritual acts that all agreed were sacramental.

What makes Christianity sacramental is that Jesus, having lived and died, rose from the dead and conquered the powers that hold humanity in thrall. The early church had a multilayered vision of Jesus' resurrection. It demonstrated the power of God over the demonic forces that ruled the world. Here there were some similarities to gnosticism. It was also a sacrifice for sin, cleansing the Christian from guilt and shame. Finally, it demonstrated the depth of God's love for his creation and pointed the way toward the kind of life God wanted people to live, a life of self-sacrifice and trusting devotion.

Charismatic Religion

Once Jesus had risen from the grave, he returned to heaven and cleared the way for the coming of the Holy Spirit. Pentecost, whatever actually took place that day, had written itself on the soul of early Christianity. Paul, in particular, made the Holy Spirit central to his sense of the message of Jesus. For Paul, the Spirit was the life of God that made a person capable of loving God and following Jesus.

Hence, Christianity would be a Pentecostal faith. That doesn't mean a lot of hooting and hollering and snake-handling, although early Christians clearly believed that the presence of the Holy Spirit in their midst released powerful abilities such as healing and prophecy, enabling the followers of Jesus to perform many of the same miraculous works that he did. What it meant was that Christianity would be marked by the experience of God as present and real in the Christian community and in the lives of individual believers.

Eschatological Religion

Jesus had left, yes, but the earliest Christian conviction displays a confidence that he would be back to finish the job. The Messiah was supposed to bring about an age of peace and justice. That clearly hadn't happened yet. The writer of the Letter to the Hebrews admits that, as yet, "we do not see everything subject to him [Jesus]," but that we do see Jesus himself. The emphasis was on hope. God had already done so much in Jesus; in time, he would completely fulfill his promises.

Christianity, then, was an eschatological faith, a religion focused not just on the future that God had planned for his creation, but on how that future was impinging on the present moment. As we'll see in the next chapter, the experience of mainstream Christians was that the church (at its best, one hopes) was the foretaste of what was coming at the return of Jesus. We've already seen, in Chapter 7, how this very attitude empowered the Christian martyrs. The willingness to put participation in the future above survival in the present was a powerful part of the early Christian ideal.

Church

We'll see in Chapter 12 how significant the gathering of Christians was viewed. The church was, in the words of 1 Timothy 3:15, "the pillar and foundation of the truth." But how is truth preserved, interpreted, and passed on intact to the next generation? The recognition of a canon of Scripture and the evolution of a symbol of faith were not considered to be enough. There had to be a way of guaranteeing that truth was public rather than private, open to everyone rather than privileged.

Tradition: Open or Secret?

Tradition was a big deal in the ancient world. The ancient truths had substance and meaning. They could be trusted. Newfangled religions were worthless. As we saw in Chapter 7, part of the apologetic enterprise was to convince the detractors of the faith that the Gospel was the most ancient of stories, not something new.

Traditions mattered within Christianity as well. The source of all truth could be localized. It was in Jesus, so whoever had access to Jesus or one of his disciples had a direct line to authorized truth. You can see some of this playing out in Paul's sometimes testy insistence that he is no less an apostle just because he received his Gospel "by revelation" rather than secondhand from Peter or James.

As we head into the second century, with the final passing away of the generation of eyewitnesses, a scramble was on to claim the traditional high ground. Gnostic teachers, wandering prophets, and bishops alike began to lay out the pedigree of their knowledge. Irenaeus is the most explicit. He had sat at the feet of Polycarp, who had studied under John the apostle. It was a royal lineage, in theological terms.

Other groups besides the orthodox crowd claimed access to tradition as well. For example, Basilides, the gnostic teacher in Alexandria, also alleged that he had inside knowledge of Christ's teachings from a fellow named Glaucias, who was "an interpreter" of Peter. Marcion asserted that he alone was upholding the essence of the Pauline teachings, saving them from their infection by Jewish ideas. The Montanists claimed to be able to access direct revelation from the Holy Spirit that could counter the holiest of texts.

What set the orthodox notion of tradition apart from the rest was that it was public in nature, not esoteric or ecstatic.

From the Source

"It is within the power of all, therefore, in every Church, who may wish to see the truth, to contemplate clearly the tradition of the apostles manifested throughout the whole world; and we are in a position to reckon up those who were by the apostles instituted bishops in the Churches, and to demonstrate the succession of these men to our own times; those who neither taught nor knew of anything like what these heretics rave about. For if the apostles had known hidden mysteries, which they were in the habit of imparting to 'the perfect' apart and privately from the rest, they would have delivered them especially to those to whom they were also committing the Churches themselves. For they were desirous that these men should be very perfect and blameless in all things, whom also they were leaving behind as their successors, delivering up their own place of government to these men; which men, if they discharged their functions honestly, would be a great boon [to the Church], but if they should fall away, the direst calamity."

—Irenaeus of Lyon, *Against Heresies*

Apostolic Succession

The idea that truth was personally guaranteed by the fact that your bishop was the latest in a line of bishops going all the way back to the apostles and to Jesus was pretty confidence inspiring. But it required that you could show your bishop's pedigree, so to speak. Suddenly the scramble was on to demonstrate connection with the apostles.

By and large, that wasn't too difficult. In the larger cities, such as Rome or Ephesus, the churches had been keeping records of their leadership for some time. How historically accurate some of these lists are is a stickier question. That mainly has to do with the fact that, early on, many of these churches didn't have a single head bishop, but rather a council or committee of leaders. Nevertheless, the mainstream church was able to show a clear line of descent, organizationally speaking, back to the apostles in a way that many other Christian teachers could not.

But as historian Justo Gonzalez has pointed out, apostolic succession was an inclusive idea at first. Rather than resting all of its teaching on this or that disciple of Jesus speaking in secret, it built itself on what it claimed was the unified testimony of all of the apostles. Churches didn't need to be able to claim apostolic succession for themselves to enjoy its benefits. They only had to agree with those "touchstone" churches that were rooted in the apostolic witness, churches that could be looked upon as authorities on the meaning of the Gospel.

The Least You Need to Know

- The compiling of the New Testament was partly a response to Marcion and his truncated Gospel.

- Early on, the church settled on the four canonical Gospels as the authoritative texts for Christian worship.

- Early Christians relied on a series of confessional statements and the rule of faith to identify their faith.

- The idea of apostolic succession asserted that the bishops were authorized conveyers of the true tradition of the church.

Part 3

Church and Culture

Okay, all this stuff about leaders and their arguments is fine, but what about the regular guy? What was it like to live as a Christian day by day? Christian faith was meant, ideally, to impact every part of a person's life. Socially, politically, and materially, Christians were supposed to live differently—or at least live for different reasons.

Part 3 explores how Christians were living out their faith in key arenas of daily life. Our first stop is the worship gathering, where Christians came together to celebrate their faith. Next, we look at Christian attitudes about sex, celibacy, and marriage. A chapter on the role of women in the Christian community is our next stop. Because Christianity was such an urban phenomenon, I'll take you on a tour of cities in the Roman Empire, and what it was like to live in them. Last, we'll talk about classical culture, music, and the arts, and how they fit into the Christian's life.

Chapter 11

The Body and the Blood

In This Chapter

- ◆ Remember to say your prayers
- ◆ Shall we gather at the river?
- ◆ To dunk or not to dunk
- ◆ Having dinner with Jesus

In the previous chapter, we looked at what orthodox Christians believed and the structures that they created—Bible, creed, and bishop—to support those beliefs. It would be a mistake, however, to suggest that Christianity was primarily a belief system. Most Christians, coming from lower-class backgrounds, were not intellectually equipped to plumb the theological depths of their faith. But just as you don't have to be a math whiz to show up for the prom, Christians didn't have to be theological geniuses to give themselves to the essential practices and disciplines of their faith.

In short, Christianity was a way of life as well as a way of thinking. In this chapter, we look at the rituals and practices that filled and shaped the lives of Christians. Taking our cue from the Jewish Temple, where things got holier the farther in you went, we'll start with daily practices and move steadily toward the central act of worship in the church, the Eucharist.

Daily Spirituality

Like all religions, Christianity developed rituals and practices that took root in daily life. Through these various disciplines, Christians were brought into the community of faith and learned to pattern their lives after the example of Jesus.

Bible reading took place primarily in the gathered worship of the church, but there were still opportunities for reading Scripture outside of church. As the New Testament writings became more widely available, it wasn't uncommon for a person or a household to have a copy of Paul's letters or one of the Gospels. Literacy was always an obstacle, since as little as 10 percent of the population could read with any fluency, but those numbers were concentrated in the city and it took only one or two people in the larger households (a slave, perhaps) to be able to read a text aloud, often over dinner. In this way, it was possible, and became increasingly common, for Christians to listen to the teachings of the apostles even when not gathered together.

The same thing could be said for other spiritual reading. The second century was a boom time for Christian writing and publishing. Even taking into consideration the loss of so many texts from this period, evidence shows that Christians were writing and printing books and other written materials in quantities far beyond their apparent size or importance within the Roman Empire. Books like *The Shepherd of Hermas*, the Gospel of Thomas, the *Infancy Gospel of James*, and *The Acts of Paul and Thecla* were widely distributed, so somebody must have been reading them.

Very early on, beginning with Matthew's account of the Sermon on the Mount, Christians defined three critical practices of Christian spiritual life: prayer, generosity in giving, and fasting. Christian communities were dedicated to prayer, and instruction in prayer makes up a good chunk of the New Testament writings. The Gospels frequently show Jesus going off to pray, either alone or with his disciples. Above all else, he gave his followers a very specific prayer to pray.

From the Source

"Before all else, the teacher of peace and master of unity desires that we should not make our prayer individually and alone, as whoever prays by himself prays only for himself. We do not say: 'My father, who are in the heavens,' nor 'Give me my bread this day.' Nor does anybody request that his debt be pardoned for himself alone, nor ask that he alone be not led into temptation and delivered from the evil one. Our prayer is common and collective, and when we pray we pray not for one but for all people, because we are all one people together."

—Cyprian of Carthage, *On the Lord's Prayer*

The Jews already had a variety of prayer practices in the first century that Christians inherited, adding their own as well. *The Teaching of the Twelve*, a church manual compiled sometime at the end of the first century or the first part of the second century, describes the Pater Noster, or Our Father (better known to some as the Lord's Prayer), and recommends that Christians pray it three times a day. The assumption is that this means morning, midday, and evening.

We'll talk more about giving in Chapter 14 when we look at the Christian care for the poor, but here we'll talk about what giving away money and goods had to do with the good of one's soul. In a famous encounter, Jesus told the "rich young man" in Mark 10:17–22, "Go, sell everything you have and give to the poor, and you will have treasure in heaven. Then come, follow me." It was a command that the young man, being quite wealthy, was unable to follow, but it gave Jesus the chance to warn those who had great wealth that it is "easier for a camel to go through the eye of a needle than for a rich man to enter the kingdom of God." Generally, the church maintained that notion at least as an ideal, if not always a reality. Paul, for example, calls greed "idolatry." The Letter of James warns the wealthy to "weep and wail" for oppressing the working man.

Fasting was a practice inherited from Judaism. According to *The Teaching of the Twelve*, Christians were to distance themselves from the practice of "the hypocrites," who fasted on Mondays and Thursdays. Instead, Christians should fast on Wednesdays and Fridays. Christians were also to fast for a day or two in preparation for their baptism, an injunction echoed by Justin Martyr and Tertullian. Fasting also seems to have been associated with the repentance of those Christians seeking readmission to the church after some grievous sin. General fasting for a day or two in preparation for Easter Sunday was widespread by the late second century.

Ecclesia

As I mentioned in Chapter 1, the word *church* is a translation of the Greek word "ecclesia." Literally, it means "the called-out assembly," a body of people summoned out of whatever they are doing to gather together for a purpose. From the beginning, the church held in creative tension two opposing notions. On the one hand, ecclesia was the word that the Septuagint used to describe the Israelite people on their way out of Egypt and moving toward the land promised to them by God through Abraham, Isaac, and Jacob. So to be ecclesia, to be the church, was to be a people on pilgrimage toward a new future.

On the other hand, as I mentioned in Chapter 1, in the Greco-Roman world, the ecclesia was the citizens of a city called together as a deliberative body to do the work of the community. So to be ecclesia, to be the church, was to be a polis, a new and alternative city. In some way, we've already seen this paradoxical approach to life in the martyrs and apologists. What was expressed individually there, here we look at collectively.

The Alternate City

Christians in the Roman Empire were faced with the confident assertion of Roman power and endurance. Rome was the "Eternal City," established in history but built to outlast the ages. What ultimately mattered, of course, was not the bricks and mortar, but the idea and ideal of Rome. But the Roman ideal had to be lived out in some form, expressed as a government and a religion alike. And Rome demanded total allegiance and obedience. There could be no second loyalty. As we've seen already, Caesar was Kyrios. Caesar was Lord.

Consequently, the Christians were on thin ice when they asserted that, in fact, Jesus was Kyrios. His kingdom was parallel to the Roman Empire, but like it in the notion that it demanded complete loyalty. They constituted an *altera civitas*, an alternate city. As such, early Christian writers pointed out, the church presented a future for humanity very different from that asserted by Rome's Eternal City. It's no surprise, then, that many of the rituals and practices of gathered worship in the church tended to subvert Caesar's claims to absolute power and authority.

From the Source

"Therefore make every effort to come together more frequently to give thanks and glory to God. For when you meet together frequently, the powers of Satan are overthrown and his destructiveness is nullified by the unanimity of your faith."

—Ignatius of Antioch, *Letter to the Ephesians*

Word to the Wise

"The Christian movement was revolutionary not because it had the men and resources to mount a war against the laws of the Roman Empire, but because it created a social group that promoted its own laws and its own patterns of behavior. The life and teachings of Jesus led to the formation of a new community of people called 'the church.' Christianity had begun to look like a separate people or nation, but without its own land or traditions to legitimate is unusual customs."

—Robert Louis Wilken, *The Christians as the Romans Saw Them*

Often these were names and titles used to address Jesus. In his letter to the church at Philippi, Paul calls Jesus both Kyrios (Lord) and Soter (Savior), both titles used for the emperor. Many of the tasks of the emperor, such as bringing prosperity and peace to the empire, are tasks that Paul ascribes to Jesus. That a person could walk into a church gathering and hear these kinds of things being said about Jesus instead of Caesar was pretty remarkable, and contributed to the Christians' sense of themselves as a separate people with a different political identity and allegiance. It also didn't do much to help their image with the non-Christian public or the imperial authorities.

The City Made Without Hands

The writer of Hebrews describes Abraham's faith by saying that he willingly risked everything because he was looking for "a city with eternal foundations, a city designed and built by God." Left to itself, the idea of the church as the alternate city could have led to an obsession with the realm of politics and possibly even armed rebellion, as it did with the Jews. But the *altera civitas* was countered by an opposing reality, the understanding that the church was only the foretaste of the coming kingdom of God. While Christians had an obligation—they would say the joy—of living by the laws of that coming kingdom right now, that didn't mean that the rest of the world was following along.

From the Source

"You have come to Mount Zion and to the city of the living God, the heavenly Jerusalem, and to innumerable angels in festal gathering, and to the assembly of the firstborn who are enrolled in heaven, and to God the judge of all, and to the spirits of the righteous made perfect, and to Jesus, the mediator of a new covenant, and to the sprinkled blood that speaks a better word than the blood of Abel."
—*Letter to the Hebrews* 12:22–24

From this standpoint, the church was an eschatological gathering living toward the future promised by God in Jesus Christ. This attitude was epitomized by the martyrs, with their unwillingness to engage this world but rather to leave it in pursuit of a better one. But the martyrs were only the tip of the iceberg. While not every Christian was ready to lay down his or her life, the gatherings shaped them into a people whose priorities were not focused on worldly success or gain. The cosmic images of worship in the Revelation of John or in the Letter to the Hebrews demonstrates what Christians hoped to be aware of when they gathered with each other. They were literally "seated … in the heavenly realms in Christ Jesus."

The Eighth Day

Jesus rose from the dead on the first day of the week, which on the Jewish calendar was Sunday. That also happened to be the first day of creation according to Genesis. Early Christians saw symmetry in the timing of these two events and right away began to gather on Sundays to worship together as a group. At least as early as the *Letter of Barnabas,* which we saw in Chapter 5, Christians were referring to Sunday as the "eighth day," the first new day of the new creation in Jesus. Where beforehand humanity was trapped in a weekly seven-day round, now suddenly, in the resurrection, something new had occurred. As a community living on the cusp of the new creation that had begun with Jesus' resurrection, the church kept Sunday as its holy day.

From the Source

"You see what he means: it is not the present Sabbaths that are acceptable to me, but the one that I have made; on that Sabbath, after I have set everything at rest, I will create the beginning of an eighth day, which is the beginning of another world. This is why we spend the eighth day in celebration, the day on which Jesus both arose from the dead and, after appearing again, ascended into heaven."

—*Letter of Barnabas*

Sunday Go-ta-Meetin'

The exact outline of a church gathering in the earliest days of the faith is hard to describe simply because there was so much variety. Certain general practices seem to have been common, however. The Book of Acts describes the early believers in Jerusalem as …

> devoted … to the apostles' teaching and to the fellowship, to the breaking of bread and to prayer …. All the believers were together and had everything in common. Selling their possessions and goods, they gave to anyone as he had need. Every day they continued to meet together in the temple courts. They broke bread in their homes and ate together with glad and sincere hearts ….

Key to the early gatherings were the apostles' teachings, the breaking of bread (a euphemism for the Eucharist, which we'll discuss in a moment), and the prayers (which we've discussed briefly already).

The earliest Christian gatherings, being almost exclusively made up of Jewish Christians, were profoundly shaped by the way that Jewish synagogues conducted their worship. So there were readings from the Hebrew Scriptures interspersed with prayers and the singing of psalms and hymns. At some point, there was a confession of faith, probably pretty simple at first, but growing in complexity over time (see the previous chapter for information about the formation of the creeds). A final prayer or *doxology* closed the gathering.

Word Knowledge

Doxology, literally "words of praise," is usually a short verse or prayer that is sung at the end of a worship gathering.

Paul gives us some small glimpses into the worship lives of his churches, especially in Corinth. Paul talks a great deal about the Eucharist, which we'll get to in a moment. In Corinth, we see the use of spiritual gifts such as prophecy and the ever-amazing "tongues" (whatever it actually was), and the confusion that was caused by the abuse of these seemingly supernatural occurrences. Corinthian worship sounds like it could be a chaotic environment, with everyone bringing a prophecy, a song, and a testimony to share, but this kind of spiritual dynamism was apparently on display in many churches.

Over time, Christian gatherings developed a more precise *liturgy*, though it still exhibited a great deal of simplicity. Pliny the Younger offered Trajan the information that he had gleaned as part of his investigation into Christianity. The Christians gather before dawn to sing a song "to Christ as to a god." Pliny writes that they follow this with oaths to live out a decent life, perhaps part of the prayers and confessions.

Word Knowledge

Liturgy comes from the word *leitourgia*, which is commonly translated "work of the people." In public use, it usually indicated the performance of a public duty, such as the philanthropic act of a wealthy benefactor on behalf of a city. In this sense of performing a public duty, the Septuagint used *liturgy* to describe the activity of the priests in the Temple. From there it was an easy jump to using it to refer to the worship being offered at the Temple. In the churches, the liturgy was recognized as the public duty of the Christians to attend to the Lord in communal worship and prayer.

Justin Martyr gives us a brief description of Sunday gatherings at the churches in Rome. The Christians gathered from all over, listen to the reading of "the memoirs of the apostles or the writings of the prophets," followed by a sermon. The people then rose to pray, after which bread and wine were brought out for the Eucharist. The president of the assembly prayed and gave thanks "according to his ability," and the people participated by assenting to his prayers (using the Aramaic word *amen*). Everyone ate and drank, and a collection of money was taken from those willing to give for the relief of the poor and the support of the widows and orphans under the community's care.

Because Christians principally met in one another's homes, the gatherings were necessarily small. Even the homes of the wealthier members were capable of hosting only perhaps 50 or 60 (the house church in Dura Europos, which we'll discuss in Chapter 14, could hold about 60 after it was renovated). This relatively small space created an intimate social environment for the early Christians to worship together in.

It was common in at least the Pauline churches to greet other Christians with "a kiss of peace." Kissing as a form of greeting was not unusual in the ancient world, not even between those of the same sex. The addition of "peace" may indicate that it was intended to signify that the believers were in harmony with one another.

That might not always have been very comfortable. Christians were a diverse bunch of people. While they were probably concentrated in the lower classes, there was still enough social variety to force people to meet folks that they otherwise might not meet. Women and men were forced into a much closer social space than was considered appropriate by most of society, and slaves often held leadership positions despite the presence of the wealthy. The many words of correction penned by Paul and other Christian writers is evidence of both the diversity of the Christian gatherings and the potential problems that could and often did arise by putting so many different people together in one room.

Initiation

By the beginning of the third century, large churches like the one in Rome already had programs in place to integrate newcomers into the Christian community. Recognizing that Gentiles were often completely unfamiliar with anything more than the bare rudiments of the Jesus story, let alone the larger context provided by the history of Israel, the church established something called the *catechumenate*. This was a process whereby a person interested in Christianity was allowed to be part of the community in order to learn about its life and to absorb its culture and message. In Rome, this process could last as much as three years. At the end of this time, if a person demonstrated seriousness about becoming fully part of the Christian community, he or she was prepared for baptism.

Baptism is one of those acts that has so many meanings and uses that it's almost impossible to mention them here. The New Testament, of course, takes seriously the origin of the ritual in the activity of John the Baptist. While there were Jewish practices involving ritual immersion in water, these were meant to be repeated frequently, even daily. John's baptism was clearly a one-time-only event. The early followers of Jesus, some of whom were previously followers of John, continued the practice of baptism during and after Jesus' life. When confronted with the question "What shall we do?" by the crowd on Pentecost, Peter tells them, "Repent and be baptized."

Word Knowledge

The **catechumenate** was the process whereby a person interested in becoming part of the Christian community joined in the community's life for a time, and with certain restrictions, until he or she was better acquainted with the doctrinal and ethical standards of Christian life and practice. The word comes from the Greek *katakeo*, which means "to echo."

Jewish Christians seem to have kept a good deal of the meaning of John's baptism, with its emphasis on a cleansing from sin in tandem with a person's sincere choice to turn his or her life in a new direction. It is with Paul that we get a much more mystical emphasis in baptism. For Paul, baptism is identification and even union with the Lord in his death, burial, and resurrection. In fact, the act of immersing a person in water was recognized as a physical reenactment of that threefold pattern. The writer of the Letter to the Hebrews, as well as 1 Peter and Justin Martyr, uses the image of enlightenment to describe the effect of baptism. John's Gospel harks back to the moment in Genesis 1:2 when the Spirit hovered over the waters of creation, as well as alluding to the womb in John 3, suggesting that baptism is about rebirth "by water and the Spirit."

In later practice, the baptismal ceremony could be quite elaborate. Even in its simplest forms, it involved the candidate reciting a confession of some kind, removing all of his or her clothes, and going naked into the water. There the person was immersed (if enough water was available) or water was poured over him or her, sometimes once and sometimes three times. The one administering the baptism said something to the effect of, "I baptize you in the name of Jesus" or "I baptize you in the name of the Father, the Son, and the Holy Spirit." Afterward, the newly baptized Christian was clothed in a white robe and led into the Christian assembly. Here, for the first time, he or she was allowed to eat and drink the Christian's sacred meal.

Eucharist

The Eucharist was the central act of worship in the church. It was originally part of a meal. As we saw in Chapter 2, table fellowship with its radical redefinition of community was one of the hallmarks of Jesus' life and ministry. The early Christian community latched on to this as they kept fellowship with one another. Even more important from the standpoint of Christian worship, the institution of the Eucharist at the Last Supper, seen as a culmination of all the acts of table fellowship, created a new act whereby the believers could continually reorient themselves to Jesus' life and message. At the same time, Jesus had told his followers at that Last Supper that he would not drink wine again "until that day when I drink it anew with you in my Father's kingdom." So each Eucharistic meal was also an anticipation of the future return of Jesus.

Word Knowledge

Agape is one of several Greek words for love. Agape is distinct from several others for having often been compared in Greek literature to divine love, love that is total and self-sacrificial. It seems that the Greeks had little use for the word, since it shows up so rarely. Christians, however, claimed it for their own. Agape is used frequently in the New Testament, especially for the love of God.

The meal setting emphasized the communal nature of the Eucharist. It is interesting that these meals were known in the Pauline churches as *agape*, a Greek word meaning "love." In fact, the early church adopted the word *agape* to describe the self-sacrificing love of God displayed in the death of Jesus. The same word was used to describe these "love-feasts." It's a bit remarkable—and telling, I think—that in the Christian community, love meant having dinner together.

As with baptism, the images used to describe the Eucharist and its meaning are far too rich to fully explore in this small space. The very word *Eucharist* points to thanksgiving as a fundamental part of this act of celebration, thanks for the gift of God that was given in Christ. Paul points to the aspect of communion when he writes about "participation" in the body and blood of Christ. The unity of the church, he argues, comes about through unity of Christ experienced because "we all partake of the one loaf." In fact, Paul's condemnation of the Corinthians for the ways that they were failing to act as a genuine community (the wealthy were bringing food but not sharing it with the poor, who had little or nothing to eat) stems precisely from this idea of communion as unity.

Originally, it appears that Christians actually observed two gatherings, possibly a result of the Jewish roots of the faith. Jewish Christians gathered with other Jews at the synagogue to participate in the readings, the prayers, and the teaching. Later, just the Christians gathered together separately to eat their communal meal and focus specifically on Jesus.

The earliest form of the Eucharist, then, was indistinguishable from the communal meals that early Christians shared. Over time, however, the ritual act became separated from the meal. Putting it in a new context, all by itself, meant that it would be experienced and understood differently. The focus came to rest more on the mystical aspects of communion with Jesus Christ through the act of eating and drinking.

From the Source

"Is not the cup of thanksgiving for which we give thanks a participation in the blood of Christ? And is not the bread that we break a participation in the body of Christ? Because there is one loaf, we, who are many, are one body, for we all partake of the one loaf."

—Paul of Tarsus, *1 Corinthians* 10:16–17

By the time Justin Martyr gives us his description of the Sunday gatherings, the meal and the Eucharist are entirely separate. This might have occurred because of the abuses. Pliny's experience suggests that the occasional bans on the meetings of voluntary associations may have stifled the meals (the Christians that Pliny meets tell him that they have stopped their meal gatherings because of the ban). Possibly it was just the logistical pain of having to organize a group meal every week. In any event, once it was no longer in the context of a meal, the Eucharist by itself became too short an act to warrant its own gathering. It was combined with the earlier gathering for readings, and the two remain joined to this day in most Christian gatherings.

The Least You Need to Know

◆ Christians observed a variety of spiritual practices aimed at bringing their life into line with the Gospel.

◆ The church was the new community of God, distinct from the rest of the people on earth.

◆ Baptism in water was the rite of initiation into the church.

◆ The central act of worship in the church was the Eucharist.

12

Single-Minded People

In This Chapter

- ◆ It's only sex
- ◆ Do you have your cloud and harp?
- ◆ Can you have sex in church?
- ◆ Married to Jesus

Nothing arouses passions, metaphorically speaking, more than disagreements over sex. To understand Christian attitudes toward marriage, sex, and singleness, we have to see them against the backdrop of their culture.

The Married State

Rome needed children. The world was a pretty vicious place, and mortality was high. Disease, disasters, and wars, not to mention the toil and trouble of everyday life, took their toll on the population of the empire. Shortly before and after the birth of Jesus, Augustus Caesar passed laws designed to, among other things, reward fertility. He was also deeply concerned about the sexual excesses of the day. Adultery was rampant and abortion was widely used to keep from having children. Under Augustus, marriage was required by law and widows were expected to remarry or face severe penalties. The state also rewarded couples that produced three or more sons. You could say that Augustus had a real focus on the family.

That didn't mean marriage was a picnic for women. Young ladies were at the mercy of their fathers until married off, usually around the age of 13 or 14, to an older husband, and then they remained part of their husband's household. Those who survived childbirth—and many did not—had no real control over their own lives until their husband's death. If they were young widows, and most were, they were required by law to remarry and place themselves again under the control of another man.

Roman Sex

Sex in the Roman Empire was considered a natural part of human life, but it created no bond of love or obligation between two people. Contrast that with the Jewish and Christian notion that sex made two people "one flesh" and united them in a way not easily or casually broken. Roman law forbade adultery on pain of death. But adultery was defined as one married freeborn person having sex with another freeborn person for free. Prostitution was not adultery, and neither was having sex with one of your slaves.

Sex was not shameful, but loss of control was. Sex was as much about power as it was desire. In fact, it was about power over desire. Self-mastery was a big deal to Romans, an ideal to strive for. Sexual excess did not fit into that ideal, so men tended to keep their sexual exploits in check, or at least under wraps. This was especially true in the case of homosexual sex, which was perfectly permissible for a man as long as he was not the passive partner. That implied a feminine nature that would have been insulting to the Roman quest to dominate.

Demographic Dilemma

The empire also suffered from a critical shortage of young women. Girls were widely regarded as a burden to the family, requiring a substantial dowry to marry off. Many newborn girls were exposed as infants, meaning that they were abandoned to die from the elements. A letter discovered in Egypt, written from a man named Hilarion to his wife, demonstrates the almost casual willingness of some families to discard girls.

From the Source

"Know that I am still in Alexandria. And do not worry if they all come back and I remain in Alexandria. I ask and beg you to take good care of our baby son, and as soon as I receive payment I shall send it up to you. If you are delivered of a child [before I come home], if it is a boy keep it, if a girl discard it. You have sent me word, 'Don't forget me.' How can I forget you. I beg you not to worry."

—A letter from a man named Hilarion to his wife Alis, 1 B.C.

Christians were opposed to exposure, and churches in the cities would often comb the garbage heaps and alleys looking for young children who had been left to die. These orphans, mostly girls, were raised and supported by the church. In part because of the Christian willingness to raise daughters, we'll see in a moment that the ratio of women to men in church was almost the opposite of Roman society at large. This would have serious implications for marriage in the church.

Body and Soul

Christian attitudes toward marriage were grounded in a larger view about the goodness and purpose of the body. Christians initially inherited Jewish convictions that the body was an organic part of the human person. There was no clear separation between body and soul in the Jewish worldview. This is crucial to realizing the importance of a concrete, physical resurrection as part of a Jewish belief in life after death. There was a murky sense of an intermediate state of the soul after death, but always with an eye toward the restoration of the human body.

Greek views of the body were quite different. Under the influence of Plato's philosophy, the Greeks asserted that the body and the soul were two distinctly different things. While the soul required the body for living, it was not synonymous with the body. Hence, for the Greeks, the body was material and temporary, while the soul was immaterial and immortal.

As Jews came into contact with Hellenistic thinking, there was an attempt to make the two views jibe with one another, usually by interpreting the Jewish view in light of the Greek. The Hellenistic Jew Philo of Alexandria adopted the body-soul distinction but warmed it a bit by locating individuality not in the soul, but in the body. The soul is sort of generic, while the body is what makes you uniquely "you."

Word Knowledge

An **ascetic** is a person who practices forms of self-denial as a means toward spiritual perfection. It's rooted in a Greek word that indicates hard work and rigorous exercise. An ascetic is a spiritual athlete, training the soul by disciplining the body.

Others tried to mesh the severely *ascetic* notions of the Syrian religious world with Greek philosophy. We see some of this in the development of gnostic thinking. The body for the gnostics was bad, a prison for the soul. Salvation, for the gnostic, was deliverance from the body. In contrast to the gnostics, Irenaeus argued that both body and soul were good, having both been made in the image of God. The body was critical to salvation since it was the arena in which sin and salvation warred with one another. It was with the sufferings of the body that Jesus Christ saved humanity, making salvation possible.

The gnostic views on the body virtually eliminated, at least in theory, the importance of sex. What mattered was the uniformly feminine nature of the soul, not the male or female illusory body that it found itself in. This actually played into the question of women's roles in church leadership. Tertullian objected to the gnostics allowing a woman to baptize or preside over the Eucharist, arguing that the sex of the body was an integral part of personhood.

Over time, the relationship of the body and soul was gradually redefined away from a Jewish view toward a perspective more comfortable to the Greek world. The Christian philosophers of Alexandria, Origen chief among them (see Chapter 15), were responsible for championing this change, but the church in the Roman Empire was largely ready to embrace it. The main difference had to do with the nature of resurrection. The new view, being more embarrassed by the idea of a physical resurrection (because who would want to come back in a body?), opted for an immaterial resurrection. All the cartoons you saw as a kid where heaven is a place in the sky where you float around on a cloud playing a harp come from right here. (See, now wasn't that worth the price of the book right there?) Sounds strange or even comic, perhaps, but it was a view that combined the Christian confidence in the significance of the body now with the conviction that the body was not meaningful in the longed-for eternal life. It was a view of the body that contributed greatly to the elevation of virginity and celibacy as spiritual ideals.

Christian Marriage

So how did Christians view marriage? By and large, they accepted the Jewish respect for marriage as a union created by and blessed by God. The Gospels record Jesus' teachings on marriage, which are sometimes viewed as rather harsh. The Law of Moses had made a provision for a man to divorce his wife (though not the other way around, apparently), and there was a wide latitude as to what grounds a man could use to put his wife away. Jesus seems to have sided with those who took a strong line against easy divorce. "So they are no longer two, but one," Matthew's Gospel quotes him as saying. "Therefore what God has joined together, let man not separate." Many of the early disciples were married, and at least some had children. Peter actually traveled with his wife, and Philip had four daughters (more about them in a moment).

Christians Against Marriage

From reading some later Christian writings, it would be easy to get the idea that they were down on marriage entirely as a distant second-best to singleness and celibacy. And it's true that there is a strong tendency to compare marriage unfavorably to virginity. On the other hand, in their apologetical writings directed at the culture at large, Christians were quick to recommend marriage as an honorable union as opposed to unbridled sexual promiscuity.

We've already noted the Encratites in Chapter 8 and their decision to avoid marriage entirely as something that keeps human beings from experiencing the fullness of God in their lives. Marcion as well taught his followers that sexual relationships, even in marriage, were inherently sinful and should be avoided.

On the other hand, there were many criticisms of groups that seemed to have gone the other direction entirely. Clement of Alexandria, for example, condemned a group called the Carpocratians, who supposedly held their wives in common (we'll meet Clement in Chapter 15). The Nicolatians, who are blasted by the risen and glorified Jesus himself in the opening chapters of the Revelation of John, were also alleged to be sexual libertines. Any number of gnostic groups were lumped into this crowd as well.

Two Cheers for Marriage

Walking a tightrope between these two excesses, early Christians were often at pains to extol marriage. Clement, the ultimate moderate in the ancient church, rejected the notion that having children was either sinful or, for that matter, something that would keep a person from living a holy or spiritual life. In fact, in order to make his point, he tells stories about some of the apostles who were married, like Peter and Philip.

Tertullian has gotten a bad rap for some of the comments that he made about women (if you don't believe me, go read Chapter 13), but he is also responsible for one of the most moving tributes to marriage ever to flow from a Christian pen. His essay *To My Wife* describes the unity in both body and spirit that attends two followers of Jesus in terms that are almost as idealistic as his comments about women are troubling.

From the Source

"How beautiful, then, the marriage of two Christians, two who are one in hope, one in desire, one in the way of life they follow, one in the religion they practice. They are as brother and sister, both servants of the same Master. Nothing divides them, either in flesh or in spirit. They are, in very truth, two in one flesh; and where there is but one flesh there is also but one spirit. They pray together, they worship together, they fast together; instructing one another, encouraging one another, strengthening one another. Side by side they visit God's church and partake of God's Banquet; side by side they face difficulties and persecution, share their consolations. They have no secrets from one another; they never shun each other's company; they never bring sorrow to each other's hearts."

—Tertullian, *To My Wife*

Christian weddings had much in common with those of non-Christians. The differences arose as the church began to insinuate itself into the process of blessing the marriages. Because Jesus was so closely identified with his church, the participation of the church in the contracting of a marriage came to be normal rather quickly.

Most of the traditional ritual trappings of the wedding ceremony were kept—the exchanging of the ring, the bride veiled in orange (yes, orange), and the joining of the hands—with the difference being that it was now Jesus rather than Juno who bonded the married couple together.

From the Source

"It is right for men and women who marry to be united with the consent of the bishop, that the marriage be according to the Lord and not according to lust."

—Ignatius of Antioch, *Letter to Polycarp*

Ultimately, what is most positive about the Christian view of marriage in the early period was how the Christians elevated marriage from a functional necessity of life that often, but not always, involved love to a union between two equal souls. Because an alternative to marriage—namely, virginity—was possible and often even preferred, marriage had become a choice rather than a mandate. Both partners entered in voluntarily, and therefore both were on an equal footing.

More than that, in the eyes of the Lord husband and wife were both of the same stature as persons. Paul had glorified marriage by referring to it as a symbol of the union between Christ and his church. While a wife was still called to submit to her husband, she did so now in Christ as a voluntary act. What was naturally expected of her by the society she lived in could now also become the means by which she could worship and glorify the Lord. Her husband, on the other hand, was hearing for the first time in his life that he was expected to love her with the same love that Jesus had for his church: a self-sacrificial kind of love. Sexual fidelity was now required of him as well, not only his wife.

Having Sex in Church

It's interesting to see how early Christians held in tension the goodness of marriage and even of sexuality, but also how they attempted to restrain sexuality even in marriage. For the most part, there is little enthusiasm in early Christian writings for sex for its own sake. Desire was a burning flame that often got out of control and could destroy lives. Better to keep it under control and not feed it too often. Even in marriage, lust was still a sin, though apparently a manageable one.

Having children was viewed as a good thing by most mainstream Christians. Folks like the gnostics and Encratites would certainly have disagreed. For many of the gnostics, such as the compiler of the *Gospel of Philip*, having children only kept the great earthly prison going. Why on earth would you want to keep adding to the misery of existence by bringing more souls into subjection to this rotten, illusory physical life? Orthodox Christians would not go quite that far, believing as they did in the goodness of creation.

> **From the Source**
>
> "Either we do not marry except to rear children, or we refuse to marry and we exercise complete self-control."
>
> —Justin Martyr, *First Apology*

Paul advised married couples in Corinth not to deprive one another sexually, lest they fall into temptation. The fact that he had to tell them that indicates that there were people for whom celibate marriages were the natural outcome of a spiritual life. We don't know if the Corinthians listened to Paul, but these spiritual marriages crop up in other places as well. In Syria, for example, the *Acts of Thomas*

> **Word to the Wise**
>
> "Christian teachings on sex and remarriage were part of a wider ethic, concerned with desire and human sin."
>
> —Robin Lane Fox, *Pagans and Christians*

portray Thomas teaching married couples to abstain from sex and lead celibate lives. It only reflects what Tatian was busy teaching in the same region at that time (the latter end of the second century). There's good evidence to suggest that this was a normal requirement for married couples coming to be baptized into the Syrian church (see the following sidebar about the Sons and Daughters of the Covenant).

The Single Life

While marriage was regarded positively among Christians, and sex at least tolerated, it was virginity and celibacy that really excited them. While Christian marriage was defined in opposition to the perceived sexual excesses of Roman society, virginity was about living the life of the angels. Jesus had said, "At the resurrection people will neither marry nor be given in marriage; they will be like the angels in heaven." Many Christians, especially in places like Syria, where the kingdom of God was considered a present reality, longed to live that resurrected life here and now. Renouncing sex was one clear way to do that.

 In Depth _____

> The Sons and Daughters of the Covenant were a loosely defined group of single men and women and married couples who, when baptized, vowed to live lives of celibacy. They did so, however, not hidden away in a monastery somewhere, but as regular members of the community.
>
> The Syriac word for the Sons and Daughters was *ihidaya*, a word that basically means "one" or "single," but with several shades of meaning. Primarily, it was used in reference to Jesus as "the one and only Son of God." The ihidaya, then, are closely associated with Jesus as they try to live their lives after his example. The word also indicates single-mindedness, an attitude of complete devotion. Finally, the literal idea of singleness, as in not being married, comes into play.
>
> So the ihidaya were folks in the Syrian church who pursued the example of Jesus with complete devotion by, among other things, living celibate lives in the midst of their communities. In doing so, it was believed that they served the rest of the church by being living examples of the Kingdom of God.

There was an accepted history of celibacy in the church from early on. Luke's Gospel tells us about Anna, a woman who lived in the Temple and who had been celibate for decades since the death of her first husband. Anna was not unusual in Palestine at the time. Other groups had established patterns of celibate living. The men of the Essene communities, particularly the ones at Qumran who are thought to be responsible for the Dead Sea Scrolls, dedicated themselves to sexual purity (celibacy) as part of their participation in the community.

Of course, Christians had the ultimate example of Jesus himself, who was not believed to have been married. His mother, Mary, as we'll see in the next chapter, had a growing reputation as having remained a virgin all her life, and this was a powerful model particularly for young women. Philip may have been married, but his four daughters were all virgins. Last but not least, there was the example of Paul, who encouraged celibacy and virginity as states of freedom for the Christian, though he was more careful than folks later gave him credit to not suggest that celibacy was spiritually superior to marriage, despite his own clear preference for the single life.

Widows and the Church

There were two ways to end up single. The first was through the death of a spouse. While men often lost their wives to complications in childbirth, women normally outlived their husbands due to the common disparity in their ages. Frequently, the husband was two or even three times his wife's age, and sometimes more. Decisions about marriage were usually made by the child's parents, so often only after the death of a spouse was a person finally free to choose whether to live a celibate life.

As noted earlier, the state penalized widows who chose not to remarry, usually by not allowing them to inherit their husband's estate. Those who suffered this loss were without support in a world that generally despised widowhood. The support, financial and otherwise, of the church for the widows was a very real help in the ancient world and made it possible for many women to embrace the call not to remarry, but rather to dedicate themselves to lives of prayer and service.

Virgins and the Church

The other way to the single life was as a young person. Christian parents faced some fairly tough obstacles when it came to finding spouses for their children. As I mentioned earlier, there were a lot more women in the Christian community than men, which meant there weren't enough prospective Christian husbands around. Christian parents were faced with the dilemma of marrying their daughters to sons from pagan families. Under those circumstances, many chose to maintain their children in virginity. For young Christian men, the situation was less difficult. Still, marriage laws limited the ability of people from different social classes to marry. A young man from a lower class might not be able to marry any of the eligible Christian girls at church because they were of a different class.

Virgins, particularly from the upper classes, also faced severe pressure to conform to the marriage laws. The choice not to marry was a political act as well as a spiritual one, and points us to another reason why Christians were regarded as a subversive people. The Christian virgins were perhaps the first to argue that biology was not destiny. Who would have thought that early Christians would have more in common with Gloria Steinem than with James Dobson?

Either old or young, many people in the church at some point found themselves in a state of sexual renunciation. This wasn't as unpopular then as it probably would be today. Because of the idealization of virginity, those who practiced such self-control were often lauded in the churches as heroes and examples. For women especially, virginity was a doorway to esteem within their community. In the next chapter, we'll look more closely at the role of women in the church, which, among others, included the ranks of virgins and widows.

The Least You Need to Know

◆ In the Roman Empire, sex and marriage were essentially functional.

◆ The shift to a view of the body as good but temporary supported the importance placed on virginity and celibacy.

◆ Christian marriage was defined in puritanical terms to distinguish it from the sexual morals of the day.

◆ Virginity and celibacy were rooted early in the church's experience, but came to be seen as spiritually superior to marriage.

Chapter 13

God's Daughters

In This Chapter

- ◆ Does God have breasts?
- ◆ Mother Mary takes on a cosmic role
- ◆ Mary was apostle to the apostles
- ◆ The ugly fate of women martyrs

Recent work in the field of church history has been instrumental in providing us with a new and more appreciative look at the role of women in the life of the early Christian community. Not only has new data from inscriptions, epitaphs, and other sources broadened our knowledge about the daily life of women in the church, but new documents (such as the Gospel of Mary) and new assessments of old documents are both filling in the historical gaps and clearing away our social blind spots regarding the activities of women in the formative period of Christianity.

The Image of God

God created man in his own image, the saying goes, and man has been returning the favor ever since. The ancient world had a multitude of images for the divine, gods and goddesses of all stripes. Judaism and Christianity are often accused of ridding the world of goddesses, putting in their place one male God. And in the words of feminist theologian Mary Daly, "If God is male, then male is God."

Are the images of God in the Bible exclusively masculine? And what do Christians do with their belief that God has taken on human form as a man? Both of these questions are significant for understanding the backdrop against which early Christian women operated, how they saw themselves, and how they were perceived by the men around them.

The Feminine Divine

While the controlling images of God in the Hebrew Scriptures—and in the New Testament, for that matter—are usually masculine, there are many exceptions. God is often described as a mother experiencing the pangs of labor (Isaiah 42:14), nursing her children (Numbers 11:12; Isaiah 49:14–15), and giving birth and caring for them (Isaiah 46:3–4; Hosea 11:1–4). At other times, God appears as a midwife (Psalms 22:9–10; Psalms 71:6; Isaiah 66:9), as a mother eagle bearing her young on her back as they learn to fly (Deuteronomy 32:11–12), and as a mother bear defending her cubs (Hosea 13:8).

Other passages demonstrate that God transcends mere gender descriptions, being equally at home with either. For example, we are told in Genesis that both male and female are created in the image of God (Genesis 1:28), at the very least implying that the feminine images God as much as the masculine. In Deuteronomy 32:18, Moses tells the Israelites, "You deserted the Rock, who fathered you; you forgot the God who gave birth to you," using masculine and feminine imagery back to back.

Some early Christian literature picked up on these themes, presenting God in feminine imagery. Early Christian writers seem especially fond of the image of God breast-feeding the church. The first letter of Peter encourages Christians, "Like newborn babies, crave pure spiritual milk, so that by it you may grow up in your salvation, now that you have tasted that the Lord is good." (1 Peter 2:2–3) Irenaeus speaks of eating the Eucharist as "being nourished as it were from the breast of his flesh" in *Against Heresies*. The Alexandrian teacher Clement also uses this image of "the milk flowing from the Father by which alone we little ones are fed."

God as the breast-feeding Father also appears in the Odes of Solomon, a set of hymns that most likely originate in Syria. The Syrian Christians didn't stop there, but went on to describe the Holy Spirit as "she." In Syriac, just as in Aramaic and in Hebrew, the word for "spirit" is feminine in gender. The Holy Spirit was associated with the conception and birth of Jesus. The Spirit encourages, nurtures, and comforts. And the Spirit is connected with the creation of new life in the world (Genesis 1:2), in Mary's womb (Matthew 1:18, 20), and in the life of the Christian (John 3:6). The Spirit also groans together with all of existence in the birth pangs of the new Creation (Romans 8:22–26). For these reasons, the Syrian Christians referred to the Holy Spirit as female until at least the fifth century.

From the Source

"A cup of milk was offered to me,
And I drank it in the sweetness of the Lord's kindness.
The Son is the cup,
And the Father is he who was milked;
And the Holy Spirit is she who milked him;
Because his breasts were full,
And it was undesirable that his milk should be ineffectually released.
The Holy Spirit opened her bosom,
And mixed the milk of the two breasts of the Father.
Then she gave the mixture to the generation without their knowing,
And those who received it are in the perfection of the right hand."
—The opening verses of *Odes of Solomon* 19

Jesus was not uncomfortable with feminine language. Once when looking out over the city of Jerusalem, Jesus cried, "O Jerusalem, Jerusalem, you who kill the prophets and stone those sent to you, how often I have longed to gather your children together, as a hen gathers her chicks under her wings, but you were not willing." (Matthew 23:37) While he famously referred to God as "Father," Jesus also described God both as a shepherd seeking lost sheep and as a woman seeking a lost coin.

Jesus broke many of the taboos of his culture, not least of which was his close involvement with women. He received financial support from a group of women who traveled with him as disciples just like the Twelve, among them Mary Magdalene (more about her in a moment). This was practically unheard of in his day. In fact, we know quite a bit about many of the women in Jesus' life, an indication that some of them may be the sources for some of the traditions that eventually made it into the various Gospels.

From the Source

"After this, Jesus traveled about from one town and village to another, proclaiming the good news of the kingdom of God. The Twelve were with him, and also some women who had been cured of evil spirits and diseases: Mary (called Magdalene) from whom seven demons had come out; Joanna the wife of Cuza, the manager of Herod's household; Susanna; and many others. These women were helping to support them out of their own means."

—Luke's Gospel 8:1–3

Spoiling the Image

Okay, there are certainly positive images of women and the feminine in the Bible, and Jesus obviously embraces the role of women in the world. Still, there's no avoiding the fact that, for at least several early Christian writers, women were a problem. Or maybe it wasn't women, per se, but one woman in particular.

In Depth

When they first met, Adam called his wife "woman" because she was "flesh of my flesh, bone of my bones" and, therefore, his equal. After the Fall, Adam gave his wife a new name. He called her Eve, which means "mother of all living." What had been a relationship of nature was now a relationship of function.

Poor Eve can't catch a break. Sure, listening to that snake wasn't the grandest idea ever, and it did manage to louse things up pretty badly, but hadn't she paid for all of that? When her husband first met her, he had called her "woman" as a sign that she was the equal partner to "man," different but the same. Now he just called her Mama. Eve was persona non grata for certain early Christian thinkers. Already in the New Testament, 1 Timothy restricts women's teaching role in the church on the grounds that it was Eve who was deceived by the serpent in the Garden of Eden, not Adam. The implication, of course, is not just that Eve is unreliable, but that all women are.

Implicit, then, in Eve's responsibility for the fall of humanity was the notion that somehow all women were complicit in the same act. It was Tertullian, with his gift for words, who gave this theological view of women its most notorious expression when he referred to women as "the Devil's gateway."

Neither Tertullian (who was married, by the way) nor any of the other early Christian writers was trying to be especially antagonistic to women, nor were they all that different from most other men, Christian or otherwise, in their age. And while they could be pretty hard on Eve—and, by implication, all women—they were also looking for a way to redeem femininity. Of course, you may not like what they came up with. You see, to counter Eve, they needed another woman to stand in her place. Just as Jesus had countered Adam, as Paul theologized in his letter to the Romans, someone needed to balance out Eve. Guess who that was gonna be?

From the Source _____

"God's judgment on this sex [women] lives on in our age; the guilt necessarily lives on as well. *You* are the Devil's gateway; *you* are the unsealer of that tree; *you* are the first foresaker of the divine law; *you* are the one who persuaded him [Adam] whom the Devil was not brave enough to approach; *you* so lightly crushed the image of God, the man Adam; because of *your* punishment, that is, death, even the Son of God had to die."

—Tertullian, *On the Dress of Women*

Mother

Of all the women associated with Jesus, by far the best known and most beloved has been his mother, Mary. Today there is no question of the important place that Mary holds in the Christian faith. But how much of the reverence and devotion modern Christians directed toward Mary was mirrored by her own contemporaries?

As the earliest witness to the Christian faith, Paul gives no indication of a special place for Mary. In fact, with one exception ("God sent his Son, born of a woman" [Galatians 4:4]), he doesn't even mention Jesus' mother. Of course, Paul's letters betray very little about the life of Jesus beyond the fact of his crucifixion, so we might not expect him to make much of Jesus' birth. It's possible that the virgin birth, if known to him, formed part of the inner core of the faith, something that was not discussed openly with outsiders.

As perhaps the earliest of the Gospels, Mark also reveals no interest in any virgin birth. He picks up with Jesus' life at his baptism by John. But Mark also contains no accounts of the resurrection, though its author certainly believed in it, so it's hard to make much out of the silence. Matthew and Luke, on the other hand, are deeply interested in Jesus' birth. It is from their Gospels that we get the story of the virgin birth.

A Cosmic Figure

By the end of the first century, however, Mary was finding higher esteem. While John's Gospel contains no birth story, per se, it is to the Beloved Disciple that the crucified Jesus entrusts his mother, a sign that she was a figure of some respect within the early Christian community. Some have detected a reference to Mary in the Revelation's description of the woman "clothed with the sun, with the moon under her feet and a crown of twelve stars on·her head" who is about to give birth to the Christ child.

Later tradition had Mary passing away quietly in Ephesus, where tradition also places the apostle John toward the end of his life. A competing tradition puts her in Jerusalem. There is no way of determining which, if either, is correct, but if Ephesus is true, it places Mary's final years right in the middle of one of the most vibrant Christian communities of the first and second centuries.

> **From the Source**
>
> "Now the virginity of Mary and her giving birth were hidden from the ruler of this age, as was also the death of the Lord—three mysteries to be loudly proclaimed, yet which were accomplished in the silence of God."
>
> —Ignatius of Antioch, *Letter to the Ephesians*

Ignatius of Antioch, coming out of Syria, gives us our next reference to Mary. Writing maybe only a decade or two after John's Gospel and the Revelation, Ignatius already has a remarkable view of Mary's role in the Jesus story. Both her pregnancy and her virginity, he alleges, were part of God's assault on the "ruler of this age," which, though once kept under wraps, should now be "loudly proclaimed."

Toward the end of the second century, reflection on Mary's place in God's salvation plan had entered a new level. Christian writers began to compare her with Eve, the disgraced wife of Adam, whose sin supposedly caused all of humanity to fall into darkness and death. Justin Martyr (we met him in Chapter 7) is the first we know of to contrast Eve and Mary. Later, picking up on Paul's argument in his letter to the Romans that Jesus was the "second Adam," Irenaeus also suggests that Mary is the new Eve. By her obedience and willingness to bear Jesus, he argues, she made up for the disobedience of Eve and opened a door for the salvation of the human race. Mary's cosmic role in the salvation plan meant that women were not merely bystanders, and provided a counterbalance to Tertullian's reminder of women's continuing guilt for Eve's sins.

So then what? Jesus was the balance to Adam, yes, but he was also a model for how to live out the new life. If Mary was the new Eve, how did that impact behavior? What kind of model was she for feminine behavior?

From the Source _____

"So the Lord now manifestly came to his own, and, born by his own created order which he himself bears, he by his obedience on the tree renewed [and reversed] what was done by disobedience in [connection with] a tree; and [the power of] that seduction by which the virgin Eve, already betrothed to a man, had been wickedly seduced was broken when the angel in truth brought good tidings to the Virgin Mary, who already [by her betrothal] belonged to a man. For as Eve was seduced by the word of an angel to flee from God, having rebelled against his Word, so Mary by the word of an angel received the glad tidings that she would bear God by obeying his Word. The former was seduced to disobey God [and so fell], but the latter was persuaded to obey God, so that the Virgin Mary might become the advocate of the virgin Eve. As the human race was subjected to death through [the act of] a virgin, so was it saved by a virgin, and thus the disobedience of one virgin was precisely balanced by the obedience of another."

—Irenaeus, *Against Heresies*

Perpetual Virgin

Written right about the same time as Justin's comments, the *Infancy Gospel of James* (sometimes called the *Protoevangelium of James*) alleged to provide a lengthy history of Mary's life beginning with her miraculous birth. Among other revelations, the Infancy Gospel alleges that Mary remained a virgin even after giving birth to Jesus. The Odes of Solomon concur, suggesting that Mary felt no pain in childbirth, possibly an allusion to the curse laid on Eve in Genesis 3 that she would experience pain in childbearing.

From the Source _____

"So the Virgin became a mother with great mercies.
And she labored and bore the Son but without pain, because it did not occur without purpose.
And she did not require a midwife, because He caused her to give life.
She brought forth like a strong man with desire, and she bore according to the manifestation, and she acquired according to the Great Power.
And she loved with redemption, and guarded with kindness, and declared with grandeur."

—*Odes of Solomon* 19

Of course, all of this theologizing focused on Mary's pregnancy. In other words, she was obedient to God by becoming a mother, but without sex. Ignatius had pointed out that it was both virginity and pregnancy that made Mary so special. But pregnancy and virginity, by and large, don't go hand in hand for most women, now, do they? By virtue of her dual role, however, Mary quickly became a model for both virgins and mothers. While these images are difficult for some to swallow now, Mary's capacity to straddle the boundaries between the domestic life of wife and mother, and the liberated world of the virgins must have been a powerful image in the day-to-day life of women in the early Christian communities.

Apostles and Prophets

Women were the first to see Jesus alive after his resurrection and the first to tell anyone about it. That simple fact continued to work on the Christian imagination as the faith grew and developed. While men seem to have been the major evangelistic names in the early church, women also played a significant role that has until recent years not been entirely celebrated.

Asia Minor was a stronghold of prophetic activity, particularly among women. At least three of Philip's four daughters, all of them prophets (Acts 21:9), were believed to have lived in the region. In Philadelphia, one of the seven cities mentioned by John in his Revelation, the prophetess Ammia developed such a reputation that, in the late second century, both mainstream Christians and Montanists were vying to adopt her as their own. Among the Montanists, Priscilla and Maximilla were the two companions of Montanus and exercised as much spiritual authority as he did. Even Tertullian mentions women in Carthage who had prophetic gifts.

Mary of Magdala

Have you noticed that Mary Magdalene has been in the news a lot the last couple of years? You can thank Dan Brown for most of that. His megahit *The Da Vinci Code* launched the second-most-famous woman in Jesus' life to superstar status, prompting an outpouring of interest and increasingly wild and even bizarre speculations about her life.

It's not that all of this attention hasn't been helpful for Mary's good name. For centuries, Mary of Magdala had a reputation in the West as a repentant whore. This came about because Mary was confused with two other women in the Gospel accounts, Mary of Bethany (the sister of Lazarus, who anoints Jesus with perfume in John 12) and the sinful woman of Luke 7:37–38. It was Gregory the Great, late in the sixth century, who merged these three women into one. He did it with the best of intentions because the Christian community had begun to read Mary's life as a metaphor for itself as sinful yet redeemed. Nevertheless, the Magdalene's image as the penitent sinner obscured her actual role in Christian history.

Prior to Mary's makeover, however, the Western church understood what the Eastern church has always held—namely, that Mary Magdalene was one of the favored disciples of Jesus and a leader in the early Christian community. It was actually a third-century Roman writer, Hippolytus, who first referred to Mary as "apostle to the apostles." As the first person to see Jesus alive after his crucifixion, Mary's testimony was critical to the early Christians. While Paul, in his list of "authorized" witnesses to the resurrection (1 Corinthians 15), nowhere mentions the women to whom Jesus first appeared, all four of the Gospels mention it. John, in particular, gives us that singularly subversive image of Jesus appearing to Mary Magdalene first (John 20).

Even opponents of Christianity demonstrate the importance of Mary's witness in a backhanded way by ridiculing Christians for depending on a woman's testimony. The writer Celsus, for example, is surely referring to Mary Magdalene when he mentions "a hysterical woman" as the basis for believing in Jesus' resurrection.

From the Source

"While he [Jesus] was alive he did not help himself, but after death he rose again and showed the marks of his punishment and how his hands had been pierced. But who saw this? A hysterical woman, as you say, and perhaps some other one of those who were deluded by the same sorcery, who either dreamt in a certain state of mind and through wishful thinking had a hallucination due to some mistaken notion (an experience which has happened to thousands), or, which is more likely, wanted to impress the others by telling this fantastic tale, and so by this cock-and-bull story to provide a chance for other beggars."

—Celsus, from Origen's *Against Celsus*

Celsus was not alone in his critique of the high level of female involvement in the early leadership of the Christian community. The Christian apologist Minucius Felix responded early in the third century to those who described Christians as "gullible women, readily persuaded as is their weak sex." The presence of women at Christian gatherings was always suspicious to outsiders, who had an easy time imagining the bizarre goings-on. As a consequence, Christians were frequently forced to account for the public behavior of women who belonged to the community in ways that had more to do with how outsiders perceived them than with any theological insight. The consequence of this was the eventual downplaying of women's involvement in the events of the Gospel, and certainly Mary was impacted by this caution.

The Apostle Junia

There are few names in the New Testament about which we know less than Junia's, and even fewer that have caused as much controversy. At the end of his letter to the Romans, Paul greets more than two dozen people by name. These are mostly former co-workers of his, fellow Christians with whom he has shared a lifetime of service in the name of Jesus. Among them he mentions "Andronicus and Junia, my relatives who were in prison with me; they are prominent among the apostles, and they were in Christ before I was." (Romans 16:7)

So where's the controversy? Well, here we have a man (Andronicus) and what appears to be a woman (Junia) who are described as "prominent among the apostles." Now, that could mean that they were well known and respected by the apostles, or it could mean that they were themselves highly regarded apostles. The translation could go either way. The amazing thing is that, if Junia is a woman and Paul is referring to these two folks as apostles, then *we have a woman being called an apostle in the New Testament.* So why is it that popular translations of the New Testament, such as the New International Version and the New American Standard, render the name not "Junia," but "Junias," which is a man's name?

Supporters of the Junias translation will tell you that the name Paul writes could go either way. Depending on how it's accented in the Greek, it could be read as Junia or as Junias. But there are no accent marks in the text. So how do you decide which is right? Well, the answer might already be obvious to you. Women can't be apostles. So if Paul is calling Junia an apostle, then Junia can't possibly be a woman. Thus, the name must be Junias. Simple, right? Well, not so much.

A search of inscriptions from monuments and epitaphs from the same period as Paul's letter turns up scores of examples of the name Junia. It turns out that it's a very common name for women in Rome. The name Junias, on the other hand, doesn't show up anywhere. Not once. It just doesn't exist.

Add to that the fact that nearly all early Christian writers who mention this text understood Junia to be a woman. The lone exception is a fourth-century fellow named Epiphanius, but he also thought that Prisca (of "Priscilla and Aquila" fame) was a man, so clearly he's not a very reliable source. Add to that the fact that, when scribes began to add accent marks to the biblical texts that they reproduced, they wrote it as a feminine name, not a masculine one. Finally, consider that every English translation of the New Testament up until the middle of the nineteenth century, including the beloved King James Version, has Junia. The evidence becomes overwhelming that we're talking about a woman. A woman who was an apostle.

In Depth

"Then another praise besides. 'Who are of note among the Apostles.' And indeed to be apostles at all is a great thing. But to be even amongst these of note, just consider what a great song of praise this is! But they were of note owing to their works, to their achievements. Oh! How great is the devotion of this woman, that she should be even counted worthy of the appellation of apostle!"

—John Chrysostom, patriarch of Constantinople (398–407) from his thirty-first *Homily on Romans*

Martyrs

Early Christians lived constantly with the possibility of arrest, torture, and execution for their faith, although realistically such assaults on the church were infrequent and tended to be local or regional (later we'll see what happened when the imperial government launched an empire-wide, active persecution of Christians).

We've talked a bit about martyrdom in general already (see Chapter 7), so here we'll focus specifically on the role that women played during these outbreaks. Again, as we've seen, outbreaks of violence against the Christian community usually focused on the leaders of the church. The fact that so many women were arrested, abused, and killed in the course of these storms is an indication of how active they were in leadership positions.

There are several documented instances both in the acts of the martyrs and in other writings of women being tried and sentenced. Pliny the Younger, for example, reports to the emperor that, in his prosecution of those accused of being Christians, he attempted to "seek the truth, with the assistance of torture, from two female slaves, who were styled deaconesses." It's worth noting, first, that Pliny would deem it worthwhile to torture a pair of women in order to discover what Christians were doing. Clearly, despite being slaves, these two unnamed women were significant leaders in their community. Second, the casual way that Pliny mentions torture only serves to reinforce the danger that Christians—and, in this case, Christian women—could face if brought before the magistrate.

That danger was heightened by the fact that physical torture was not the only means by which officials could punish women accused of being Christian. There was also the threat of rape, and we know of numerous instances in which Christian women were forced into brothels either in lieu of a death sentence or as a sadistic way to maximize the humiliation of their prosecution before their execution. Tertullian is the first to mention such an incident, but similar stories come from other early Christian writers like Hippolytus of Rome and Cyprian of Carthage. The Christian historian Eusebius relates not only information that he had collected from past sources, but also the abuses that he had witnessed with his own eyes during the Great Persecution under the emperor Diocletion (we'll talk about that in Chapter 16).

Clearly, Christian women faced dangers from persecution not shared by men, yet they continued to take up leadership roles in the church, despite the fact that this would draw attention to them. Their bravery was inspired by famous women who modeled true martyrdom. If men had Stephen or the apostles Peter and Paul to look up to, women had Blandina and Perpetua.

Blandina

Blandina was a slave woman who was tortured and executed as part of the slaughter of Christians in Lyons and Vienne in 177 (remember this from Chapter 7). When the report of her death began to circulate among the Christian communities, Blandina became both a hero and a model.

From the Source

"Blandina was hung on a post and exposed as food for the wild beasts let loose in the arena. She looked as if she was hanging in the form of a cross, and through her ardent prayers she stimulated great enthusiasm in those undergoing their ordeal, who in their agony saw with their outward eyes in the person of their sister the One who was crucified for them, thus convincing those who believe in Him that any man who has suffered for the glory of Christ has fellowship forever with the living God. As none of the beasts had yet touched her she was taken down from the post and returned to the gaol, to be kept for a second ordeal, that by victory in further contests she might make irrevocable the sentence passed on the crooked serpent [Satan], and spur on her brother Christians—a small, weak, despised woman who had put on Christ, the great invincible champion, and in bout after bout had defeated her adversary and through conflict had won the crown of immortality."

—Eusebius, *Church History*

In their description of Blandina's death, the authors of the account quoted by Eusebius make clear that she had become for those who watched a representative of Christ. In her, "a small, weak, despised woman," Christ had become visible for all to see. She especially encouraged her fellow Christians who were suffering with her.

Perpetua

One of the most significant accounts of martyrdom from the late second century, and one that we saw already in Chapter 7, was that of Perpetua and Felicity. While we've already talked about the larger issues of martyrdom to which this text speaks, I did say that we would come back to it to talk about what it has to tell us about the experience of women specifically.

Vibia Perpetua, to give her full name, was arrested along with several other catechumens during Septimius Severus's persecution of the Christians (details in Chapter 16). She was a young Roman matron and mother to a newborn son who had not yet been weaned. The other woman in the group, Felicity, was a slave girl who was eight months pregnant. Afraid that she would be kept out of the arena because she was with child (even the Romans had scruples about killing pregnant women in the arena), she asked the others to pray that she would give birth before the day arrived. She did, and was able to join her fellow prisoners when they faced their execution.

As mentioned before, the account includes part of the diary of Perpetua. It is, quite simply, the earliest text that we have written in a woman's own words and from her own perspective. That alone makes it enlightening and exciting. Perpetua comes across as a strong, committed person. Her determination to bear witness to Christ with her life is deeply compelling, all the more so because it comes at such a high price. Not only is she to be put to death, but she is burdened by the fate of her newborn son.

That highlights an important point about both Perpetua and Felicity. They were both mothers. In a Christian world where virginity and celibacy were deeply admired, here were two women who clearly were sexual persons. When they were dragged out into the arena to face the animals, they were presented to the crowd naked. "The people shuddered, seeing one a tender girl, the other her breasts yet drooping from her late childbearing. So they were called back and clothed in loose robes." Apparently the crowd didn't mind killing them as long as they couldn't see how vulnerable they were.

In addition to the relationship with her son, we are privy to Perpetua's struggles with her father, who desperately tries to convince her to perform the necessary offering and escape the death penalty. In their first meeting, he uses logic and anger, trying first to reason with her and then ordering her to obey him. She refuses. Then he tries to shame her, asking her what her son will do without her. When that doesn't work, he kneels in front of her and weeps. For all of this, Perpetua is unmoved. The implication is that her father is the only member of her family who is not Christian, and this is why he can't see the glory in what she is doing.

Interestingly, Perpetua's husband is never mentioned. We hear about her encounters with her son and her father, but not the father of her son. It's possible that he is a pagan and has divorced her, but we hear nothing of it. He might be dead, but she is never described as a widow. In the end, his identity remains a mystery and his absence unexplained.

Widows and Virgins

We've already talked about those who chose to live a life of celibacy either before or after having married. Here we'll focus briefly on the implications for the place of women in the early Christian community. It seems that there were three such orders or organized communities within the larger church composed entirely of women. Two are common everywhere, and that's the virgins and the widows. The third seems to have been common in the eastern part of the empire but not in the West, and that was the deaconesses.

Virgins

We've already taken a general look at virgins, so we won't spend too much time here. The development of an order of virgins was a lengthy process. Throughout most of the period that we're looking at in this book, a celibate lifestyle was a matter of individual piety, although certainly supported by the church. Frequently, pairs or groups of such ascetics would get together to form a common household.

For women, the freedom from marriage and childbearing could be liberating. At the same time, as we saw in the last chapter, the choice of whether to marry was not usually up to a child, especially not to a daughter. While some entered a life of celibacy without choice, others did so voluntarily. These were the widows.

Widows

It's clear in the New Testament that early in the life of the church, Christians were taking upon themselves the responsibility of caring for the marginalized, the poor, and the needy. This was a day with no government welfare worth speaking of, so if you had nobody to care for you and no money to fall back on, you were in pretty deep trouble.

The group of people who epitomized this need were the widows. They were exactly what their name sounds like, women whose husbands had died. Initially, support for the widows was part of the charitable function of the church. But soon the widows became a sort of order in the church, where women who received support from the church could be freed from other responsibilities in order to devote themselves entirely to the work of service and hospitality. Widows were often found visiting the sick and those in prison, as well as the wives of pagan husbands who were unable to receive male ministers as visitors.

Deaconesses

The first deaconess is mentioned in Paul's letter to the Romans. In fact, she delivered the letter. Phoebe hailed from Cenchrea, a sort of suburb of Corinth. She is described as a deaconess or, more generally, a servant of the church in Cenchrea. He urges them to give her whatever help she needs for some unnamed task because "she has been a great help to many people, including me." The word *help* here indicates that Phoebe has been a patron to the church and to Paul. That means that she is a woman of independent means who has provided money and assistance to other Christians, including Paul.

Aside from another possible reference in 1 Timothy 3, the New Testament has nothing more to say about women serving as deaconesses. By the beginning of the second century, however, it is clear that deaconesses are beginning to perform an organized role in the church. So the two slave women tortured by Pliny in 112 were described as deaconesses (actually, *ministrae* in Latin, which is the rough equivalent).

The function of the deaconess, like the deacon, had three basic parts. Deaconesses were responsible for the charitable work of the church, distributing food, clothing, and funds as necessary. They were often called upon to instruct the catechumens and prepare them for baptism. Finally, during the worship gatherings, the deaconesses were assistants to the presbyters and bishops. They were especially visible during baptisms. Since Christians were baptized naked, a man could not perform the baptism directly. The bishop worked through the surrogacy of the deaconess, who led the female catechumen into the water and administered the act of baptism.

Over time, the office of deaconess disappeared. As more people were baptized as infants, there was less need for deaconesses in baptism. While women still offered leadership within their own gender-specific communities, the nearer Christianity got to being an acceptable faith, the easier it was for men to exclusively fill the roles that once women had performed alongside them.

The Least You Need to Know

- Both the Bible and early Christian literature display a certain openness to feminine images of God.

- Mary the mother of Jesus was interpreted as the counterpart of Eve.

- Women functioned as apostles and prophets in much of the first and second centuries.

- Women provided important role models for martyrs and servants throughout the Christian community.

14

The Urban Plunge

In This Chapter

◆ The city's not so bad—as long as you don't inhale

◆ Who needs a Christian plumber?

◆ Christians hip deep in disease

◆ The church has a home of its own

If you went looking for Christians in the second century, you had to look for them in the cities. Although there were Christian communities in the countryside, the cities were the center of gravity for Christian expansion. That only stands to reason, as the cities were the center for nearly everything important in the Roman Empire. That doesn't mean, of course, that cities were wonderful places. In fact, they were quite the contrary.

Urban Life in the Empire

When talking about life in Roman cities, one is tempted to use Thomas Hobbes's famous summation of human life as "solitary, poor, nasty, brutish, and short." Cities of the Roman Empire were very difficult places to live, filled with vice, filth, disease, ethnic violence, and every type of crime imaginable. The only thing they had going for them was that living anywhere else was often worse.

Living Space

Ancient cities were remarkable for the number of people they could cram into a small space. Most ancient cities occupied just a few hundred square acres, while populations rarely exceeded 20,000 or 30,000. A handful of cities had higher numbers. In Antioch, for example, 150,000 people packed themselves into two square miles. That's more than 100 people per square acre, five times the density of Chicago, Boston, or Miami. The average density for cities in the empire was probably much higher, approaching 200 people per square acre.

New folks moving into the city looked for work and for housing close to others who looked and spoke like them, so you found ethnic groups and people of the same occupation clumping together in the same parts of the city. Rodney Stark points out that there were 18 separate ethnic enclaves in the city of Antioch. Clashes between these different districts were frequent and violent.

The streets were narrow and crowded, and tended to meander all over the place rather than run in a straight line. Juvenal's description of trying to walk down the street will resonate with anyone who has ever sat in a traffic jam. Most people lived in apartment-style tenements made of wood. There were few regulations regarding construction, and the few that existed were rarely observed or enforced, so buildings had a tendency to fall apart under stress, such as from an earthquake or even a serious windstorm. Fire was a constant danger.

From the Source _____

Though we hurry, we merely crawl;
We're blocked by a surging mass ahead,
  a pushing wall
Of people behind. A man jabs me,
  elbowing through, one socks
A chair pole against me, one cracks my
  skull with a beam, one knocks
A wine cask against my ear. My legs are
  caked with splashing
Mud, from all sides the weight of
  enormous feet comes smashing
On mine, and a soldier stamps his
  hobnails through to my sole.

—Juvenal, *Satire III*

Living in the cities was an assault on the senses. And good luck trying to get any sleep at night. The noise from wagons passing through the streets, slamming doors, people fighting, and the like must have been endless and, at times, overwhelming. Graffiti was everywhere, on every surface, displaying advertisements, news of local events, even pornography. Graffiti was the World Wide Web of the ancient world.

The overcrowding problem was made worse by the large areas set aside for public space in Hellenized cities, which squeezed the population into an even smaller area. Temples, forums, and the like provided people with a place to go to escape their squalid living conditions—but they were swarming with people, too. Privacy under these conditions was nearly impossible.

Filth, Squalor, and Games of Chance

Private residences were uncomfortable. Livestock like chickens and goats lived with people in their homes. There were no fireplaces, so all cooking and heat came from open charcoal stoves called braziers. Smoke would have filled the rooms, making breathing difficult. Windows helped, but only by replacing smoke with draft and humidity. Mold and mildew were everywhere.

You can bet that the smell was hideous. There were no sewers to speak of, only the occasional latrine. Instead, urine and feces were often dumped directly into the street. There was no running water, so every gallon had to be carried out from smelly public cisterns by hand. With little water for bathing and limited access to public baths, things could get pretty ripe. Insects, drawn by the filth and standing water, were a frequent torment. The combination of man and beast, mold and mildew, smoke and excrement must have been overpowering. It's no wonder that churches later used incense in their gatherings.

All of this meant that public health in the cities was a disaster. Nobody knew anything about germs, so disease was rampant. Hazards abounded, so scars and loss of limbs were not at all unusual. Sickness was a nearly constant phenomenon. Seeing someone in perfect health would have been uncommon. As a result, even under normal circumstances, the populations of the cities were constantly in need of replenishment from the rural areas. Fires, floods, earthquakes, epidemics of disease, and war only upped the ante.

> **Word to the Wise**
>
> "Any study of how Christians converted the empire is really a study of how they Christianized the cities."
> —Rodney Stark, *Cities of God*

Crime was abundant in the ancient city. Just about anything was available, for the right price. There was no real police force to speak of, and no courts of law for average folks to turn to in need. More often than not, if you wanted to get away with it, you did, unless someone stronger came along. In almost any city in the empire, you were gambling with your life to go out and walk the streets at night.

And if the Romans had a favorite pastime, it was gambling. Games of chance abounded, and you could bet on just about anything with just about anyone. An especially favored subject for betting was the horse races at the Circus Maximus. Ever watch the chariot race in the movie *Ben Hur?* Then you know exactly what I'm talking about. And the crowds were, if anything, even rowdier than they were in that movie. Riots could and did break out among fans of different riders.

Public Life and Duties

Roman society was built on a class system. At the very top of this steep pyramid were the aristocrats, the wealthy, and the elites. Below them were merchants, petty government officials, artisans, and other freeborn men. The next rung down the ladder included freedmen and freedwomen. These were former slaves who had either been given their freedom or acquired it by purchase. Freedmen took their former master's family name as their own—but they weren't entirely free. They were still counted as clients of their former master, which points out the importance of patronage in the Roman world.

The patron-client system was half of the heart of social relationships in the Roman Empire (the other half, family relationships, we've already seen in Chapter 12). Every morning, a patron held court, usually in the atrium of his house. All of his clients, people who were in a subservient position to him, came to visit to offer their assistance to the patron. Clients were expected to work on behalf of their patron's business or political interests. In return, the patron safeguarded his clients, provided them with financial assistance, and offered advice and even legal protection. If it sounds a lot like *The Godfather*, then you're right on. The structure of the mafia is one continuing example of the old patronage system.

Slavery

The bottom rung on the social ladder was slavery. Roman slavery was a little different from what Westerners are used to because it was not primarily based on race, and, because it wasn't racial, slavery wasn't genetic. If you bought or were given your freedom, your children were free from any stigma. Slavery was entirely about the power of one person over another. In Rome, a slave was not legally a person. Slaves were property, no different from a pot or a chair, and were entirely subject to the authority of their master.

While slaves had no rights, they were still able to exert a great deal of power in Roman society. Partly that's because there were so many of them. In Rome, they might have been one fifth of the population. Slave labor was a backbone of the Roman imperial economy. Also, slaves were quite often placed in important positions of responsibility. Unlike wage-earning hired hands, slaves could usually be trusted.

A slave's situation could vary greatly. You could find them from the homes of the wealthy, where life was comfortable, all the way down to hard-labor situations like mines and rock quarries, where life span was measured in months rather than years. Some slaves were purchased specifically for their specialized skills, such as teachers, engineers, accountants, and the like. A pedagogue was a slave in charge of raising and tutoring the young children of a family, a fact that figures in Paul's letter to the Galatians, where he describes the Law of Moses as the pedagogue who led the believer to Jesus (Galatians 3:24).

The New Testament documents, especially the letters of Paul, have much to say to and about slaves. The letter to Philemon, the only personal letter in the entire Pauline collection, is entirely about a runaway slave whom Paul is returning to his master. The problem is that both master and slave are now Christians. Should a Christian master treat his slaves differently because of his faith? Does a Christian slave have a different attitude toward his master because of his religion? These were important questions for early Christians living in a world where slavery was so prevalent.

Religion in the Marketplace ... and Back Alley

As I mentioned in Chapter 1, there's no way to disentangle religion from the shape of urban living in the Roman Empire. Each ethnic group that populated the city brought its gods and goddesses with it. Temples could be found anywhere, and shrines to this god or that were built at every street corner and in every alley.

Magic and religion went hand in hand. Curses were considered very powerful, especially if they involved some kind of sacrifice. Many people wore amulets with incantations to protect them from harm or to draw health and prosperity. There were practices for seeking out omens regarding the future. Many people reserved a place in their home for statues representing household deities and family spirits. These were honored and revered with small offerings and prayers. Members of the household looked to them for blessings on major life events like births and marriages. These and many other folk practices were everywhere and were considered entirely understandable.

That's because, for most people, religion was a matter of transaction. The desire was not normally to draw close to a deity personally, but to acquire some kind of benefit, preferably at the least personal cost. The covenantal aspect of both Judaism and Christianity was in many ways unique in late antiquity.

Word Knowledge

A **cult** is usually a negative thing these days, but really it just means any religion that expresses its beliefs through ritual acts. Cultic acts are things that worshippers do as part of their religion, as distinct from what they believe.

The more formal aspects of religious life that you might encounter in the cities included the observances of the civic *cults*. Cities usually had a patron deity of some kind. For example, in Ephesus, the goddess Diana or Artemis was profoundly significant, so much so that challenging her worship, even indirectly, got Paul into deep trouble (Acts 19:23–41). The civic cults were deeply entwined with the daily activities of city government. An attack on the cults was perceived as an attack on the government.

The Church and Public Life

Because so much of public life involved participating in pagan rituals and practices in one way or another, Christians often found themselves withdrawing into their own communities. As we saw in Chapter 6, this was a fundamental part of the criticism of Christians. Writers like Celsus could not fathom a religion that, because of its exclusivity, made Christians unavailable for public service and participation.

Word Knowledge

An **aedile** was a government official in Roman cities. They were generally responsible for public works, public events, and often for public security.

Although it's true that Christians were generally unable to be involved in public roles, it wasn't always the case. Many Christians did perform civic roles despite the concerns that came with them. The church in Corinth, for example, included Erastus among its members. Archaeological evidence suggests that he was an *aedile*, one of the four most important figures in the city. Essentially, he was in charge of public works.

Most occupations were open to Christians, though fidelity to faith could be an obstacle. We have inscriptions indicating that Christians were boat owners and woodworkers; there was even a Christian athlete named Helix. There were butchers, bakers, and, yes, even the occasional candlestick maker. Marcion, we know, had a family business in maritime shipping. The high level of literary activity in the Christian community meant that there were certainly openings for scribes, bookmakers, and distributors.

Some occupations, on the other hand, were more difficult to operate in. Many Christians shied away from military service, partly because it involved killing and partly because, like many public roles, it could involve sacrifices to the gods. There were occasional exceptions, but these were mostly individuals who were already soldiers when they converted.

The theater was another field generally considered forbidden. There is a fascinating letter from Cyprian of Carthage, a third-century bishop we'll meet in Chapter 16, to a church under his care. Apparently, a Christian convert who formerly worked in the theater was trying to make a living by teaching acting. The elders of the church consulted Cyprian to get his input. Cyprian responded by forbidding the actor from continuing in his field, suggesting that instead he be willing to accept the church's financial support. If the congregation can't afford it, Cyprian continues, then his own church would chip in the money to help the fellow.

From the Source

"Nor let anyone excuse himself that he himself has given up the theater, while he is still teaching the art to others. For he cannot appear to have given it up who substitutes others in his place, and who, instead of himself alone, supplies many in his stead; against God's appointment, instructing and teaching in what way a man may be broken down into a woman, and his sex changed by art, and how the devil who pollutes the divine image may be gratified by the sins of a corrupted and enervated body. But if such a one alleges poverty and the necessity of small means, his necessity also can be assisted among the rest who are maintained by the support of the Church; if he be content, that is, with very frugal but innocent food."
—Cyprian of Carthage, *Letter 60*

A large number of early Christians were slaves, which had all sorts of implications for their participation in the faith. A slave was under the control of his or her master.

If the master was pagan, this could present difficulties for the slave. The slave's owner might forbid the slave to participate in this new, illegal religion, and the consequences could be severe. At the same time, working for a pagan master might involve tasks that were wrong for a Christian. It could be especially difficult for female slaves, who were considered sexually available to their masters.

The apostle Paul was not opposed to slaves buying their freedom if they could, but he encouraged them to focus on what he considered to be more important matters. Paul seems to have believed that, in Christ, the slave could be utterly free even though bound. There was also concern that slaves would be more interested in gaining their freedom than in their spiritual condition. Ignatius of Antioch, in his letter to Polycarp, writes that Christians who are enslaved "should not have a strong desire to be set free at the church's expense, lest they be found to be slaves of lust." His comment shows that Christians were eager to provide for those who were most helpless, often at great expense or even at the cost of their own lives, but not without due consideration for the worthiness of the person seeking the church's assistance.

Christians and the Poor

In the middle of the fourth century, after Christianity had finally been legalized, the emperor Julian fumed in a letter to pagan priests, "… the impious Galilaeans support not only their own poor but ours as well …." His frustration with the charitable behavior of early Christianity in comparison to the less compassionate followers of the pagan religions reveals one of the most important characteristics behind the spread of the Christian faith. Christians were motivated by their religion to provide aid and comfort to the poor, the sick, and the marginalized in the cities. Julian was not the first to realize that this humanitarian side of the Christian faith both contributed to the good of the social order and won many converts to Christianity.

As the old saying goes, charity begins at home. Already in the New Testament, Christians were holding up the ideal of supporting one another in times of need. Paul spent a tremendous amount of time and energy organizing an aid offering from the various churches that he had founded to go to the church in Jerusalem, which was suffering at the time. In one of the few records of actual numbers available to us, the bishop of Rome wrote a letter to the bishop of Antioch in 251, telling him that the Roman church was supporting "over fifteen hundred widows and persons in distress." Those would include folks like the former actor whom Cyprian was so ready to provide for.

From the Source

> "Even if we have a kind of treasury, this is not filled up from a sense of obliga-
> tion, as of a hired religion. Each member adds a small sum once a month, or when he
> pleases, and only if he is willing and able; for no one is forced, but each contributes
> of his own free will. These are the deposits as it were made by devotion. For that sum
> is disbursed not on banquets nor drinking bouts nor unwillingly on eating-houses, but
> on the supporting and burying of the poor, and on boys and girls deprived of property
> and parents, and on aged servants of the house, also on shipwrecked persons, and
> any, who are in the mines or on islands or in prisons, provided it be for the cause of
> God's religion, who thus become pensioners of their confession. But the working of that
> kind of love most of all brands us with a mark of blame in the eyes of some. 'See,' they
> say, 'how they love one another'; for they themselves hate one another; 'and how they
> are ready to die for one another'; for they will be more ready to kill one another."
>
> —Tertullian of Carthage, *Apology*

That care could often be extended in extraordinary ways. In 165, an epidemic (probably of the measles) struck the empire as soldiers returning from war in the East
brought back infection. The disease spread like wildfire and killed indiscriminately.
Anywhere from a quarter to a third of the population of the Roman Empire died. One
hundred years later, a similar plague erupted at the height of the Decian persecution
(more about that in Chapter 16). In both cases, Christians remained in the cities to
care for their own and for others who were struck down by the disease. Many victims,
Christian and otherwise, survived when they otherwise might not have. More important, as far as their public witness might be concerned, Christians were willing to risk
infection themselves to remain and care for others in the harshest of conditions. That
was not something easily forgotten.

Here's the Church, Where's the Steeple?

I've stressed how much of one's life would be lived out in public in a Roman city. It
isn't surprising, then, that little escaped notice. Rumors traveled fast, and anything
new was worth passing along. You can bet that a new religion that was attracting numbers of new members would get talked about.

The Book of Acts describes Paul's attempts to communicate his faith through a variety
of venues. We see him in the synagogues of the diaspora communities, in Tyrannus's
lecture hall in Ephesus, and in the tent-making shop. Each of these venues would have
brought him into contact with a different part of society. Once contact was made with
interested people; however, the focus often changed to the household.

Given the household nature of early Christianity, it makes sense that they would first begin to gather primarily in houses. This presented a problem for poorer members of the churches—who were a large chunk of the group—as their living quarters were almost certainly too small to host even a small group of fellow believers. Typically, then, the wealthier members of the congregations opened their homes to the rest.

We don't have too many examples of these house-churches and how they may have evolved physically to provide space for the growing communities of Christians. The prime example is a converted house in the city of Dura-Europos, a border outpost situated in the Syrian desert along the Euphrates River. Dura-Europos was lost after the Romans abandoned it in 257 after a Persian siege, after which the city was covered by sand and mud. It was rediscovered in 1920 and excavated by the British.

Sometime between 230 and 250, one of the town's private residences was converted for use by a Christian community. One of the back rooms, large enough to hold about 60 people, was set up for worship gatherings. A separate room designed to look similar to a tomb housed the baptismal font. The walls of this room were painted with frescoes depicting the Good Shepherd and, significantly, the women coming to Jesus' tomb on Easter morning.

The house-church at Dura-Europos is evidence of a community that was growing numerically and capable of sustaining a facility entirely for its own use. That it was located on the edge of the empire is even more remarkable and hints at what kind of facilities other, larger Christian churches may have utilized.

Cities were difficult places to live in. At the same time, cities were where change was happening, where new values and new opportunities could be explored. In the country, you would always be what you were right now, but the cities opened the door to advancement.

The Least You Need to Know

- ◆ City life was filled with difficulties and dangers.
- ◆ Despite their tendency to withdraw, Christians were involved in many aspects of social life.
- ◆ Christians were most visible in the city because of their charity, especially in times of death and disaster.
- ◆ The church was beginning to develop physical spaces of its own for worship gatherings.

Chapter 15

Jerusalem and Athens

In This Chapter

- ◆ Alexandria sets the stage for a Christian philosophy
- ◆ The man of steel
- ◆ Did Jesus sit for a portrait?
- ◆ Archaeologists find a musical blast from the past

It was Tertullian, in *The Prescription Against Heretics*, who wrote, "What indeed has Athens to do with Jerusalem? What agreement is there between the Academy and the church? What between heretics and Christians? … Away with all attempts to produce a mottled Christianity of Stoic, Platonic, and dialectic composition!" His intent was not to discard all reasoned approaches to Christian thinking, but to attack the ways that certain teachers in the church were forcing Christian beliefs and practices into the mold of non-Christian philosophy.

Tertullian certainly spoke for the masses of simple folk who filled the churches of North Africa where he lived, but the future of Christian theological discussion would rest on the efforts of those who did seek to find a rapprochement between the academy and the church. Cultural experimentation in philosophy, the arts, and music pushed past the boundaries established by leaders in the church to contribute to the creation of a distinctly

Christian cultural life right at the time when the church was moving from being an underground movement to being an "alternative city."

The Christian Philosophers

We've already talked about the apologists and their attempts to make Christianity palatable to an audience steeped in the basic assumptions of Greek philosophy. Their purpose, however, was not primarily constructive. In other words, they weren't trying to create a Christian philosophy so much as they were trying to demonstrate that Christianity was actually the goal of all pagan philosophy. You still get the feeling when you read Justin Martyr, probably the most philosophic of the apologists, that philosophy is as much a tool for attaining to Christian faith as anything else.

The gnostic teachers also are not the source of a genuinely Christian philosophy. They were busy creating what amounted to an apocalyptic form of Platonic philosophy, as oxymoronic as that sounds. While the difference between them and men like Clement and Origen was often a matter of degree, by and large the gnostic teachers succeeded in fashioning not a Christian philosophy, but Greek philosophy with some Christian characteristics.

Word to the Wise

As in Philo's time, the concept of the Logos would prove the most hopeful means of establishing common ground between Greek and biblical ideas of the universe. To succeed in Alexandria and indeed in much of the Greek-speaking world, Christianity would have to be articulated in Platonic terms."

—W.H.C. Frend, *The Rise of Christianity*

Alongside the gnostics in Alexandria was a group of Christian teachers who were reaching out to create a genuinely Christian system of philosophy. They were forced to walk a very narrow tightrope between using philosophy for apologetic purposes as Justin did and adapting Christianity to Plato the way the gnostics did. Whether they were successful is still debated, but the end result of their efforts had a decisive effect on the shape of future Christian thought and life.

Pantaenus

His student Clement called him "the Sicilian bee," so it's possible that Pantaenus was from Sicily. Other evidence suggests that he originally came from Palestine, though this is less likely. A devotee of Stoicism, Pantaenus converted to Christianity in Alexandria and formed a unique partnership with the bishop of the city, Demetrius, a fairly simple man with close ties to the masses of Christians in the Egyptian churches.

At Demetrius's invitation, Pantaenus took over the task of catechetical education, opening a school for the purpose of communicating the tenets of Christian faith to new believers. We know that he brought Christianity and philosophy into meaningful dialogue with each other because it was precisely this that drew in his students, one of whom we'll meet in just a moment.

As we saw in Chapter 5, later in his life, Pantaenus was invited to travel to India and enter into a dialogue with Hindu scholars. It appears that he took that trip, the results of which I've already mentioned. It seems that he returned, but we don't know when or what happened to him afterward. While he was gone, the school that he founded became the responsibility of one of his greatest students, Clement.

Clement of Alexandria

Perhaps a native of Athens, Clement was born around 150 and traveled widely in search of philosophical teachers. His final journey took him to Alexandria, where he fell under the spell of Pantaenus. For a while he worked alongside his teacher in the catechetical school, and he became its head when Pantaenus left for India.

 In Depth

> Clement authored three important works, designed to be read as a trilogy:
>
> *Protrepticus* (*Exhortation to the Greeks*): Intended to persuade non-Christian Greeks to convert to Christianity.
>
> *Paedagogus* (*The Teacher*): A work of moral theology, where Clement presents his picture of the perfect Christian as the "true gnostic." This work begins with a refutation of gnostic teachings.
>
> *Stromata* (*The Miscellanies*): Clement's attempt to delve more deeply into speculative theology. Only seven chapters remain, of which Chapters 4 and 7 are of particular interest regarding Clement's view of the gnostics.

Clement operated the catechetical school until the persecution started by Emperor Septimius Severus in 201. During that time, he labored intensively to reach out to the educated Greek elite of the city, making Christianity palatable to a body of people steeped in the conceptual language of Plato and the Greek philosophers. Several of his students went on to become leaders in the church, both in Alexandria and elsewhere.

In Clement's Alexandria, there was a distinct split in the churches. On one hand were the elite, largely Greeks, who were well educated and attracted to the systematic religious philosophy of the gnostics. On the other hand, the majority of Christians were native Egyptians, who experienced Christianity as a system of beliefs and ethical behavior, and had little patience for speculative theology.

Clement attempted to create a middle way between these two camps. He affirmed the gnostic desire for illumination through knowledge. He recognized that all Christians were not created equal, that some were more advanced than others. But rather than accept the gnostic's prescription for knowledge as a sudden experience, he described the "true gnostic" as the Christian who found the knowledge of God through a lifetime of consistent moral growth leading to spiritual maturity.

 In Depth

> Clement authored a work titled *Who is the Rich Man that Shall Be Saved?*, in which he softened Jesus' command to the "rich young ruler" in Mark 10:17–31 to give away his wealth to the poor. For Clement, in contrast to others such as Tertullian, wealth was not an absolute evil to be removed from a person's life. Rather it was to be stewarded well, and the church was a school for learning that stewardship.
>
> Interestingly, Clement's reaction to the story of the "rich young ruler" in Mark's Gospel is a polar opposite to that of the famous monk Antony, who obeyed that same text as literally as he could (we'll meet Antony in Chapter 18). In many ways, the moderate Clement and the absolute Antony exemplified the divisions in the Egyptian church between the Greek elite and the native Egyptian masses.

In 203, with the outbreak of violence against the church under Septimius Severus, Clement was forced to flee Alexandria. The persecution, as we'll talk about in Chapter 16, was directed at catechumens and those responsible for teaching them, which included Clement. He took refuge with a former student who was now a bishop in Cappadocia (eastern Turkey) and died sometime around 211 or 212.

When Clement left, Demetrius was pressed to find someone else to head up the catechetical school. It had to be someone brilliant, dedicated to the faith, and, probably most important, crazy enough to take on a task that would mean flirting with arrest and even death. He settled on a 17-year-old prodigy, a young man with an iron will and a mind like a steel trap. His name was Origen.

Origen

I've already mentioned that we can't understand Christianity as a whole without looking at Jesus, and that Gentile Christianity is impossible without Paul. Now it's important to point out that there is no way to grasp the future developments of Christian theology without getting to know Origen of Alexandria. Origen's prodigious intellect and uncompromising religious zeal combined to remake the boundaries of Christian thinking about the Jesus story.

Childhood and Early Life

Origen was a mixed-race child, a real no-no in Egypt at the time. His mother was an Egyptian, his father a Greek, and it was against the law for them to marry. His parents, particularly his father, Leonides, were ardent Christians, and Origen was raised with a profound knowledge of the Bible. At the same time, Leonides made sure that Origen was well educated in the literary classics and in philosophy. So we can already see that Origen's origin was a mash-up of cultures and ideas. He grew up convinced that Christianity and philosophy could be melded, as evidenced by his own childhood.

When Septimius Severus's persecution broke out in 202, Leonides was arrested and taken away for execution. The young Origen was determined to follow his father, but his mother stopped him by hiding his clothes. Apparently he didn't mind dying, but he didn't want to do so naked.

Everything that we know about Origen's early life points to the intense zeal and passionate intellect that he displayed throughout his later career. In the wake of his father's death, Origen accepted Bishop Demetrius's invitation to take over the catechetical school after the departure of Clement. To support himself, he sold his father's library for an annuity, which provided him with a stipend just barely enough to live on, exercising frugality and living an ascetic lifestyle. As the persecution raged on, Origen visited those who were arrested, openly supporting and encouraging them, but he managed to never get arrested with them.

Origen became a tremendously popular teacher. Eventually his students became so numerous that Demetrius made him give up his attempts to court martyrdom and focus on his teachings. During this period, according to later rumor, Origen took very literally Jesus' suggestion in Matthew 19:12 that "some make themselves eunuchs for the kingdom of heaven's sake" and castrated himself.

Days of Labor

The next three decades were a period of feverish activity for Origen. He persuaded a wealthy man named Ambrose to give up his interest in Valentinian gnosticism. In thanks, Ambrose agreed to be Origen's patron and publish all of his writings. From that time on, Origen had a team of stenographers available to him so that he could dictate his works, and the equivalent of a publishing house prepared to reproduce all of his books (by hand, of course) for distribution. This partnership lasted Origen's entire career and is part of the reason he became so influential.

But what exactly was Origen publishing? Slowly, Origen had moved away from teaching the more basic students at the catechetical school. His interests turned to more academic work, though with a practical goal. There was a huge commentary on John's Gospel to write, as well as commentaries on several other scriptural books and treatises on a variety of subjects.

The first major project was the *Hexapla*, literally "sixfold," a pioneering work in what scholars now call textual criticism. In it, Origen attempted to put together a critical text of the Hebrew Scriptures. By putting the Hebrew text side-by-side with a transliteration and four Greek translations, Origen attempted to provide the church with an answer to Jewish arguments that Christians were misreading the Old Testament. At the same time, Origen wanted to provide the church with a single unified version of the Old Testament so that Christians everywhere would be preaching and teaching from the same foundation.

During this same period, Origen began work on his *On First Principles*, an attempt to put forward a Christian system of philosophy. The book demonstrates the challenge presented by trying to bring together Christian doctrine and Platonic philosophy. Origen was dedicated to the church and to the rule of faith, and equally dedicated to a Platonic view of the world. Taking his cue from the Platonic view of human beings as body, soul, and spirit, Origen took the method of analogical reading one step further. He proposed that every text of Scripture had several meanings: one literal, one moral, · and one spiritual. With this technique, he was able to delve beneath a given passage of Scripture to find deeper meaning, as well as link passages that might not otherwise seem connected.

In 215, Origen's patron, Ambrose, was forced to relocate to Caesarea in Palestine, where he took up permanent residence. When Origen visited him, he was warmly received by the church there. Origen's frequent travels, growing celebrity, and speculative theology began to cause problems for him in Alexandria. He and Demetrius clashed frequently. Finally, while on his way to debate a gnostic teacher in the region, Origen visited Caesarea again, where the bishop appointed him as a presbyter. Demetrius went ballistic, denouncing what he viewed as an encroachment on his authority as Origen's bishop. The rift became final when Origen, tired of the constraints of life in Alexandria and encouraged by the acceptance he received in Caesarea, relocated to Palestine permanently.

Coming into His Own

By 233, while Alexander Severus was still alive and at war with the Persians, Origen had taken up permanent residence in Caesarea. His first order of business was to begin writing again. With the continued patronage of Ambrose, who once again supplied him with stenographers and copyists to publish his manuscripts, Origen settled in and resumed work on his *Commentary on John*, now in its sixth volume, and also penned a treatise *On Prayer*.

Also, as he had in Alexandria, Origen began to take on students, introducing them to his own understanding of Christianity as the highest expression of philosophy and instructing them in his methods of reading Scripture allegorically.

Origen's new duties also included the regular opportunity to speak in church, a task that Demetrius in Alexandria had restricted to presbyters and bishops alone. Eschewing high-sounding rhetoric, Origen explained the chosen text verse by verse and often word by word, focusing where possible on the simplest meanings and avoiding the speculative theology that appeared in some of his written works. Over 200 of Origen's sermons remain in existence today, which offers a glimpse of his exegetical talents and pastoral insight.

 **In Depth**

Prior to Origen's commentary on John's Gospel, the only available commentary on that text was by Heracleon, a gnostic. Origen wrote his commentary in part to address some of his disagreements with the gnostics. Heracleon's commentary no longer exists independently, but large chunks of it are preserved in Origen's book.

Origen continued to travel as well and was invited to attend synods and gatherings as a consultant on doctrinal issues. He accompanied Bishop Alexander of Jerusalem and his own bishop, Theoctistus of Caesarea to Bosra, a significant city east of the Sea of Galilee, to attend an examination of Bosra's bishop, Beryllus. Beryllus rejected the idea of Christ's preexistence and denied that he possessed a divine nature of his own apart from that of God the Father. Origen justified his friends' faith in him by persuading Beryllus to renounce these views. It was an example of how Origen was fast becoming a significant spokesperson for the Christian faith.

The death of Alexander Severus and the onslaught under Maximinus caught Christians by surprise. Origen, who had dealings with Alexander's mother, Julia Mammaea, would have rightfully been concerned about his own safety, but as in Alexandria the danger fell not on himself, but on those whom he cared for. His patron, Ambrose, and Protectetus, a presbyter with whom they were friends, were both either arrested or feared imminent arrest. As he had done with his father, Origen took pen in hand to encourage his friends. His *Exhortation to Martyrdom* embraces the notion of martyrdom as a heroic act.

The essay is a model of Christian Platonism. For the Christian, martyrdom is a supreme test of the resolve to desire spiritual things above worldly things. "I think that they love God with all their soul," he writes, "who with a great desire to be in union with God withdraw and separate their soul not only from the earthly body but also from everything material." At worst, Origen argued, martyrdom will only free us from the limitations that bodily existence places on us, allowing us to behold Christ in his wholeness.

Thankfully, neither Ambrose nor Protectetus was called on to make that sacrifice. If they were even arrested, they were soon set free. Maximinus's persecution passed quickly, and his reign shortly ceased as well.

Caesarea

In Caesarea, Origen continued to take on students. Around 245, one of them— tradition says that it was Gregory the Wonderworker—wrote a *panegyric* or speech of praise about Origen and his time studying with him. This *Speech of Appreciation* offers us a window into the methods and the content of Origen's teaching. Gregory's laudatory address to his teacher provides us with a wealth of information about the curriculum Origen devised for these students. Since Origen's influence on his students was so deep and long lasting, the description of his program of study outlined in Gregory's speech deserves a lengthy look.

Word Knowledge

A **panegyric** was a speech of praise, usually expressed in enthusiastic and even hyperbolic language.

The speech adheres closely to the style of a panegyric, sprinkled with allusions to Plato and using lofty and, at times, almost divine language to describe the person being honored. Distinctly Christian terminology is avoided in favor of language more typical of the philosophers. Christ is referred to as the Logos, a common philosophical term, and the Christian faith is called "the barbarian philosophy." All in all, it is a polished piece of rhetoric, though to modern ears it may sound grandiose and flattering in the extreme.

Gregory begins by describing the circumstances that brought him to Origen. Sometime shortly after Origen relocated to Caesarea, two brothers from Pontus on the Black Sea arrived in town escorting their sister back to her husband, who was an aide to the governor of Palestine. Their intentions were to proceed to Beirut and enroll in the famous law school there to continue their studies. Instead, they happened to meet Origen, who spoke so profoundly about Christ that the brothers decided to stay and study with him. Gregory describes Origen's impact on him at that first meeting:

> I was persuaded to give up all those objects or pursuits which seem to us befitting, and among others even my boasted jurisprudence,—yea, my very fatherland and relatives, both those who were present with me then, and those from whom I had parted. And in my estimation there arose but one object dear and worth desire,—to wit philosophy, and that master of philosophy, that divine man.

In Depth

Gregory Thaumaturgus (or Wonderworker) was a native of Pontus in northern Asia Minor, born in 213. He became a Christian when he and his brother, in Caesarea to learn law, ran into Origen instead. After studying with Origen for seven years, Gregory returned to Pontus, where he was appointed bishop of New Caesarea, his hometown. Legend states that the church Gregory led began with 17 Christians, but by his death, only 17 pagans were left in town. For 30 years, Gregory was bishop, during which time he earned his title, Wonderworker, for all of the miracles that were attributed to him. He died in 270.

The second half of the speech delves into the course of study that Gregory and his brother engaged in with Origen. As was customary at the time, Origen's students actually lived with him, an arrangement that obviously limited the number of students he could take at one time. Origen had devised a seven-year course of study; Gregory had completed five of those years but was unable to complete the final part.

Gregory notes that Origen's preeminent concern is with the Scriptures, even joking that everyone dreamt about the Bible all night because they had studied it so passionately all day long. Still, Origen considered the study of philosophy to be the best means of preparing for the study of Scripture. His students studied the standard areas of philosophy—logic or dialectics, physics, and ethics. The pinnacle of Origen's curriculum was theology, which was the last discipline to be studied.

Lessons began with logic. Origen would adopt a calm, sober demeanor, taking care not to indicate in his teaching which ideas he considered sound and which he rejected. The intent was to school his students to accept ideas based not on authority—because the instructor considered them correct—but on the basis of their own serious reflection. In particular, Origen encouraged his students to be careful of accepting ideas that were elegantly stated, a common fault in the rhetorical education of the day.

Afterward came physics, the study of the natural world. Origen was well acquainted with the natural sciences and considered thoughtful examination of creation to be a helpful entry point into consideration of higher spiritual realities. Chief among these sciences was astronomy.

Ethical considerations followed the standard cardinal virtues outlined by the philosopher Plato. These are prudence, temperance, justice, and courage, to which Origen added piety. Origen was careful to redefine these virtues in Christian terms, seeing Christianity as the ultimate expression of the moral and ethical principles described by the various philosophical schools. Chief among Origen's criticisms of the non-Christian philosophers was that they were unable to live up to the ethical system they espoused. Gregory makes it clear that, unlike others, Origen was diligent to practice what he preached.

Theology was the final, crowning area of study. Origen's method was to teach all of the major systems of philosophical thought, with the exception of atheism, pointing out both their strengths and their weaknesses. Again, his intention was to keep his students' minds open to all possibilities rather than getting tied down to only one way of thinking. This was the precondition to a serious study of the Scriptures.

What becomes clear is that Origen was not running a simple catechetical school like the one he led in Alexandria. Gregory's panegyric limits itself to a discussion of those Christian truths that can be expressed philosophically. Apparently, Origen was running a kind of missionary outreach, a school directed at young pagans who demonstrated an interest in Christianity. Origen's goal was to demonstrate to them that Christianity was the highest expression of everything that the Greek philosophers struggled to define. At the same time, he encouraged their moral and ethical growth in practical terms.

Death and Legacy

When Decius's persecution broke out against the church (see Chapter 16), Origen himself was not executed. However, he suffered tremendously in prison, where he was tortured repeatedly in the hopes that, as a high-profile Christian leader, he could be made to publicly recant. He remained faithful, however, and was eventually released when the persecution ceased after Decius's death in 251. His body broken and his health shattered, Origen limped on quietly for another three years or so and died in the city of Tyre sometime around 254 at the age of 69.

The tenor of Origen's life was one of the qualities most of his contemporaries admired, even those who rejected much of his thinking. Already during his own life-time, some had given Origen the nickname Adamantios, meaning "man of steel." He needed that strength because by the time his life was winding down, he was already spending a good bit of his time defending himself from attacks on his orthodoxy.

As I've mentioned, Origen had a direct and lasting impact on the theological develop-ment of Christianity for at least the next century or two. Inevitably, however, his spec-ulative nature caught up with him, and later church councils condemned many of his works, largely due to the extremism of those whom he inspired. Nevertheless, Origen frequently cropped up at key moments of later Christian history, and his example demonstrates that theological speculation and zealous faith in the core teachings of the church can go hand in hand, however fitfully.

Art

The urban landscape of the ancient world boasted a riot of images, from the scrawl-ing graffiti on nearly every surface and the statuary of family idols and shrines, all the way up to the fine art mosaics and frescoes fashioned for businesses and wealthy households. Even the money was marked by the image of the emperor. These images served more than aesthetic purposes. In a largely illiterate world, without television or the Internet, painted and sculpted images were the principal means of communicating ideas. Eventually, Christians needed to express their message in visual forms.

The Difficulties of Christian Art

Since Christians were such a small segment of the population of the Roman Empire—estimates range from as low as 8,000 to 50,000 at the end of the first century, in an empire with a population of 45 million to 60 million—physical remains are almost impossible to discover. Locating evidence of Christian art anytime in the first century would be the ultimate needle in a haystack.

At the same time, early Christians had inherited the Jewish distrust of visual images. The Second Commandment specifically forbade the making of "graven images," and Christian leaders throughout the period objected to the making of Christian images. Tertullian, Clement of Alexandria, and the church historian Eusebius—not the type of men to agree on much—seem to be unified in their belief that Christian imagery was absolutely off-limits.

The Beginnings of Christian Art

Despite that, the third century, in particular, saw an explosion of Christian artwork. Only a few examples survive, but they are enough to suggest what must have been available at the time, particularly to the wealthy. I have already mentioned the phenomenal paintings discovered in the house church at Dura-Europos (in Chapter 14), which included images of various versions of a beardless Jesus walking on the water with Peter and healing the paralyzed man. There is also the Good Shepherd, a relatively common image, and the much more specifically Christian fresco of the women coming to the tomb on the morning of the resurrection.

The famous catacombs of Rome boast some of the earliest Christian artwork. These underground tombs were tunneled out as a place for Christians to be buried, as their belief in bodily resurrection made them uncomfortable with cremating their dead. The oldest of the tomb systems, the catacombs of St. Callixtus, were first constructed in the middle of the second century and continued to serve Christians until well into the fourth century, at which point it was safe to have Christian cemeteries above ground.

 In Depth

By the way, if you feel sorry for Alexamenos, whoever he might be, a nearby inscription in a different handwriting insists, "Alexamenos is faithful." Good for him.

Interestingly, the earliest image of Jesus may not even come from a Christian. A bit of graffiti, discovered on the wall of a building in Rome that once housed young boys learning to be imperial pages, portrays a donkey-headed figure on a cross with a man standing in front and the words "Alexamenos worships his God." It's difficult to date, though most scholars put it at sometime during the third century.

Music

Early Christians continued to use the Psalms from the Hebrew Scriptures as the music of their worship. Early in the life of the Christian community, new songs were created either from scratch or as modifications of preexisting Jewish music. Paul reminds the Christians in both Ephesus and Colosse to sing to one another "with psalms, hymns, and spiritual songs," and several passages in the New Testament, especially Philippians 2:5–11, seem to be examples of such songs.

The Odes of Solomon are the earliest Christian hymnbook of which we know. We've seen portions of them in previous chapters. Probably composed in Syria sometime at the end of the first century or the beginning of the second, the *Odes* give us a fascinating glimpse at how Christians were exploring how to express their faith.

From the Source

O Gracious Light
pure brightness of the everlasting Father in heaven.
O Jesus Christ, holy and blessed!

Now as we come to the setting of the sun,
and our eyes behold the vesper light,
we sing praises, O God:
Father, Son, and Holy Spirit.

You are worthy at all times
to be praised by happy voices,
O Son of God, O Giver of life,
and to be glorified through all the worlds.

—*Phos Hilaron* (from *The Book of Common Prayer*)

Unfortunately, while we have the text of most of these songs, the musical side of things is largely lost. In fact, most everything that we know about early Christian music we have to infer from later developments. We do have the insight from Pliny's report to the emperor in 112 that Christians, as part of their gatherings, "sing responsively a hymn to Christ as to a god." The text of the phenomenal *Phos Hilaron*, or *Hail Gladsome Light*, first appears in Justin Martyr's *Dialogue with Trypho*, written around 150. It is the oldest Christian hymn still in use, and it gives us some idea of how Christian music was sung. Finally, a fragment of a document discovered at Oxyrhynchus in Egypt contains both part of the text and musical notation for a Christian hymn. The hymn was written down late in the third century, though the hymn itself may be older.

From the Source

… Let it be silent
Let the Luminous stars
not shine,
Let the winds and all the noisy rivers die down;
And as we hymn the Father, the Son and the Holy Spirit,
Let all the powers add "Amen, Amen"
praise always, and glory to God,
The sole giver of
good things,
Amen, Amen.

—From the papyrus fragment Oxyrhynchus, 1786

The Least You Need to Know

◆ Pantaenus and Clement founded the catechetical school in Alexandria to communicate the Jesus story to elite Greeks.

◆ Origen created a system of Christian philosophy and shaped Christian theology for centuries to come.

◆ Despite some warnings, early Christians expressed themselves artistically.

◆ Early Christians had a large body of music to use as part of their worship, but most of it is inaccessible now.

Part 4

Kingdom and Empire

In this last part, we'll get Constantine on the throne and the church in the driver's seat, but there are some trade-offs to being in charge. Having once been victims of "the world," Christians now found themselves running it. Whether that was a good thing has been a matter of tremendous debate ever since. We'll see how the seeds of early Christianity continued to grow and blossom through time, along with the challenges of being a dominant force in Western culture. Vast numbers of people in Asia, Africa, and Latin America have been moving to a vibrant Christian faith at the same time Christianity is declining in the West. Our journey ends with a survey of world Christianity and the surprising similarities between the present moment and the ancient church.

Chapter 16

The Great Persecution

In This Chapter

- ◆ An emperor tries a new attack
- ◆ The first empire-wide assault on Christianity
- ◆ Purity or love?
- ◆ The most vicious persecution of all

Heading into the third century, Christians were experiencing a period of peace and growth. While Christianity was still illegal, Trajan's policy of not seeking out Christians was still widely observed. This meant that most persecutions during the latter half of the second century were local in nature. As long as Christians were able to maintain good relations with their neighbors, not much would happen.

The rules changed in the third century. Septimius Severus, distracted by a series of civil conflicts and wars in Britain, attempted to unite the increasingly diverse and divergent population of the empire. His policies paved the way for later imperial persecutions. By the end of the third century, the conflict between Rome and the church would reach its ultimate climax.

Septimius Severus

Septimius Severus faced an insurmountable task. The Roman Empire had become almost impossible to rule. Rome was constantly threatened by the barbarian hordes of the north and frequently upset by economic distress and ethnic conflict within, but the increasingly obvious danger was coming from dissidents within the military. As the emperor became less a figure of awe and more a regular politician—even a military dictator—the more liable he was to see revolts and mutinies.

Severus sought to create unity in the empire by fostering an overarching faith in Sol Invictus, the Unconquered Sun. By tying the worship and faith of all the religions and sects in the empire into this one blanket religious confession, he sought to give people something that they would have in common. But as with emperor worship, there were two very obvious flies in the ointment: Jews and Christians. Neither group was willing to make obeisance to the sun, even in the face of imperial sanction. Severus, eager to stop the growth of both groups, made conversion to Judaism or Christianity punishable by death.

Killing the Catechumens

Earlier persecutions had tended to focus on the leaders of the Christian community. Essentially pagan in their outlook, Roman authorities were used to facing religious institutions with a professional hierarchy of priests and a larger body of believers. If you take out the priests, they reasoned, the believers really have nowhere to go with their faith. They hadn't reckoned on the essentially nonhierarchical nature of Christian spirituality, which recognized different roles but called for a vital and uncompromising faith from all of its adherents.

This time, Rome took a different tack. Severus decreed that it was converts who would be punished. This meant that the full weight of the legal system would come down not on those in leadership, who might be expected to demonstrate great tenacity in their faith, or even on the population of the churches at large. Instead, it was the catechumens, those brand new to the faith, and their teachers who would be prosecuted. The implementation of this empire-wide persecution had the added effect of amping up the same sort of localized harassment to which Christians had always been subject. The effect was an increase in the level of terror in Christian communities.

North Africa was especially hard hit by the new decrees. During this persecution Origen's father was killed, and his mentor and friend Clement, as head of the catechetical school, became a target and was forced to flee from the city. In Carthage, Perpetua and Felicity were killed, along with their fellow catechumens. In Europe, legend has it that Irenaeus suffered martyrdom under Septimius Severus, but there is no way to confirm that tradition.

For all of its difficulties, Severus's persecution finally petered out, for reasons unknown. Perhaps there was just general weariness with all of the death and disruption. And, truth be told, martyrdom only served to nurture the church. Christian communities were strengthened by their losses, to the bewilderment of the imperial authorities. Even attacking what might be considered the weakest link in the chain, the novices in the religion, did not have the desired effect. Tertullian was right. The blood of martyrs was the seed of the church.

Fall of the Severines

In any event, the empire was about to slip into the worst crisis of its history. Septimius Severus's three successors, Caracalla, Elagabalus, and Alexander Severus, ruled with relative success. Though they continued their predecessor's policy of unified worship, seeking to unite the empire behind one religious confession, they largely put aside the use of coercion and left the church virtually untouched. Christians were freer than at any time before to participate in public life, and many of them, including Origen, were on friendly terms with Alexander and Julia. Legend even has it that Alexander Severus had added Jesus to the other gods on his private altar. It's not exactly conversion, but it's at least tolerance.

Alexander and his mother may have been too soft for the times, unfortunately. The Severine dynasty had long relied on military might to sustain their rule, at a devastating cost to the other institutions of Roman life. Septimius Severus had advised his successors to "enrich the soldiers, and scorn all other men." He and his sons had nearly bankrupted the empire in order to shower the army with riches. It was a system that couldn't last.

Alexander, with the guidance of his mother, had been slowly chipping away at the army's stranglehold on power. The two of them returned a greater share of power to the people of Rome, particularly to the Senate. At the same time, they cut the army's pay and did their utmost not to get bogged down in costly wars. These policies were healthier for the empire, but the loss of funds and the lack of opportunity for plunder eroded the army's morale and fed into the general feeling of discontent with the direction that the empire was taking.

Alexander made camp outside the fortress city of Mainz on the Rhine River, apparently unaware of the murmuring and mutiny that lay just beneath the surface of the army's discipline. On the advice of his mother, and eager to avoid another costly war like the one he had just concluded, the young emperor began negotiating a settlement with the Germans. An understanding was soon reached. In exchange for an annual payment from Rome, the Germans would pack up and go home.

Before the agreement could be implemented, however, word reached the army that Alexander had talked, and paid, his way out of a fight. Instantly, the grumbling and complaining turned into naked hostility. The soldiers began to talk among themselves, reciting all of Alexander's mistakes and shortcomings. "A real emperor," they told one another, "would hammer the Germans and make them beg for peace." "And he wouldn't let his mother run everything for him." "He's tight-fisted when it comes to us, but he sure is generous to our enemies."

The open contempt for Alexander escalated until finally someone suggested that Rome, and certainly the army, would be better off if Alexander Severus were replaced by a man better suited to lead an army. They had just the person in mind.

In the middle of March 235, the soldiers mustered onto the camp parade ground in full military regalia, as if preparing for their regular drill. When their commander, a mountain of a man named Gaius Julius Verus Maximinus, stood up to lead them, they suddenly surged forward and, throwing a purple cape over him, proclaimed him their emperor. In all likelihood, Maximinus was aware of their plans. His first response, whether sincere or not, was to refuse, whereupon his men drew their swords and threatened him with death if he did not accept the honor they were bestowing on him. Wisely, Maximinus accepted. The soldiers stormed Alexander's tent, murdering the emperor, his mother, and their entourage.

In Depth

During this period, from 240 to 277, Mani began to teach in Persia. Combining elements of Zoroastrianism, Buddhism, Christianity, and some gnostic concepts, he created a new faith called Manicheism. Mani set out deliberately to create a universal faith by combining the different threads of religious insight in human experience into one form of spirituality. Far from being a starry-eyed dreamer, Mani laid out administrative plans for a religious organization, sent out missionaries, and wrote extensively—not only religious prose, but hymns and poetry. Manicheism posed a significant challenge to Christianity beginning in the fourth century, counting among its adherents Augustine of Hippo, who later became a Christian and one of the most important thinkers in Western culture.

With the death of Alexander Severus, the empire slipped into a 50-year crisis. From 235 until the rise of Diocletian in 285, Rome had 26 emperors, only one of whom managed to die of natural causes. Some never even set foot in the city of Rome during their brief tenure. Almost all of them were soldiers, or at least were propped up by their reliance on the military, earning this group the collective title "Barracks Emperors." The utter lack of stability shattered faith in the imperial system and widened the many cracks in Roman society.

Decius and Valerian

Maximinus launched a very brief persecution of the Christians, but he was the exception. The aged bishop of Rome, Pontianus, was deported to the very unhealthy region of Sardinia, along with his archrival, Hippolytus, who had been on good terms with Julia Mammaea. Others suffered as well, including Origen's patron, Ambrose. However, for all the tension, the persecution was aimed not at Christianity as a religion so much as it was directed at individual Christians who had relationships with the murdered Alexander or his mother. If anything, Maximinus's pursuit and punishment of Christians testifies to the extent of the spread of Christianity early in the third century and foreshadowed the growing influence Christians would have in the empire in later years.

For the better part of a generation, Christians were largely overlooked as the various emperors and emperor-wannabes clashed, schemed, and assassinated one another. The reign of Philip the Arab was especially comfortable. Philip and his wife were not only tolerant of Christians, but actually encouraging.

 In Depth

> Philip the Arab (ruled 244–249) has sometimes been called the first Christian emperor of Rome. The story goes that when he returned from the war with Persia, during which he instigated the murder of Gordian III, Philip wanted to join the church in Antioch for its Easter vigil, which would indicate that he had been baptized. However, the bishop prevented this because of his sins. Philip was directed to repent and make penance, which, as the story goes, he cheerfully did. While it might explain the kind treatment that Philip extended to Christians, it is unknown if the story is accurate.

Philip was succeeded by Gaius Decius, a very traditional Roman with very traditional values. Among those values was the conviction that properly worshipping the gods guaranteed the safety and prosperity of the Roman Empire. Christianity, growing in every part of the Empire, posed a clear danger to that conviction. Decius's persecution, the first empire-wide attack on the church, was deviously clever. Rather than target Christians specifically, he issued a decree early in 250 that all citizens across the empire be required to appear before a government official and offer a sacrifice to the gods and the divinity of the emperor, for which they would receive a certificate. The emperor sought to draw Romans back to their pagan roots in the hopes of restoring the unity of the empire.

In Rome itself, the persecution seems to have had limited appeal. Racial and religious tolerance ran deep in the Eternal City, and many pagans found the whole affair distasteful. There were a handful of martyrs, including Bishop Fabian, but the persecution fizzled out as soon as Decius left Rome to fight in the north.

The true strength of Decius's assault on the church was felt in the east, where a militant anti-Christian sentiment already seethed under the surface. As soon as Decius's ascension to the throne was announced abroad, local persecutions began breaking out across northern Africa. Bishop Babylas of Antioch and Bishop Alexander of Jerusalem, a friend of Origen's, were both killed, and Origen himself may have been arrested at this time. If not, he certainly was when the imperial decree reached the outlying provinces. With imperial sanction, the prosecution of Christians became brutal.

From the Source

"And with them there were four women. Ammonarium, a holy virgin, the judge tortured relentlessly and excessively, because she declared from the first that she would utter none of those things which he commanded; and having kept her promise truly, she was dragged away. The others were Mercuria, a very remarkable old woman, and Dionysia, the mother of many children, who did not love her own children above the Lord. As the governor was ashamed of torturing thus ineffectually, and being always defeated by women, they were put to death by the sword, without the trial of tortures. For the champion, Ammonarium, endured these in behalf of all."

—Dionysius the Great, bishop of Alexandria, describing some of the martyrs during the Decian persecution

Decius's persecution exposed the weakness of the church after years of prosperity. Christians had lost the sense of themselves as a heroic band of pilgrims. When the decree was announced in Antioch, thousands of Christians surged forward in their eagerness to absolve themselves. In one North African town, there were so many applicants on the appointed day that the officials had to ask many of them to return the next day. A handful of Christians were able to fraudulently purchase certificates, and others just attempted to lay low and not draw attention to themselves. In the end, it was not the number of people killed that made the persecution so horrendous, but the difficulty of dealing in the aftermath with those who complied with the decree and then wanted to return to the church once the threat of punishment was lifted.

 In Depth

> Just as the persecution kicked into high gear, there was another outbreak of disease similar to the Antonine Plague that had so ravaged the empire in the late second century. Thousands died in Rome every day, and throughout the empire the effects were devastating and demoralizing. Pagans blamed the epidemic on the Christians, and this reinforced the assault on the church by intensifying the local persecutions.

The Lapsed

The persecution under Decius ended in 251 with the death of the emperor. His successor, Gallus, dropped the edict, and things calmed down, though there were still local outbreaks of violence. When the dust began to clear, however, that's when the real problems began. Always in previous persecutions there were some who, under threat, *apostatized*. But Decius's persecution had caught the Christian community flat-footed, and many had renounced the faith.

In some cases, like the city of Carthage in North Africa, it may have been the majority of the Christians. Now many of those people were clamoring to get back into the church. The situation was unprecedented in its scope.

The problem was compounded by the fact that a new kind of martyr came out of the Decian persecution. Because Decius was trying to break people rather than kill them, many people were arrested and tortured but never executed. In previous persecutions, the number of such persons, called *confessors*, was

Word Knowledge

An **apostate** is a person who abandons a group, cause, or belief system. To apostatize, obviously, means to become an apostate.

A **confessor** is someone who has suffered for his or her confession of faith in Christ but who lives through the ordeal. They were considered martyrs because they had been prepared to die.

relatively small. If you made it that far along the martyrdom trail, you could pretty well expect to end up going all the way. Under Decius, however, the number of confessors was quite large.

So more people lived. Is that a bad thing? Well, no, of course not, but it did confuse things. Because of the close relationship between the martyr and Christ in the eyes of the church, many people who were seeking forgiveness for egregious sins would go to the martyrs who were in prison. Usually, with the martyr's seal of approval on someone's repentance, they were allowed back into the church, by which I mean they were allowed to receive the Eucharist again. This caused conflicts occasionally when martyrs and bishops came to different conclusions about whether a person should be allowed back into the church, but the number of martyrs was often relatively low and they usually weren't around long enough to be too much of a disruption to order.

Ah, but now there was a whole new crop of martyrs, and they were going to stick around for quite a while. As masses of people began clamoring to receive pardon from the confessors, the bishops started to see their own authority flying out the window. They no longer had any control over who was coming to the table of the Lord. The whole controversy began to heat up very quickly, and something had to be done. Two of the most important names during this crisis were Cyprian of Carthage and Novation.

Novation

Novation was a presbyter in Rome who was absolutely against letting the lapsed back in. When Pope Fabian died during the persecution, an election was held to replace him. Most people voted for Cornelius, who was in favor of full acceptance of those who repented. The minority of presbyters who agreed with Novation, however, elected him as their own bishop.

 In Depth

Today, we associate the title "Pope" exclusively with the bishop of Rome. Where did the title come from?

In the early church it was common practice to refer to spiritual leaders as "father." In Latin, the word was "papa." Over time, in the Western church, the title became limited to bishops. In 1073 it became limited to the bishop of Rome alone. The word "papa" came into English as "pope," the title with which we are familiar.

So now there were two bishops in Rome. The two sides continued to harden their position over time. Novation received some support from around the empire, but not enough to make a huge difference. Setting up an alternative church structure, the Novationists actually lasted for several centuries.

Cyprian of Carthage

Cyprian may have been a late bloomer, spiritually speaking. From a wealthy family in the North African city of Carthage, he had an excellent education and had even studied rhetoric. He converted to Christianity only when he was about 40, around 245. In that, he was following in the footsteps of his favorite theologian, "the master" Tertullian. He swiftly rose through the ecclesiastical ranks and was named bishop of Carthage in just three or four years.

From the Source _____

"Whoever is separated from the Church and is joined with an adulteress is separated from the promises of the Church, nor will he who has abandoned the Church arrive at the rewards of Christ. He is a stranger; he is profane; he is an enemy. He cannot have God as a father who does not have the Church as a mother."

—Cyprian of Carthage, *The Unity of the Catholic Church*

When the Decian persecution broke out, Cyprian ran for his life. He consistently claimed that he was obeying a vision from God and that he was trying to preserve some ability for the church to continue to function. If he had stayed and died, there would have been chaos, he claimed. His critics were unmoved, calling him a coward and an apostate. They even went so far as to accuse him to the church hierarchy in Rome, which issued a mild rebuke.

When the persecution ended, controversy erupted over how to deal with the lapsed. A group of confessors had begun to pardon everyone they could, allowing hundreds back into the church that they had so recently abandoned. From his safe haven, Cyprian argued that the lapsed should not be allowed to return right away. Instead, the decision about whether to readmit should be put off until everyone's emotions had had a chance to calm down.

Word Knowledge

A **schism** is a break between two factions within a larger community.

You can imagine how well that went over with everyone who had lived through the crisis, coming from Cyprian off in his undisclosed location. Some of Cyprian's presbyters aligned themselves with the confessors, and all of a sudden there was a full-fledged *schism* going on.

Cyprian called a synod to decide the matter. Bishops from around the region arrived and eventually settled on a way of dealing with the lapsed. The agreement put an end to the immediate break in the church, in which a splinter group aligned with the Novationists in Rome had elected one of Cyprian's critics as bishop of Carthage. That didn't last very long, largely due to the public reaction to Cyprian's tremendous self-sacrifice in the face of the epidemic that was just beginning to break in the city.

In 258, there was another brief suppression of the church under Valerian, a friend of Decius, when he became emperor after Decius's death, but it ended swiftly when he was taken prisoner during a war against the Persians. Nevertheless, it was enough to kill several celebrated Christians, including Cyprian of Carthage. Afterward, there were 40 years of peace.

The Great Persecution

Toward the end of the third century, the empire finally began to get back on an even keel. The new emperor, Diocletian, had completely reorganized the imperial system, bringing stability to Rome for the first time in over 50 years. Diocletian understood that the empire had grown too large for one man to administrate. So he set up a system, a "team" of emperors. There were two men with the title Augustus, and two more junior emperors with the title Caesar. In the East, Diocletian was the Augustus and Galerius was his Caesar. In the West, Maximian was Augustus, with Constantius Chlorus as his Caesar.

Yeah, I know, a lot of names. Diocletian wanted to create a system that would avoid all of the bloodshed and revolution as one would-be emperor fought another. So his system was designed so that when the Augustus died, his Caesar would take his position as the new Augustus, and then he would appoint a new person to be his junior partner, and so on, and so on. It was a nice idea, but the whole thing was held together with bailing wire and Diocletian's personality.

You would have thought things were just fine. Christians were growing as a segment of the population, prospering from four decades without significant violence.

Of the three emperors, only Galerius had ever shown any kind of hostility toward Christianity. Why, Prisca and Valeria, Diocletian's wife and daughter, were both Christians themselves. What could possibly go wrong?

Galerius Attacks the Church

There were problems with the army. Many Christians did not feel that it was appropriate for them to serve in the military. Some soldiers who became Christians tried to leave military service. In both cases, Galerius came to the conclusion that Christians were a threat to the stability of the empire's military might. They were unreliable, at a time when the reliability of the army was very important. Galerius decided that only a purge of all Christians from the army would do. He convinced Diocletian to support him. The idea was just to get rid of the Christians, but things got a little rough, particularly in legions under Galerius's command.

In 303, Galerius raised the heat a notch. He persuaded Diocletian that the army wasn't enough. He wanted a purge of all Christians from whatever office they might hold, and he wanted to limit the growth of Christians in the empire. To that end, Diocletian issued an edict that required Christians to hand over copies of their sacred writings to be burnt. Church buildings were to be confiscated and destroyed. Many Christians refused, and they were executed as a result.

What followed was a tit-for-tat escalation of the persecution. Someone set fire to the royal palace, not once, but twice. Later, disturbances and riots convinced both Galerius and Diocletian that the Christians were out to get them. Each time they responded with greater levels of violence until finally all Christians everywhere were required to sacrifice to the gods or face execution. It was the worst persecution that the church had ever faced.

From the Source

"… in view of our most mild clemency and the constant habit by which we are accustomed to grant indulgence to all, we thought that we ought to grant our most prompt indulgence also to these, so that they may again be Christians and may hold their gatherings, provided they do nothing contrary to good order. But we shall tell the magistrates in another letter what they ought to do.

"Wherefore, for this our indulgence, they ought to pray to their God for our safety, for that of the republic, and for their own, that the republic may continue uninjured on every side, and that they may be able to live securely in their homes."

—from *The Edict of Galerius*, April 30, 311

The End of Persecution

In 305, Galerius forced both Diocletian and Maximian, the two Augustuses, to resign. He and Constantius took their place. It was a short-lived affair. In 311, Galerius became seriously ill and, thinking that the Christians had sent their god after him, issued an Edict of Toleration, ending the ban on Christians and asking them to pray for him. It didn't help much. Galerius was dead five days later. Across the empire, Christians came out of hiding, out of prisons and rock quarries and mines where they had been sent, and praised their God.

The political situation was still very rocky, and the situation for the Christians perhaps even more precarious. But things were about to change in a way nobody could have predicted. Up in the northern reaches of the empire, governing Gaul and Britain, the son of Constantius Chlorus had been biding his time and waiting for an opportunity to make his move. The death of Galerius opened the door for Constantine.

The Least You Need to Know

◆ The attempt to attack the catechumens ended with growth for the church.

◆ The Decian persecution humbled the church by causing so many to defect from the faith.

◆ Cyprian defended the prerogatives of the bishop and the unity of the church.

◆ The Great Persecution under Diocletian and Galerius was unable to destroy the Christian community.

Chapter 17

"In This Sign, Conquer!"

In This Chapter

- ◆ The man of the hour
- ◆ Christian sign language
- ◆ He's a referee with a big stick
- ◆ There can be only one

The last chapter ended with the culmination of the official, empire-wide persecution of the church, the Great Persecution. We also saw the death of Galerius, the main instigator of that persecution. The empire, reorganized around two new senior and two junior emperors, was still in a rocky state. In the wake of such a vicious assault, so was the church. Both were looking for an end to violence. What they got was something else entirely.

Constantine

Flavius Valerius Aurelius Constantinus—or Constantine, as he is known to history—was born in 280, the son of Constantius Chlorus and an innkeeper's daughter named Helena. Constantius divorced Helena when his son was 12 years old in order to marry the daughter of Maximian, who was then the emperor of the western half of the empire. It was a political marriage that gained Constantius the status of junior emperor.

The political intrigue and maneuvering of those years was quite intricate. Constantine's father was finally named the senior emperor or Augustus of the western empire in 305, but he died a year later in Britain. When Constantine arrived to join his father, the army stationed there proclaimed him Augustus in his father's place, but he ended up being appointed junior emperor instead. Constantine then holed up in the northwestern quarter of the empire, which included Britain, modern-day France and Germany, and Spain. The region had suffered tremendously through the third century, despite its rich potential, but it afforded Constantine the largest army in the empire. During the six years that followed, Constantine bided his time, ruling his provinces with an iron hand and promoting stability.

The death of Galerius in 311 created a great power vacuum. None of the remaining rulers had any real interest in holding on to the imperial structure that Diocletian had created (refresh your memory by reading Chapter 16). Constantine allied himself with Licinius, his counterpart in the eastern empire, and waited while his co-rulers plotted and schemed against him and one another.

Chi-Rho

In 312, Constantine was prepared to strike. Gathering his armies, he crossed the Alps and attacked the forces of the western Augustus Maxentius. The two finally clashed just outside of Rome, beside the Milvian Bridge. During the lead-up to the battle, it seems that the still-pagan Constantine may have been receiving bad omens from the gods that he consulted, and Maxentius had a number of perceived advantages going for him (the day of the battle, for instance, was the fifth anniversary of Maxentius's ascension to Augustus). He was also better positioned for the fight. Constantine was casting about for divine help in the fight to come, someone on high who could give him a much-needed edge.

Word Knowledge

Chi-Rho is the merging of the two Greek letters Chi (X) and Rho (R), which are the first two words in the Greek spelling of Christ. From very early in the history of the church, this shortened way of writing Christ was used.

And here's where history and legend collide in ways difficult to untangle. We know that Constantine ordered his soldiers to paint the *Chi-Rho* on their shields and to make a banner that would display this ancient symbol of Jesus Christ. The following day, when they went into battle against Maxentius, Constantine's army would be flying the Christian flag, so to speak.

Why would he do such a thing? And why would his army follow him? There are actually three different versions of the story behind Constantine's sudden act of dedication. One version comes from Lactantius, a Christian scholar that Constantine had made tutor to his son Crispus. Lactantius writes that Constantine had a dream the night before the battle that caused him to paint the Christian symbol on his soldiers' shields.

The other two versions come from the Christian historian Eusebius of Caesarea. In the first, a bare-bones version, Constantine simply has a vision in which he sees the sign and the words, "In this, be victorious." Years later, in an oration praising Constantine, Eusebius gives a much more elaborate version that, he claims, Constantine swore was true. In this version, Constantine was praying for divine guidance when he saw a sign in the heavens. In fact, his entire army saw it with him. In a dream that night, Christ himself appeared to explain the vision to Constantine.

From the Source

"And while he was thus praying with fervent entreaty, a most marvelous sign appeared to him from heaven, the account of which it might have been hard to believe had it been related by any other person. But since the victorious emperor himself long afterwards declared it to the writer of this history, when he was honored with his acquaintance and society, and confirmed his statement by an oath, who could hesitate to accredit the relation, especially since the testimony of after-time has established its truth? He said that about noon, when the day was already beginning to decline, he saw with his own eyes the trophy of a cross of light in the heavens, above the sun, and bearing the inscription, 'Conquer by This.' At this sight he himself was struck with amazement, and his whole army also, which followed him on this expedition, and witnessed the miracle."

—Eusebius of Caesarea, *Life of Constantine*

On October 28, 312, carrying aloft the sign of the cross, the Roman army under Constantine marched into battle. The Milvian Bridge was out of action, and a temporary pontoon structure had been built next to it to allow Maxentius to get his troops across. Maxentius was in a stronger position, since Constantine had to get across the bridge in order to enter Rome.

Maxentius made the mistake of bringing his troops across the river to engage Constantine. When the two forces clashed, Constantine was able to push Maxentius's army back to the river. But the only way across, the pontoon bridge, was too narrow to accommodate all of Maxentius's men in one mad rush. The entrance to the bridge became a bottleneck that made it impossible for Maxentius and his army to retreat, and Constantine's army crushed them. Maxentius's body was later discovered in the river, where he had drowned in a desperate attempt to swim to the other side. Rome belonged to Constantine. It was only the western half of the empire, but it was a start.

God Politics

Writers have debated the validity of Constantine's conversion to Christianity almost since it happened. Was he genuinely moved by a spiritual conversion, or was he just a shrewd politician who could sense which way the wind was blowing? His conversion was just about the last thing that the church expected. Christians, weary from the years of persecution, were happy to see in Constantine a protector and friend. But was he a brother?

 In Depth

> Constantine's mother, Helena, also converted to Christianity along with her son. She made a very famous pilgrimage to Palestine in 327–328, toward the end of her life. During her journey, she visited all of the holy sites associated with Christianity.
>
> Legend has it that Helena was responsible for the recovery of the True Cross, the actual cross on which Jesus died. She had chosen a site to excavate for a church to commemorate the place where Jesus had been crucified. When digging started, three pieces of wood were discovered. Believing one of them to be the Cross, they were each touched in turn to the body of a sick woman. The third cross healed the woman, indicating that it was the True Cross.
>
> There's no actual evidence that Helena had anything to do with the Cross. These stories actually come from almost a century after the fact. It is true, however, that the church of the Holy Sepulcher was completed in 335 and that almost right away there are references to the display of the True Cross.

Constantine was raised in a pagan household, educated within the imperial system, and surrounded almost his entire early life by people hostile to the Christian faith. How on earth did he ever end up a Christian? Was it as simple as a vision or a dream? Everything about Constantine's vision could have been understood as a sign from Apollo, a god that Constantine's family had a close connection to. Why did he see these signs and the dream that followed (assuming that they had happened as Eusebius describes) as originating from the Christian God?

One of Constantine's first actions when he succeeded his father was to restore confiscated property to the churches in the lands that he controlled. Shortly afterward, Constantine's entourage included a Spanish bishop named Hosius. How he ended up in Constantine's orbit we don't know, but he quickly became Constantine's right-hand man when it came to dealing with Christians. Some scholars believe Hosius was instrumental in helping Constantine interpret his vision/dream through a Christian lens. If Constantine had confided in Hosius, the bishop surely would have steered Constantine in that direction.

Constantine adopted the Christian banner while it was still more of a liability than a benefit. The strength of the church was in the eastern half of the empire, not the West. Rome was still proudly pagan. Supporting the Christians wasn't really the smart play, so what moved him to do it? In the ancient world, the separation between political realities and religious convictions was difficult to separate. Gods were viewed as constituencies to be approached and placated as much as any other political force in a society.

That Constantine was willing to honor the God of the Christians did not require, as yet, that he dismiss all other gods. And no god could keep him from doing what was necessary to maintain his hold on political power once he had achieved it. So calling Constantine's faith into question for the many later acts of political brutality (the murder of his first wife, Fausta, and their son Crispus, for example) really misses the point. Constantine didn't convert to Christianity so much as he became its patron and, in so doing, hoped to win the favor of the Christian God for his imperial ambitions. Only at the end of his life—on his deathbed, in fact—was he finally baptized. Until then, for all of his impact on the Christian community, Constantine was officially nothing more than an interested bystander.

Donatism

Meanwhile, the Christians—hey, you remember the Christians, right? It's so easy to get caught up in the political and military action that we forget that the church wasn't just sitting around while all of this was taking place. The prospect of having a Christian emperor also opened up the possibility of getting official sanction for one's particular brand of Christianity. Suddenly, Christians began looking to Constantine to help mediate their internal disputes. Almost as soon as he set foot in Rome, Constantine was forced to deal with one particularly thorny problem, an issue that would test his tolerance and demonstrate his willingness to use force to create unity in the Christian community.

The Donatist controversy was another dispute about how to handle Christians who had abandoned their faith during the recent persecution and now wanted back into the church. Whereas the confessors, those who had suffered but not been killed, during Cyprian's day were all for letting the lapsed Christians back in, this new generation was much more rigorous. They wanted to keep out not just those who had sacrificed to the gods, but even those who had cooperated in any way with the imperial authorities. When the bishopric of Carthage opened up, the two sides of the controversy elected two different bishops. The leader of the strict group was named Donatus, hence Donatism.

In Depth

Donatists accused many church leaders of being *traditores,* a word that means "to hand over," a reference to the fact that some church leaders had complied with the order to hand over copies of the Scriptures and other church possessions. Interestingly, we get two very common words from *traditore. Tradition* means to hand something on to the next generation. *Traitor* means to hand over another person.

The conflict touched on some really difficult theological questions. The Donatists alleged that the sacraments offered by a priest or bishop who was impure were not valid. That included those who had cooperated with the authorities. Well, that put in jeopardy everyone's salvation because how could you know the state of a man's soul when, for instance, he baptizes you? Is the baptism valid? Is the Eucharist valid?

Social and economic issues were at work as well. Christianity had been strong in North Africa for 200 years, but its strength had primarily rested on the lower classes, most of whom were natives. The upper classes, who tended to avoid Christianity because of the frequent persecutions, tended to come from a Latin background. The conversion of Constantine made Christianity safe for the wealthy and powerful, and they flooded into the churches. So the masses of Donatists (as opposed to the leaders) were as aggravated by the changing makeup of the Christian community as they were by theological debates.

The disagreement was threatening to engulf the entire church. There could be only one bishop of Carthage. Bishops from around the empire jumped into the fracas, most everyone in opposition to Donatus. Constantine tried to intervene, but the Donatists would have none of it. They viewed the empire as a corrupting force. When persuasion wouldn't work, Constantine dispatched troops to Carthage in 317. For the first time, Christians used the power of the state against other Christians. It set a very bad precedent for the future and didn't really work out that well. The Donatists were more determined than Constantine gave them credit for. After five years, he was forced to call off his soldiers. The Donatist movement persisted for a least a century.

One Empire, One Emperor

Constantine and his counterpart, Licinius, met in 313 in Milan, where the two entered into an alliance sealed by the marriage of Licinius to Constantine's sister. Among the other matters agreed to, the two issued the Edict of Milan. It officially ended any persecution of Christians in the lands controlled by either man and restored all property that had been taken from Christians. Galerius's edict, issued two years earlier, had actually been more important when it came to stopping the harassment of Christians, and persecution was still the norm in lands controlled by the other co-ruler, Maximinus Daia. Still, it demonstrated to Christians that Constantine was serious about putting the violence to an end.

While they were still meeting, news came that Maximinus had attacked Licinius's territory. Licinius marched straight into battle and defeated Maximinus, who died a few days later. The empire was now split between the two brothers-in-law, Constantine and Licinius. There was hope that the connection between the two would mean that the war and instability was over, but neither man was willing to settle for just half of an empire.

After whittling away at Licinius's territory for several years, in 322 Constantine launched an all-out invasion of the East. Licinius was a very superstitious fellow. He genuinely feared the sign of the cross on the shields of Constantine's soldiers and refused to launch a frontal assault against it. Not surprisingly, their general's expectations of defeat infected the morale of his troops, and Licinius lost the day. It was a definitive defeat. Later, Constantine's sister eventually negotiated the surrender of her husband to her brother. Licinius abdicated and went to live in the country, where shortly thereafter he was murdered.

By 324, Constantine was the unquestioned ruler of the Roman Empire. He reigned for another 13 years, until his death in 337. While he was not responsible for all of the changes that came about as a result of his favoring of Christianity, Constantine presided over one of the truly important turning points in human history. We'll see in the next chapter some of the consequences of his decisions.

From the Source _____

"When I, Constantine Augustus, as well as I, Licinius Augustus, fortunately met near Mediolanurn (Milan), and were considering everything that pertained to the public welfare and security, we thought, among other things which we saw would be for the good of many, those regulations pertaining to the reverence of the Divinity ought certainly to be made first, so that we might grant to the Christians and others full authority to observe that religion which each preferred; whence any Divinity whatsoever in the seat of the heavens may be propitious and kindly disposed to us and all who are placed under our rule. And thus by this wholesome counsel and most upright provision we thought to arrange that no one whatsoever should be denied the opportunity to give his heart to the observance of the Christian religion, of that religion which he should think best for himself, so that the Supreme Deity, to whose worship we freely yield our hearts, may show in all things His usual favor and benevolence .... When you see that this has been granted to them by us, your Worship will know that we have also conceded to other religions the right of open and free observance of their worship for the sake of the peace of our times, that each one may have the free opportunity to worship as he pleases; this regulation is made that we may not seem to detract from any dignity or any religion."

—Excerpt from _The Edict of Milan_, 313

The Least You Need to Know

◆ The rise of Constantine was as unexpected by his contemporaries as it seems to us now.

◆ Constantine didn't convert to Christianity as much as he became Christianity's patron.

◆ His attempt to persuade and then to eliminate the Donatists foreshadows Constantine's later attempts to unify Christians.

◆ With the defeat of Licinius, Constantine was in a position to shape the future of the entire Roman Empire.

Chapter 18

The Thirteenth Apostle

In This Chapter

- ◆ Christians adapt their theology to the new Rome
- ◆ An emperor calls a council
- ◆ Thousands flee to the desert … seeking martyrdom
- ◆ A new Rome for a new empire

It should come as no shock to any of us that, in the wake of Diocletian's attack on Christianity, and living in the shadow of the earlier persecutions of Decius and Valerian, the ascension of Constantine and the end of official sanctions against the church should strike the early Christians as a moment of direct, divine intervention. Seemingly in a moment, the Roman Empire began to be a Christian empire. That many Christians, particularly the bishops, reached out to support Constantine owes as much to a sense that they had reached a divinely appointed moment as to anything in Constantine's own behavior. Certain figures, in particular, threw their support behind Constantine, helping to make the case for understanding his imperial ambitions as sanctioned by heaven.

Imperial Theology

Constantine had himself a fan club of one in Eusebius of Caesarea. Eusebius was a bishop and historian, perhaps the most educated Christian of his day. He also developed a fascinating view of the new Christian emperor and was largely responsible for an imperial theology that interpreted Constantine as a chosen servant of God akin to one of the apostles. By championing this view, Eusebius helped to set the course for the next 15 centuries of Western history. Not bad for a guy who started life as a librarian.

Well, more than just a librarian. Origen had spent the final years of his life in Caesarea and had left his extensive library there. Pamphilus of Caesarea was the custodian of Origen's library and spent a good deal of his time not only studying the texts, but acquiring new ones to expand the library's holdings. One of Pamphilus's students was Eusebius, who was so dedicated to his teacher that he afterward insisted on being known as Eusebius of Pamphilus.

Eusebius, like Pamphilus, spent a great deal of his time traveling around the empire looking for sources of information about the history of the Christian faith. He lived a common life with Pamphilus and several fellow students, spending their days in study and writing. During this time, Eusebius began work on his most important work, *Church History*, an attempt to bring together all that he had discovered about the origins and development of the Christian faith into one work. For modern historians, it is invaluable. In it, Eusebius preserves much that otherwise would have been lost to us. In fact, a good deal of what you've been reading in this book ultimately derives, directly or indirectly, from Eusebius's scholarship.

In 303, the Great Persecution reached Caesarea. Eusebius watched as, over the next four years, many of his companions—including his mentor, Pamphilus—were arrested, tried, and executed. Eusebius himself lived under almost constant threat and may have had to flee the city on several occasions. The situation eased in 311 when Galerius backed off. The following year, Constantine and Licinius issued the Edict of Toleration, and the persecution was over.

By the time Constantine defeated Licinius to unite the two halves of the empire, Eusebius had been elected to the bishopric of Caesarea, a post that brought with it oversight of all of Palestine and helped Eusebius play an important role at the Council of Nicaea, which we'll look at in the next section. At the council, Eusebius felt common cause with Constantine's pursuit of a church unified and at peace with itself. His support for that program, despite wavering a bit on the theological issues at the heart of the council's deliberations, made him a favorite of Constantine's court.

From the Source

"But Constantine, the mightiest victor, adorned with every virtue of piety, together with his son Crispus, a most God-beloved prince, and in all respects like his father, recovered the East which belonged to them; and they formed one united Roman empire as of old, bringing under their peaceful sway the whole world from the rising of the sun to the opposite quarter, both north and south, even to the extremities of the declining day.

"All fear therefore of those who had formerly afflicted them was taken away from men, and they celebrated splendid and festive days. Everything was filled with light, and those who before were downcast beheld each other with smiling faces and beaming eyes. With dances and hymns, in city and country, they glorified first of all God the universal King, because they had been thus taught, and then the pious emperor with his God-beloved children."

—Eusebius of Caesarea, *The Church History*

In the final edition of *Church History*, Eusebius made his most enduring contribution to the Christianization of the empire and, more important in the long term, to the legitimacy of the notion that the state could be genuinely Christian. Eusebius crafted the account of the history and development of Christianity in such a way as to make the rise of a Christian emperor seem to be the very culmination of God's plan. With little patience for the kind of thinking that looked for an any-moment-now return of Jesus, Eusebius saw in Constantine's rise the climax of everything that pagans longed for but could not obtain except in Jesus, and his references to Constantine's rule are painted in messianic language. In doing so, he was articulating what many of the Christians in his day felt, particularly those who had watched friends and loved ones die under imperial persecution: a new age had dawned, and "all fear ... was taken away from men."

The Council of Nicaea

No such thing as separation between church and state had ever existed in Rome. Although there were women and men whose sole function was to serve the gods, the political leadership of the empire was also supposed to be involved in offering sacrifices, seeking omens and portents, and otherwise making sure that the civil government didn't go around offending any hot-tempered deities. Augustus had adopted the title *pontifex maximus*, the highest religious position in the Roman system of gods, and the emperors owned it from then on. So the concept of political involvement in religious matters was a given in Roman life.

> ### Word Knowledge
>
> **Pontifex maximus,** or "supreme bridge-builder," was the head of the College of Pontiffs in Rome, the apex of Roman religious life. From Augustus on, it was a title and a role adopted by the emperors. Bridges were serious business in Rome, and they had a certain religious significance all their own, but they were also metaphors. In essence, the pontiffs were those who built bridges between the world of humans and the world of the gods. In the late 300s, the emperor Gratian abandoned the title in favor of Pope Damasus I, and from that time it has become one of the hereditary titles of the bishop of Rome, the pope.

That reality didn't change just because the religion in question happened to be Christianity. Constantine was not shy about entering into religious disputes, though he was careful not to be heavy-handed. Still, nothing demonstrates the change that was coming in the new empire, and the critical way that political power began to enter into religious disputes, better than the council that Constantine called to end the fight over Arianism.

Roots of the Debate

It all started with a disagreement between Alexander, the bishop of Alexandria, and one of his presbyters, a very popular fellow named Arius. (Hence the name Arianism, but you saw that coming, didn't you?) The main point on which the two clashed had to do with the ultimate nature of Jesus as the Word of God. Put simply, Arius believed that the Word of God was not eternal, but had been the very first thing created by God. Alexander argued that to agree with Arius meant that Jesus, the Word in the flesh, was not divine and, therefore, could not be the Savior. It was a bit more complicated than that, of course, but those are the essentials.

The fight became public, with people taking sides like fans at a soccer match. In fact, given the occasional riots that broke out between supporters of the two men, it *looked* a lot like a soccer match. They even had theme songs; Arius, in particular, had composed a ditty or two to encapsulate his views. It may be hard for us to imagine a theological argument being that popular an issue, but there you go.

Alexander removed Arius from his positions. Arius responded by writing letters to friends around the empire, including his friend Eusebius, the politically connected bishop of Nicomedia, the capital of the eastern half of the empire and the site of Constantine's summer palace. Alexander drew on his own connections, and pretty soon the entire Eastern church was in turmoil.

The Emperor's Invitation

Constantine's goal was unity in the empire. His support for the Christian community was directed toward that purpose. The fight between Arius and Alexander threatened to spill over into a full-scale theological war, pitting bishop against bishop and sending their supporters into the streets to riot. That was the last thing that the emperor needed. When his personal representative, Bishop Hosius of Cordoba, was unable to bring the two sides together, Constantine decided to call a universal council of bishops to address the problem. Every bishop in the church was invited to attend and was provided with travel expenses and accommodations out of the imperial treasury. Somewhere between 250 and 300 showed up, each with a retinue of assistants, making the final count something like 1,500 people. Most of the bishops came from churches in the eastern part of the empire, where the fight over Arius's teachings was particularly severe. Western churches, less numerous than Eastern Christians and less passionate about divisions over philosophical questions, attended in much smaller numbers.

What an experience it must have been for the bishops who attended. Little more than 10 years earlier, they had been subject to arrest, torture, and death at the hands of the imperial authorities. Many bore the personal scars that commitment to their faith had earned them during that decade of Diocletian's attempt to destroy the church. And here they stood as, attended by pomp and splendor, the emperor Constantine entered the council chamber to welcome them. It must have felt like whiplash.

The Council Debate

At the council, three main factions quickly emerged. The first were those who supported Arius, chief among them Eusebius of Nicomedia, who had championed Arius's case from the start. Because Arius himself was only a deacon and not a bishop, he was not permitted to speak during the council's deliberations. Instead, Eusebius was the voice of Arius's position.

Opposing Arius's supporters was a small but zealous group led by Alexander of Alexandria (say that 10 times fast). This group felt that Arius's position constituted a devastating blow to the very heart of the Christian understanding of the relationship between God and Jesus, and therefore undermined the foundations of Christian faith itself. In Alexander's entourage was another deacon from Alexandria named Athanasius. Like Arius, Athanasius was unable to participate in the debate, but he certainly had opinions on the matter. Athanasius later became patriarch of Alexandria and the preeminent champion of the orthodoxy that emerged from Nicaea.

The last group—the largest, in fact—were those bishops who fell in the middle. You could call them the moderates, if you wish, although that doesn't necessarily characterize their position. Instead, many of them were present to hear for the first time the particulars of the case. These bishops were primarily focused on finding a compromise that would heal the bitterness that had developed in the midst of the conflict. They were looking for a way to move forward on what they considered to be more important matters.

For that reason, the moderates seemed to have been prepared to give Arius and his supporters the benefit of the doubt, and weren't all that thrilled with the harsh tone coming from Alexander's party. As the council opened, it looked like Arius might have the upper hand, until Eusebius of Nicomedia rose to explain Arius's views.

You have to understand that the bishops at Nicaea were not voting on whether Jesus was divine. There were different traditions about how exactly to word it, but belief in the divinity of Jesus was as mainstream as it got in the Christian community. What was at stake at Nicaea was whether Arius's explanation of the relationship between the Father and the Son was legitimate.

Eusebius of Nicomedia had entered the council confident that a simple explanation of his views, which mirrored Arius's, would be sufficient to garner the support of the other bishops and that the matter would be concluded quickly. Things happened quickly, alright, but not the way he expected.

As Eusebius laid out his arguments, the mood in the council chamber turned ugly. Certainly, Alexander's party was dismissive, but the shock must have come as the moderates suddenly realized that the issue before them was not simply a matter of semantics or of church politics run amok. The suggestion that the Word of God was a created being, even the very first created being, drew howls from those present. Eusebius's voice was drowned out by the cries of "Heretic!" and "Blasphemer!" According to accounts, his speech was ripped out of his hands, torn to shreds, and stomped into the ground.

Defining the Faith

What had been a hopeful atmosphere eager for reconciliation now turned purposeful as the bishops started looking for the clearest way to express their rejection of Arius's views. They tried sticking to scriptural language only, but found that it left them unable to plainly exclude the ideas that Arius had put forward. Another approach was needed, and the bishops settled on the establishment of a creed.

The church historian and bishop Eusebius of Caesarea (not to be confused with Eusebius of Nicomedia) presented the creed that his church used when it baptized people. Most of the wording will be familiar to you from Chapter 10, where we talked about creeds and the rule of faith. At the behest of Constantine, the bishops added a line to the effect that Jesus was "of one substance with the Father." The intent was to be clear that there was no difference between the Father and the Son in terms of their divinity. The bishops were also at pains to assert that the Son was not in any way a creation of the Father. The Nicene Creed is today recognized by every branch of the Christian faith.

From the Source

The Nicene Creed

We believe in one God, the Father Almighty, Maker of all things visible and invisible.

And in one Lord Jesus Christ, the Son of God, begotten of the Father the only-begotten; that is, of the essence of the Father, God of God, Light of Light, very God of very God, begotten, not made, being of one substance with the Father; by whom all things were made both in heaven and on earth; who for us men, and for our salvation, came down and was incarnate and was made man; he suffered, and the third day he rose again, ascended into heaven; from there he shall come to judge the living and the dead.

And in the Holy Spirit.

But those who say: "There was a time when he was not;" and "He was not before he was made;" and "He was made out of nothing," or "He is of another substance" or "essence," or "The Son of God is created," or "changeable," or "alterable"—they are condemned by the holy catholic and apostolic Church.

This is the original form of the Nicene Creed that came out of the Council in 325. Later, in 381, the Council of Constantinople expanded the original creed to include, among other things, a fuller section on the Holy Spirit. This Nicene-Constantinopolitan Creed, without the condemnations tacked on to the end, is the one that is familiar to Christians around the world today.

Arius and his ideas were condemned. Those who wouldn't sign off on the creed, which ended up just being two guys, were stripped of their office as bishop. Even Eusebius of Nicomedia signed, although with great reluctance and mainly to save his position. But don't feel too bad for him. A few years later, he was able to worm his way back into Constantine's good graces. Eventually, he convinced the emperor to reinstate Arius, who died the night before he could enjoy his renewed status.

Eusebius made sure that the imperial authorities promoted Arianism, not the Nicene orthodoxy. He even managed to get most of his rival bishops exiled, including Athanasius. When Constantine was finally baptized on his deathbed, it was Eusebius of Nicomedia who performed the ceremony. Eusebius exemplified the opportunities and dangers of the new close association between the emperor and the bishops.

Church and State

Constantine's role in the council demonstrated how much things had changed. While deacons and even presbyters were unable to contribute to the discussions, the unbaptized Constantine was allowed to openly lobby the bishops to accept the language of "one substance."

Constantine's involvement with the bishops extended beyond the council. While the bishops themselves were limited to pronouncing a religious sanction against those who were committed to Arius's cause, Constantine could do far more. Along with the bishops' ruling, Constantine brought civil charges against the recalcitrant Arius and whoever supported him. Constantine used his civil authority to punish those who wouldn't join him in his quest to unify the Christian community.

For the first time, the power of the state was brought to bear in order to support one group of Christians against another. It was a preview of coming attractions. For the next 15 centuries, the uneasy marriage between the church and the state would create tremendous opportunities for intolerance and violence.

Retreating to the Desert

Once Christianity had been legalized, and with the clear support that Constantine began to lavish on the Christian community, the churches began to grow by leaps and bounds. Not everyone thought that this was such a great idea. Some Christians saw the threat of persecution and even martyrdom as a way to keep out the riff-raff, to maintain a high level of commitment. After all, you don't casually join up with a group when it can get you killed, right?

In the wake of Constantine's rise to power, the possibility of bearing witness to one's faith through suffering and death was largely gone. Zealous Christians began casting about for another way to live out their faith, a new form of martyrdom. They took ascetic living to a new level by leaving behind their communities and retreating into the wilderness of Egypt, Palestine, and Syria. Just when thousands began streaming into the church, thousands more began building cities in the desert.

Anthony the Hermit

There's no way of knowing who invented *monasticism*. Solitary hermits are a part of nearly every religious tradition and go back thousands of years. In early Christianity, however, one person is regarded as the exemplar of the hermit's calling: Anthony.

A native of Egypt, Anthony was born in a small village on the shores of the Nile River. His wealthy parents died when Anthony was still a fairly young man, leaving him all of their money and a younger sister to care for. He expected to just live off his inheritance for the rest of his life, but one day he walked into church just in time to hear a reading from the story of the rich young ruler in Matthew's Gospel: "If you would be perfect, go, sell what you possess and give to the poor, and you will have treasure in heaven."

> **Word Knowledge**
>
> **Monasticism** comes from the Greek word *mona-chos*, which means "solitary" or "alone." Monks pursued solitude and silence as an essential way of life, but it goes beyond that. The word also carried the notion of single-minded devotion, that the monk was focused entirely on the pursuit of spirituality at all costs.

Anthony, hearing those words directed at him, turned right around and obeyed. He sold off his properties, set aside enough to care for his sister, and gave the remainder to the poor. Eventually, he got rid of even the small amount that was left, placing his sister in the care of a household of virgins, and struck out for the desert.

He didn't charge out into the deep desert right away. The first few years he spent living with an elderly man on the edge of town. As I said, Anthony wasn't the first to live out this life. Many people were already living ascetic lives of one kind or another. After several years with this mentor, Anthony found an abandoned cemetery where he could live in relative isolation. Some people occasionally brought him some food, but otherwise he was left alone to wrestle with his demons—literally, it seems, as Athananius tells us that Anthony physically fought with evil spirits sent to tempt and torment him.

Over time, Anthony moved into more desolate places, seeking solitude. By this time, however, he had acquired a reputation as a holy man. Sick people came to him for healing, and others began to seek him out to learn the desert life from him. It drove Anthony crazy, and eventually he agreed to be available to those who were seeking him if they would leave him alone most of the time. He spent the majority of his life as a kind of spiritual coach, teaching spiritual athletes how to struggle toward God.

Near the end of his life, sometime around 356, Anthony and a pair of his students went out into the desert alone. He died there and left strict instructions that his companions never reveal where they had buried him. His one possession, a ratty old cloak, he sent to Athanasius.

Anthony's story was written up by Athanasius, which points out the close connection that could and did exist between the ascetics in the desert and the clergy in the cities. Athanasius's *Life of Anthony* was extraordinarily popular and served to advertise the kind of life that Anthony lived to people all over the empire. While Anthony and his contemporaries went into the desert prior to Constantine's conversion, it was the Christianization of the empire that spurred a wave of women and men to flee to the desert. Anthony's example showed them one way of doing that.

Pachomius and the Communal Life

Not everyone was cut out for the life of a solitary monk. Even those who pursued the hermetic life tended to live in loose-knit groups rather than being entirely isolated from all human contact. As more people moved into the desert in search of spiritual perfection, it was natural that more community-oriented forms of monasticism would emerge. The most important of these new communities was led by a former soldier. If Anthony exemplified the life of the hermit, Pachomius exemplified the communal life.

Born around 286 in southern Egypt, Pachomius was pressed into military service as a young man. The story goes that while he was being kept under lock and key, and not very happy about his lot in life, a group of Christians regularly came around with food and encouragement. Pachomius was so moved by this act of charity that, when he was suddenly released from military life, he became a Christian himself.

Pachomius lived with a mentor to try to learn to live as a monk. While he longed for solitude, it never quite seemed to fit. When his brother John joined him, Pachomius set about creating an actual monastery, a community of monks who were bound together by a common rule of life. Their first attempt failed because, the monks complained, Pachomius was too strict. So he tried again, this time with an even more demanding rule. The new community worked and quickly grew. By the end of his life, Pachomius oversaw about a dozen monastic communities, each housing several hundred people.

The Pachomian experiment combined the desire for desert solitude championed by Anthony with the older tradition of ascetic households. It preserved the possibility of Christian community as an alternative to worldly society where even the church seemed to have become part of the established order of things. At the same time, Pachomius made the desert portable. Monasteries could be formed anywhere, expanding the reach of the monastic life beyond those few who could handle the depth of solitude Anthony exhibited.

Out of the Desert

The immense popularity of the desert lifestyle spread throughout the Roman Empire. While many came to Egypt to live, even more came to visit, looking to these "desert saints" for spiritual advice and direction. When they returned to their homes, they brought the desert way of life back with them. While some attempted to re-create the monastic life as they saw it in Egypt, others adapted their ascetic discipline to the urban world.

> ### Word to the Wise
>
> "Christians reveled in the suffering of their monks, and they celebrated their acts of self-mortification just as fervently as an earlier age had commemorated the sacrifice of the martyrs. Indeed, it was precisely the martyr's role as exemplary Christians which these desert athletes inherited, their scorn for the things of this world and their willingness to make the ultimate sacrifice testifying to the strength of their commitment and putting the seal of purity on their faith just as surely as it had for those earlier spiritual warriors. By no coincidence, tales of the desert saints began to circulate during Constantine's reign, later to be set down in writing by, among others, bishops like Athanasius and Theodoret of Cyrrhus. Like the martyrologies that Christians listened to in church, these saints' lives simultaneously inspired Christians and validated their faith."
>
> —H.A. Drake, *Constantine and the Bishops*

Strangely enough, it was often the bishops who most embraced the new phenomenon. Earlier church leaders had often found martyrs and confessors to be a real pain, accusing them of using their popular spiritual authority to sidestep the regular hierarchy of the church. The difference seems to come with the times. The bishops were as concerned as others about the influx of ill-prepared people into the church. Those who found the desert spirituality attractive were usually women and men looking for a deeper life of faith, precisely the kind of people that a bishop would depend upon for the strength of the community. At the same time, bishops like Athanasius would find that these new monastic communities made excellent shock troops in the increasingly violent debates that rocked the church in the years after Constantine's conversion.

Nova Roma

Already during his war with Licinius, Constantine had noticed the strategic value of the city of Byzantium. Located astride both the land route between Europe and Asia and the seaway connecting the Black Sea to the Mediterranean, Byzantium was an ideal location for the capitol of the eastern half of the Roman Empire. Constantine, however, saw in it something more. He saw an opportunity to escape the legacies of Rome altogether and redefine them to suit himself.

Constantine was a masterful politician who understood well the value of symbolism. Byzantium wasn't large enough to serve as the "New Rome" that Constantine hoped to build, so he stole a page from Roman legend. The story goes that Romulus, the founder of Rome, had marked out its boundaries with a plow. Constantine took his entourage into the fields around Byzantium and began to mark out its new walls with a spear. The finished city would sit on 7 hills like Rome, have 14 districts like Rome, and have a Senate like Rome.

However, there weren't enough materials available to build the massive city that Constantine envisioned. The emperor was forced to cannibalize temples and public facilities from around the empire. He used statues of the gods to decorate the public squares, in the process undermining their power. They didn't seem all that fearsome removed from their temples and shrines.

From the Source

"All these edifices the emperor consecrated with the desire of perpetuating the memory of the apostles of our Saviour. He had, however, another object in erecting this building: an object at first unknown, but which afterwards became evident to all. He had in fact made choice of this spot in the prospect of his own death, anticipating with extraordinary fervor of faith that his body would share their title with the apostles themselves, and that he should thus even after death become the subject, with them, of the devotions which should be performed to their honor in this place. He accordingly caused twelve coffins to be set up in this church, like sacred pillars in honor and memory of the apostolic number, in the center of which his own was placed, having six of theirs on either side of it."

—Eusebius of Caesarea, *Life of the Blessed Emperor Constantine*

Not everything was recycled, of course. Constantine populated the city with churches of every shape and size. When Constantine dedicated the city on May 11, 330, he decreed that no sacrifices were to be offered in any of the pagan temples and no festivals held. All worship offered was Christian. The transition was complete. From now on, with a few blips along the way, the Roman Empire would be a Christian empire with a new Christian capital named after its Christian emperor: Constantinople.

When he died, Constantine was buried in the Church of the Holy Apostles in Constantinople, his tomb surrounded by statues of the twelve apostles. That's how he saw himself, perhaps, at the end: the thirteenth apostle. By moving the capital of the empire to the East, Constantine unwittingly saved it from destruction when the western half of the empire was overrun by the barbarian hordes. By vacating Rome, Constantine created a vacuum that would eventually be filled by the bishop of Rome, the pope. In the East, the Roman Empire (later known as the Byzantine Empire) endured until 1453, when it was finally sacked by the Ottoman Empire of the Turks.

The Least You Need to Know

- ◆ Constantine's ascension prompted the creation of a new imperial theology.
- ◆ The Council of Nicaea defined Christian faith and strengthened the relationship between the church and the state.
- ◆ The sudden popularity of Christianity caused many Christians to seek a stricter way of living their faith.
- ◆ Constantine crowned his new Christian empire with a Christian Rome.

Chapter 19

The Once and Future Faith

In This Chapter

- ◆ To the ends of the earth …
- ◆ The end of Christendom
- ◆ Will the real Jesus please stand up?
- ◆ Look who's coming to dinner

And so we end our tale. The history of early Christianity takes an abrupt turn with the rise of Constantine and the empire's embrace of the church. The process was slow, never entirely completed, and always fraught with stresses, but the Christianization of the Roman Empire established a marriage between the church and Western cultural life that remained almost unchallenged for more than a millennium. During that time, the conditions that most Christians lived under were in many ways radically different from those that greeted Christians in the first three centuries after Jesus.

Over the past 200 years or so, however, that marriage has been on the rocks and a divorce appears inevitable. At the same time, out in the so-called "two-thirds world," Christianity has suddenly been growing by leaps and bounds, often without any input from the churches of the West. One of the purposes of this book has been to demonstrate that, during its first three centuries, the early church was an urbanized, racially and socially diverse group of people who would have been as much or more at home in the slums of Karachi or the crammed tenements of Shanghai or even the secularized streets of Amsterdam than in the well-churched gated suburbs of Houston. While history rarely repeats itself, similarities do arise. Today Christianity looks more like it did during those first three centuries than at any other time since.

Outward Bound

While I have mentioned briefly the various other directions that Christianity spread in its initial years, you would be justified in thinking that we have spent the vast majority of this book talking about the church in the Roman Empire. While the empire was the center of most Christian expansion in the period prior to Constantine, Christianity moved outward from Palestine in all directions, particularly in the fourth through the seventh centuries.

Asia

If you think that Constantine's Roman Empire was the first political power to embrace Christianity, think again. That honor goes to the kingdom of Armenia. One of the many border kingdoms between Rome and Persia that I mentioned back in Chapter 5, Armenia occupied a triangle of land just east of Cappadocia in Asia Minor, where the Black Sea, the Caspian Sea, and the Mediterranean meet. In 301, Armenia made Christianity its official religion. The story is pretty remarkable.

The fellow responsible for this event is Gregory the Illuminator. Gregory's father had assassinated the king of Armenia, a fellow named Chosrov. To save his life, the young Gregory was whisked away to Cappadocia while the rest of his family was wiped out in retaliation. There he became a Christian. As an adult, Gregory resolved to return to his native land in order to share the Gospel. The king of Armenia, a son of Chosrov named Tiridates III, seized the opportunity to get revenge for his father. Gregory was arrested and tortured over a period of years, but eventually he was able to convert a number of people to Christianity, including Tiridates himself. The king established Christianity as the official religion, and Gregory is still regarded as the patron saint of Armenians to this day.

We've already talked about the Christian community that took shape in Edessa (back in Chapter 5). Out of Edessa, the first Christian communities in Persia were founded. Eusebius confirms that there was, at the Council of Nicaea, a certain "John of Persia" who as a bishop was representing Persia and India. By the beginning of the fifth century, a line of churches and monasteries were strung out like pearls on the trade route between Edessa and India, starting in Basra at the southern end of modern-day Iraq and moving around the coast of the Persian Gulf into modern-day Iran and down to Bahrain.

Under the Parthian Empire, Christianity was tolerated well enough. In fact, during many of the later systematic persecutions of the church in the Roman Empire, Persia was one place that Christians could flee to and be relatively safe. When the Parthians were displaced by the Sassanids, however, things changed. The Sassanids were intent on reestablishing Zoroastrianism as the religion of the state, and they didn't take kindly to the growing Christian community.

It didn't help when Constantine began to prepare for war with Persia and had the assistance of the bishops in the empire. Suddenly, every Christian in Persia was suspected of being allied with Rome, and for more than 50 years, the entire second half of the fourth century, they were systematically hunted down and slaughtered. Estimates run as high as 190,000 dead over the course of half a century. Christianity continued to grow in Persia until the seventh century, when the Persian Empire was overrun by the armies of Islam. The church survived, but under the constraints of living in Muslim society.

The Christians in Persia had established a vast network of churches, eventually sending out an official mission to the heart of China. We actually knew nothing about this Chinese church until 1623, when farmers digging in a field discovered a stone monument memorializing the arrival of Christians in 635. The mission, under the leadership of Bishop Alopen, was able to establish a presence in X'ian, the capital of the T'ang Dynasty. The monument itself had been fashioned in 781, which means that the Persian Christians had been operating in China for almost two centuries. Christianity went into decline with the end of the T'ang Dynasty at the beginning of the tenth century, and while scattered Christians still remained, they had ceased to be a cohesive community.

 In Depth

> In recent years, BBC broadcaster Martin Palmer located the remains of a Christian monastery in Lou Guan Tai, the birthplace of Daoism. The Da Qin (literally "of the West") monastery consists of a seven-story pagoda that is still intact, a cemetery, and traces of a monastery. Inside the pagoda, two relief sculptures were discovered that are believed to portray the birth of Jesus and the prophet Jonah.

Africa

Ethiopians date the founding of their church to the encounter between Philip and the eunuch recorded in Acts 8. Whatever the fate of the newly baptized eunuch, historians generally date the introduction of Christianity in Ethiopia to the beginning of the fourth century. Two brothers, Frumentius and Edesius, were on a voyage along the Red Sea with their uncle when their ship was attacked while in port in the kingdom of Axum (roughly modern-day Ethiopia). Taken prisoner, they eventually befriended the king, who made them tutors and advisors to his young son.

The brothers remained in Ethiopia, and eventually Frumentius was able to contact the bishop of Alexandria, Athanasius, with a request that he send a bishop and priests to care for the new church. Athanasius promptly ordained Frumentius a bishop and sent him back to Ethiopia. The Ethiopian church continues to exist today.

By the third century, churches existed all along the coast of North Africa, from Egypt to Morocco. Carthage, home to Perpetua, Tertullian, and Cyprian, was one of the most important, as was Alexandria. The city of Hippo later hosted Augustine, one of most important Christian writers of all time. Conflicts within African Christianity (such as the Donatist controversy discussed in Chapter 17) weakened the unity of the Christian communities and helped to make possible the conquest of North Africa by the Muslims in the seventh century.

The British Isles

Christianity made it to Britain no later than the end of the second century, though it was confined to the Roman-controlled population south of Hadrian's Wall. Three Christian bishops were present in 314 at the Council of Arles. In the fifth century, Augustine of Hippo got into a huge fracas with Pelagius, a British monk, over the nature of salvation and grace.

The famous St. Patrick, also a British Christian, began working in Ireland in the middle of the fifth century. There were already Christians in Ireland at the time. Later the monks of Ireland returned the favor, founding monasteries in England and preaching the Christian message. They were joined later by Augustine the Lesser, who was sent by Gregory the Great, the first medieval pope.

Christendom

Still, for all of that expansion, the center of gravity for Christianity remained inside the boundaries of the old Roman Empire. After the fall of Constantinople to the Muslim armies in 1453, this became especially true of the western half of the empire. Here a unique relationship formed between the church and the state that we call Christendom. It was an uneasy partnership between the church and society whereby Christianity gained a privileged place in European life and the church would serve as chaplain to the king, and eventually to the state.

Beginning with the Enlightenment in the eighteenth century, that partnership has eroded. Christianity has very slowly been dethroned from its place as the social glue of Western society. This process has taken place much faster in Europe than in the United States, but the same trends are at work in both places. Whether rejected outright as in a large part of Europe or whether reduced to the privacy of conscience as in America, Christianity is losing its place as a public truth.

The clearest indication of this trend is the way that the Christian message no longer shapes the imagination of the Western world. Christian language and ideas are not the lingua franca for social conversation, political thought, or moral controversy. Instead, they form one of many options available to Westerners. Where once you could take for granted that nearly everyone you met had at least the basic elements of the Jesus story, that is no longer a given.

Word to the Wise

"In a London school a teenager with no church connections hears the Christmas story for the first time. His teacher tells it well and he is fascinated by this amazing story. Risking his friends' mockery, after the lesson he thanks her for the story. One thing had disturbed him, so he asks: 'Why did they give the baby a swear-word for his name?'"

—Post-Christendom.com

With the loss of that common Christian heritage has come a loss of shared convictions. Just as Christians in the West can no longer assume that everyone knows what they believe, they can also no longer assume that everyone shares their values. The point here is not to give a full diagnosis of the end of Christendom. That would take a book by itself. Rather, I want to explain how the breakdown of Christendom has made the study of early Christianity more relevant than ever before.

The loss of a consensus (more or less) about the meaning of the Jesus story is one of those changes. Christendom allowed the church to suppress those alternative versions of Jesus, such as Marcion's or the gnostics'. The loss of Christendom means the end of the monopoly on Jesus. One very public example of that is the so-called quest for the historical Jesus.

The Jesus Quest

The religious wars of the seventeenth century had shattered both the political and moral power of Christianity in the eyes of the intellectual elite of Europe. The centrality of the nation-state was on the rise, and the clergy, while still significant, lost their almost monopolistic power to control the direction of European culture as a whole. Instead, new forms of knowledge and certainty were sought, and the power of human reason became the new foundation of truth.

The Enlightenment brought its new rationalism to bear on every subject imaginable, and religion was no exception. A wave of new scholars and writers attempted to reinterpret Christian teachings through the lens of Enlightenment principles, mainly by eradicating any hint of the supernatural or the miraculous from the Gospel accounts. Some did so to destroy Christianity, or at least the church, while others did it to save one or both. Jesus was too important to be left alone, but the picture of Jesus traditionally presented by Christians was no longer fit for a new age of science and humanism.

For nearly 250 years now, scholars and theologians have sought to assess the sources that we have for the life of Jesus, and various attempts have been made to reconstruct his life and teachings. This process is often referred to as the "quest for the historical Jesus," and scholars generally break it down into three periods, the First Quest, the New Quest, and the Third Quest.

The First Quest

While all scholars are dependent on those that come before them, the "First Quest" essentially begins with the writings of H. S. Reimarus. Reimarus described Jesus as a failed revolutionary who never intended to die. After Jesus' death, his followers stole his body and constructed around their fallen leader a myth of divinity, a story that culminated with Jesus triumphantly returning from the heavens. Since Reimarus, these twin themes—of Jesus as a revolutionary figure and of the early Christian belief in the imminent return of Christ in power—have continued to impact studies in both Jesus and the early church.

The First Quest culminated with the publishing of Albert Schweitzer's landmark *Quest of the Historical Jesus* (1906). Schweitzer argued that scholars had been presenting portraits of Jesus that were more in line with the scholars' own beliefs than with the world that Jesus had actually inhabited. Schweitzer's Jesus was neither a revolutionary nor a sage, but rather an apocalyptic prophet who set about preparing his followers for the imminent, cataclysmic end of history when God would finally overthrow the kingdoms of men in place of his own reign. At the end, Schweitzer asserted, Jesus headed to Jerusalem to be crucified in order to force God's hand. While ultimately a failure on his own terms—for the kingdom of God did not suddenly appear—Jesus' spirit of radical devotion continues to inspire and challenge humanity.

No Quest

Schweitzer's apocalyptic Jesus was difficult for many people to swallow. Nobody knew what to do with him. Reflecting on the earthly life of Jesus did not fit in well with the theological currents of the early twentieth century. The theme could easily have been taken from one of the early writings of the apostle Paul: "even though we once knew Christ from a human point of view, we know him no longer in that way." (2 Corinthians 5:16)

Nobody epitomized that attitude more than Rudolph Bultmann. One of the most significant theological voices of the twentieth century, Bultmann had no use for Schweitzer's historical quest. Bultmann's approach to the New Testament was two-pronged. On one hand, he believed in the need to demythologize the texts, essentially eliminating anything of a supernatural character up to and including resurrection. There was no need to prove miracle stories wrong one by one because all of them were wrong on their face.

Word to the Wise

"I do indeed think that we can now know almost nothing concerning the life and personality of Jesus, since the early Christian sources show no interest in either and are moreover fragmentary and often legendary."
—Rudolph Bultmann, *Jesus and the Word*

Second, and more important, Bultmann believed that the Gospels were the products of the Christian community's faith rather than historical biographies. Early Christians were little interested in the facts of Jesus' life. Instead, they were passionate about the living Jesus, what Martin Kähler had called "the Christ of faith," who was not bound by historical data. What early Christians experienced as part of their present faith in Jesus, Bultmann believed, they projected back onto the historical Jesus.

> **Word to the Wise** _____
>
> "The early Church absolutely and completely identified the risen Lord of her experience with the earthly Jesus of Nazareth and created for her purposes, which she conceived to be his, the literary form of the gospel, in which words and deeds ascribed in her consciousness to both the earthly Jesus and the risen Lord were set down in terms of the former."
>
> —Norman Perrin, *Rediscovering the Teaching of Jesus*

The New Quest

It was left to Bultmann's students, rebelling against their teacher in time-honored fashion, to initiate what they called "the New Quest." Beginning in 1953, with Ernst Käsemann's lecture "The Problem of the Historical Jesus," the New Quest accepted Bultmann's methods but not his conclusions. They firmly believed that it is possible to find our way to some historical picture of Jesus. The New Quest scholars asserted that the principal sayings of Jesus were reliable historical data, but that the narrative framework that the early church composed around them was a later addition.

The best-known outgrowth of the New Quest is, of course, the Jesus Seminar. The semischolarly gatherings honchoed by Robert Funk famously (or infamously, depending on your perspective) voted on the historicity of the sayings of Jesus. The Jesus Seminar played into the perennial American fascination with Jesus, showing up in news magazines and exposing scholars like John Dominic Crossan and Marcus Borg to the general public.

New questers are more likely to accept noncanonical texts as their sources for a historical picture of Jesus. The Gospel of Thomas is a particular favorite, along with lots of speculation about the Q (remember all of this from Chapter 10?). While they differ wildly in the picture of Jesus that they draw, New Questers are united in their rejection of Schweitzer's wild-eyed prophet talking about the end of the world. Instead, their Jesus is a wise sage, a wandering Cynic philosopher dispensing wisdom, a political anarchist with a lot of pithy sayings.

The Third Quest

The so-called "Third Quest" is harder to nail down than the previous two. It's not a movement of scholarship, per se, so much as a set of characteristics common to the work of certain historians. Third questers tend to be much more committed to the idea of seeing Jesus in the context of first-century Palestinian Judaism. In particular, they tend to see Jesus as Schweitzer did, through an apocalyptic lens. They definitively reject the historical skepticism common among New Quest scholars.

The name most widely associated with the Third Quest is that of N.T. Wright. Currently the Bishop of Durham in the Church of England, Wright is a never-ending fountain of books and articles. Of most importance to the quest are the thick volumes of the *Christian Origins and the Question of God* series, originally projected at five volumes (until in the middle of the series Wright dashed off an impromptu 800-page tome dealing with questions about the resurrection). Wright argues for a "pincer" approach to the historical Jesus. Taking seriously both first-century Judaism as the context in which Jesus worked and the portrait of Jesus in the Gospels that the early church produced, Wright works forward from the first and backward from the second to get at what kind of person Jesus must have been.

The work of both Third Quest and New Quest scholars, especially as they have escaped the academy and impacted the general public, demonstrates how the old way of reading the Jesus story is no longer valid for many Christians and non-Christians alike in the Western world. The historical Jesus quest is just one symptom of the gradual unraveling of traditional Christianity as the Big Story of Western civilization.

Global Christianity

While the West has been witnessing the slow disintegration of Christendom, throughout the twentieth century, quietly and without much fanfare, Christianity has been experiencing a degree of expansion not unlike what we saw earlier in this chapter. New, indigenous forms of Christian faith have exploded into view. At the end of the twentieth century, Western Christians woke up to discover that the center of gravity of the Christian faith had shifted to Africa, Asia, and Latin America, and a new global Christianity, which has always been present in one form or another, became undeniable. We began this chapter talking about how Christianity continued to expand outside the boundaries of the Roman Empire. We end it seeing how Christianity has expanded beyond the limits of Western civilization.

Just to give you an idea of what I'm talking about, let me throw around a few numbers. At the beginning of the twentieth century, a little over 100 years ago, there were about 10 million Christians in Africa. As of this year, that number is somewhere in the neighborhood of 400 million. While the number of Christians in Europe and the United States has steadily dwindled in proportion to their populations, the percentage of Asian Christians has soared. When Western missionaries were booted out of China in the 1950s, there was grave concern about the fewer than one million Chinese who had converted to Christianity. After decades of indigenous leadership, Christians in China number in the tens of millions. Nobody knows the exact figure because no one is sure how to count the vast number of illegal house churches that abound throughout China.

Word to the Wise

"The domestic tasks of Third World Theology are going to be so basic, so vital, that there will be little time for the barren, sterile, time-wasting by-paths into which so much Western theology and theological research has gone in recent years. Theology in the Third World will be, as theology at all creative times has always been, about doing things, about things that deeply affect the lives of numbers of people."

—Andrew Walls, *The Transmission of Christian Faith*

The numbers aren't the only impressive shift in the current state of Christianity. Because so many of these new churches were founded not by Western missionaries but by native leaders, there has been an explosion of "local theologies," new ways of appropriating the Jesus story that have continuity with the history of the church but address the concerns and questions of the given culture. In a sense, we are seeing the same leap that took place as the Jewish Jesus movement made the transition to a Hellenized Gentile Christianity, except now we're seeing it happen in several different cultures simultaneously. In the process, these new local theologies are taking Christianity in directions as unfamiliar and disconcerting to Western Christians as the activities of Paul were to the Jewish Christians in Jerusalem.

Word to the Wise

"African and Latin American Christians are people for whom the New Testament Beatitudes have a direct relevance inconceivable for most Christians in Northern societies. When Jesus told the 'poor' they were blessed, the word used does not imply relative deprivation, it means total poverty, or destitutions. The great majority of Southern Christians (and increasingly, of all Christians) really are the poor, the hungry, the persecuted, even the dehumanized."

—Philip Jenkins, *The Next Christendom*

For Christians and non-Christians alike, the shifting trends in the Christian world will have long-term impacts. It is already clear that, by the middle of this century, the wealthy Western powers, including the United States, will largely be in the hands of secularized, nonreligious societies. Meanwhile, Christianity is growing by leaps and bounds in areas that are highly urbanized, poverty stricken, and often politically unstable.

What will that change mean for the future of an increasingly globalized economy and for the future of international peace and justice? Will the Christians of the "two-thirds world" be able to bring the kind of relief and self-sacrificial service that made Christianity so attractive in the cities of the Roman Empire? How will Christians in the West deal with their increasingly marginal status? What is remarkable is how the experience of Christians around the world now mirrors that of Christians in the earliest centuries of the church's existence. There are profound comparisons to be drawn between the early Christians and our contemporary situation, if we are willing to see them.

The Least You Need to Know

- Christianity continued to expand outward beyond the boundaries of the Roman Empire.

- With the Enlightenment, the partnership between Christianity and Western culture began to unravel.

- The quest for the historical Jesus demonstrates that Christians are no longer able to dominate the interpretation of Jesus.

- Christianity has spread beyond the boundaries of Western civilization, so much so that its greatest strength now lies in the "two-thirds world."

Glossary

aedile   A government official in Roman cities. They were generally responsible for public works, public events, and often for public security.

agape   One of several Greek words for "love." Agape is distinct from several others for having often been compared in Greek literature to divine love, love that is total and self-sacrificial. It seems that the Greeks had little use for the word, since it shows up so rarely. Christians, however, claimed it for their own. Agape is used frequently in the New Testament, especially for the love of God.

agrapha   Individual sayings of Jesus not found in the New Testament Gospels.

allegory   A story in which certain concrete characters or places represent something other than themselves; not intended to be taken literally, but figuratively, as a means of pointing to a deeper truth.

apocryphal   Jewish and Christian writings that were not included in either the Old or New Testament.

apologist   A word derived from the Greek *apologia*, which means "to make a defense" or "to explain." 1 Peter 3 encourages Christians to always be ready to give an apologia for their faith. An apology, then, is not a way of saying sorry so much as it is an explanation for something.

apostate   A person who abandons a group, cause, or belief system. To apostatize, obviously, means to become an apostate.

ascetic   A person who practices forms of self-denial as a means toward spiritual perfection. It's rooted in a Greek word that indicates hard work and rigorous exercise. An ascetic is a spiritual athlete, training the soul by disciplining the body.

baptism   To immerse in water. Many religions have such a ritual act.

bishop   Sometimes translated "overseer," a position of leadership in the Christian community. The Greek word is *episkopos*, from which we get words like *Episcopal*. While the development of this office is a matter of great debate, it's clear that by the middle of the second century, bishops have attained dominance as the highest authorities in the Christian community.

canon   Originally a ruler or measuring stick. In literary terms, it refers to a list of writings considered essential and foundational for a given culture, subject, or group. They are the literature against which everything else is measured. A text that belongs to a canon is called *canonical*.

catechumenate   The process whereby a person interested in becoming part of the Christian community would join in the community's life for a time, and with certain restrictions, until he or she was better acquainted with the doctrinal and ethical standards of Christian life and practice. The word comes from the Greek *katakeo*, which means "to echo."

Chi-Rho   The merging of the two Greek letters Chi (X) and Rho (R), which are the first two words in the Greek spelling of "Christ." From very early in the history of the church, this shortened way of writing Christ was used.

circumcision   The surgical removal of the foreskin from the end of the male genitalia. Yes, it's just about as bad as it sounds. In the Law of Moses, every Jewish boy was supposed to be circumcised on the eighth day after his birth.

codex   The earliest form of the modern book. It is a series of pages stacked and bound together at one edge, and often given a cover. While technically any book is a codex, the term tends to be reserved for handwritten works dating from the first century up until the dawn of printing in the late Middle Ages.

confessor   Someone who has suffered for his or her confession of faith in Christ but lives through the ordeal. They were considered martyrs because they had been prepared to die.

creed   From the Latin word *credo*, meaning "I believe." It's a confession of belief.

cult   Usually a negative thing these days, but really it just means any religion that expresses its beliefs through ritual acts. Cultic acts are things that worshippers do as part of their religion, as distinct from what they believe.

deacon   From the Greek *diakonos*, which means "to serve." Possibly based on the Seven led by Stephen in the Acts, deacons were the officers of the Christian community responsible for providing relief for the poor and indigent, visiting the sick and imprisoned, and assisting the elders of the church at the worship gatherings.

diaspora   Greek word meaning "dispersion," like a farmer scatters seeds in a field. In terms of Jewish history, it refers generally to all of the Jewish communities located outside of Palestine.

Diatesseron   Literally means "through the four." It was an attempt by Tatian to create a single, harmonized version of the Jesus story by weaving together the four New Testament Gospels, Matthew, Mark, Luke, and John. In the process, Tatian smoothed over some of the differences in those four narratives. He also edited key passages in the Gospels that dealt with sex and celibacy in the Christian life so that they would better support his encratite views. The *Diatesseron* was the most popular version of the New Testament in Syria for two centuries.

docetism   From the Greek word *dokeo*, which means "to seem, to appear." It was the idea that Jesus did not have an actual body, but only appeared to.

doxology   Literally "words of praise," usually a short verse or prayer that is sung at the end of a worship gathering.

Ebionite   From a Hebrew word that means "poor ones." Like many group designations in early Christianity, it originally began as a reference to a characteristic trait rather than a specific sect. In this case, it may derive from the same teaching of Jesus on spiritual poverty that found its way into the Gospels. For example, in the Gospel of Matthew, Jesus says, "Blessed are the poor in spirit ..." (in the Gospel of Luke, he simply says, "Blessed are the poor ..."). Only later, after the fall of Jerusalem, did the term become associated with those Jewish Christians who still observed Torah.

ecclesia   Greek word originally referring to the popular assembly in Athens where citizens made communal decisions about law and government. It was adopted by Christians as a term for the body of people who gathered together to worship Jesus, and translates into English as "church."

Encratite   A term for Christians who refused to marry or engage in sexual relations, out of a belief that sexuality itself was evil. The word comes from the Greek *enkrateia*, which means "continence" or "self-control."

eschatology   One of those big theological words that carries a lot of conceptual weight. It literally means "the study of last things." Generally, it refers to the ultimate purpose or end of all things, and particularly the human race; that meaning also tends to include the events that will bring about that ultimate end, so you get a lot of end-of-the-world kind of talk in eschatology.

gentile   The word that the Bible uses to describe non-Jews. The Greek word in the New Testament writings is *ethnoi*, meaning "nations, peoples" (it's where we get words like *ethnic* and *ethnicity*). So if it means "nation," why is it translated "gentile"? Because when the Greek New Testament was translated into Latin, *ethnoi* was translated into the Latin word *gentilis*, which means "belonging to a tribe."

gnostics   Got their name from the Greek word *gnosis*, which means "knowledge." Literally, they are "ones who know."

Hellenism   Literally means "to make Greek." In practice, it refers to the way that the Mediterranean world in the aftermath of Alexander the Great absorbed, or was absorbed by, core aspects of Greek ideals.

Hellenistic Jews   Another way of differentiating Jews native to Palestine from those who were rooted in the diaspora. Hellenistic Jews were far more comfortable with the Greek language and generally had a better relationship with non-Jews.

incarnation   Literally means "in flesh." It's a theological term for the idea that God became a human being in Jesus of Nazareth.

liturgy   From the word *leitourgia*, which is commonly translated "work of the people." In public use, it usually indicated the performance of a public duty, such as the philanthropic act of a wealthy benefactor on behalf of a city. It was in this sense of performing a public duty that the Septuagint used liturgy as the word to describe the activity of the priests in the Temple. From there it was an easy jump to using it to refer to the worship being offered at the Temple. In the churches, the liturgy was recognized as the public duty of the Christians to attend to the Lord in communal worship and prayer.

Markan priority   The theory that Mark's Gospel was written first and was used by Matthew and Luke to compose their own Gospels.

martyr   From a Greek word that means "witness." Early on, however, the word became exclusively associated with those whose witness led to their deaths.

Matthean priority   The dominant theory for most of Christian history, it is the belief that Matthew's Gospel is the source for the common elements in the Synoptics.

monasticism   From the Greek word *monachos*, which means "solitary" or "alone." The monk was someone who pursued solitude and silence as an essential way of life, but it goes beyond that. The word also carried the notion of single-minded devotion, that the monk was focused entirely on the pursuit of spirituality at all costs.

panegyric   A speech of praise, usually expressed in enthusiastic and even hyperbolic language.

paraclete   Translated variously as "advocate," "comforter," and "counselor," from the Greek word *paracletos*, which literally means "one called alongside." Describes the role of the Holy Spirit in the lives of Jesus' followers. As such, it appears exclusively in the Gospel of John.

passion   From a Latin word that means "suffering," with the sense of being acted upon. Passion involves vulnerability to harm. Words *passive* and *patience* belong to the same family of words.

Pax Romana   Latin for "peace of Rome" and refers to the period of Roman history between the rise of Augustus Caesar in 27 B.C. and the death of Marcus Aurelius in A.D. 180. It was roughly 200 years of relative peace and predictability in the lives of most of the residents of the Empire.

polis   Usually translated into English as "city" or "city-state." It is the basic unit of Greek political identity. From it we get English words like *political* and *politician.*

pontifex maximus   "Supreme bridge-builder," the head of the College of Pontiffs in Rome, the apex of Roman religious life. From Augustus on, it was a title and a role adopted by the emperors. In essence, the pontiffs built bridges between the world of humans and the world of the gods. In the late 300s, the emperor Gratian abandoned the title in favor of Pope Damasus I, and from that time it has become one of the hereditary titles of the Bishop of Rome, the Pope.

presbyters   Also mentioned in the New Testament, where the word is usually translated "elder" or "elders." At first, this office seems to have been synonymous with the office of bishop. Over time, and certainly by the beginning of the second century, the bishop appears to have become the first among the presbyters. Eventually, the presbyters were seen as the agents of the bishop, appointed by him as his helpers. The word *priest* is derived from *presbyter*, and that's how most presbyters are referred to today.

proselytes   Converts to a religious faith. Specifically, this Greek word was a way of referring to foreigners who decided to live in Israel, either living as Jews or abiding by certain basic laws as resident aliens. In the New Testament, proselytes are converts to Judaism.

pseudonymous   Writings that were forgeries, written by someone other than the person to whom they were attributed.

recapitulation   "To sum up or summarize." Theologically, the idea that Jesus recapitulated human experience, that he lived every aspect of human life and, in so doing, made human existence holy.

repent   In the New Testament, a translation of the Greek word *metanoia*, which literally means "to change your mind." The emphasis is not on guilt or sorrow, though these may accompany repentance. Instead, the summons to *metanoia* is an invitation to reconsider the direction of your life and thinking. The presumption that one's way of living will change as a consequence of this self-reflection is also implied.

rule of faith   From the Latin words *regula fidei*. It's one of several phrases used to indicate a core body of teaching that summarizes the essential truths of the Jesus story as it was perceived by the mainstream church starting at least at the beginning of the second century.

sacrament   Often called a visible sign of an inward grace. The idea is that physical acts, rituals, and elements can carry the love and mercy of God, and make it available to people in their day-to-day existence. In early Christianity, baptism and Eucharist were two ritual acts that all agreed were sacramental.

schism   A break between two factions within a larger community.

Septuagint   The Greek translation of the Hebrew Scriptures produced in the second century B.C. and widely used by Greek-speaking Jews. The name, odd as it may sound, is Latin for "seventy," often abbreviated LXX (the Latin numeral 70). The title is a reference to the 72 scholars who supposedly produced the original version, a Greek translation of the first five books of the Bible, called the Pentateuch. Other scriptural texts were added over time. The Septuagint was held in great esteem. Jews and, later, Christians considered it as inspired as the original. Both the Jewish historian Josephus and the Christian apostle Paul used the Septuagint in their writings when they quoted from Scripture. In Western Christianity, the Septuagint was finally displaced by the Latin translation called the Vulgate, but Eastern Christians, for whom Greek has remained a living language, still use the Septuagint.

sesterce One fourth of a denarius, which was a typical day's pay for a laborer in the Roman Empire.

Shavuos The Hebrew name for the harvest festival that takes place 50 days after Passover. Christians refer to it as Pentecost. Shavuos is both the celebration of the end of the grain harvest, at which time a presentation of bread was made in the Temple, and a commemoration of the giving of the Mosaic Law at Mt. Sinai following the escape from Egypt.

Further Reading

The Apostolic Fathers in English, 3rd Edition, translated by Michael W.
   Holmes (Baker, 2006).

Holmes has done us a service by updating these translations of the earliest Christian texts outside of the New Testament. Here you will find many
of the books that I've mentioned, including the letters of Ignatius and
Polycarp, and *The Shepherd of Hermas.*

Eusebius: The Church History, translated by Paul L. Maier (Kregel, 1999).

For understanding early Christianity, there may be no single source more
important than Eusebius. *The Church History* is filled with information that
would have been completely lost if Eusebius hadn't told us about it, and
some of the stories he relates are simply extraordinary. This edition by Paul
Maier tames Eusebius's sometimes flourishing prose and makes him much
easier to digest.

The Rise of Christianity, by W. H. C. Frend (Fortress, 1984).

Okay, I admit it, this one's a long shot, but if you're really interested in
digging into early Christian history, this is one book that you're going to
want to get to know. At over 1,000 pages, they should sell this book by the
pound. It's an in-depth treatment, to be sure, but it's worth the effort if

you're serious. If the sight of page numbers into the four digits gets your blood pressure up, try out Henry Chadwick's less paper-intensive *The Early Church*. Works that include more than just early Christianity are also worth looking at. Consider Justo Gonzalez' *The Story of Christianity Vol. 1* or the very readable *Church History in Plain Language* by Bruce Shelley.

The Rise of Christianity, by Rodney Stark (HarperOne, 1997).

No, that's not a mistake. It's another book titled *The Rise of Christianity*, but this is one that you can lift with one hand. Stark is a sociologist who specializes in the spread of new religions, so when he applies his modern theories to the development of early Christianity, he comes up with some eye-opening conclusions. Other worthwhile works that have taken a sociological approach to early Christianity are Wayne Meeks's singular *The First Urban Christians* and Bruce Winter's *Seek the Welfare of the City*.

Who Is Jesus?, by John Dominic Crossan and Richard G. Watts (Westminster, 1996).

A champion for the revisionist reading of the Jesus story, Crossan combines a warm Irish wit with keen scholarly instincts. If you want to understand the arguments for approaching the New Testament with a deeply skeptical eye, Crossan's *Who Is Jesus?* is about as painless an introduction as it gets. If you feel like moving on to something meatier, try his *The Birth of Christianity* or the more recent *The Historical Jesus*.

The Challenge of Jesus, by N. T. Wright (InterVarsity Press, 1999).

In an academic world where the big-selling names—Crossan, Borg, Erhman, and the like—tend to discount the traditional Christian story, Wright stands out as a defender of historical Christianity. *The Challenge of Jesus* summarizes Wright's views in a fairly accessible fashion. If you want to step down a bit more, try his *Simply Christian*, or if you really want a challenge, take on the multivolume *Christian Origins* and the *Question of God* series. Wright has been authoring (including the landmark *Jesus and the Victory of God*, the book on which *The Challenge of Jesus* is based). For a comparison between the contending perspectives on Jesus, check out *The Meaning of Jesus: Two Views*, co-authored by Wright and Marcus Borg, who, it turns out, are good friends.

Guide to Internet Resources

Christian Classics Ethereal Library
www.ccel.org

Early Christian Writings
www.earlychristianwritings.com

Gnostic Society Library
www.gnosis.org/library.html

The Formation of the New Testament Canon
www.infidels.org/library/modern/richard_carrier/NTcanon.html

The Tertullian Project
www.tertullian.org

Internet Resources for the Study of Judaism and Christianity
ccat.sas.upenn.edu/~jtreat/rs/resources.html

The Ecole Initiative
www2.evansville.edu/ecoleweb/

Creeds of Christendom
www.creeds.net

From Jesus to Christ
www.pbs.org/wgbh/pages/frontline/shows/religion

Index

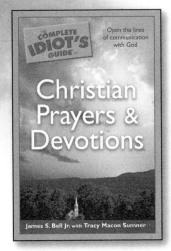

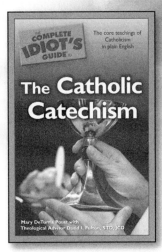
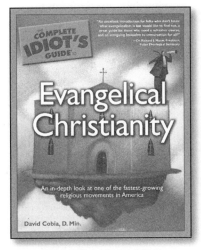
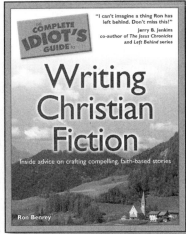

Check out these BEST-SELLERS

READ BY MILLIONS!

978-1-59257-115-4
$16.95

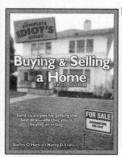

978-1-59257-458-2
$19.95

FULL COLOR!

978-1-59257-566-4
$22.95

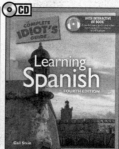

978-1-59257-485-8
$24.95

978-1-59257-480-3
$19.95

978-1-59257-469-8
$14.95

978-1-59257-439-1
$18.95

978-1-59257-483-4
$14.95

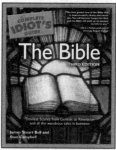

978-1-59257-389-9
$18.95

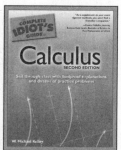

978-1-59257-471-1
$18.95

978-1-59257-437-7
$19.95

978-1-59257-463-6
$14.95

978-0-02864244-4
$21.95

978-1-59257-335-6
$19.95

978-1-59257-491-9
$19.95

More than **450 titles** available at booksellers and online retailers everywhere

ALPHA

www.idiotsguides.com